Second Language Classrooms

Research on teaching and learning

Craig Chaudron
University of Hawaii at Manoa

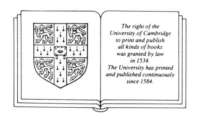

The right of the
University of Cambridge
to print and publish
all kinds of books
was granted by law
in 1534.
The University has printed
and published continuously
since 1584.

Cambridge University Press
Cambridge
New York   Port Chester
Melbourne   Sydney

Published by the Press Syndicate of the University of Cambridge
The Pitt Building, Trumpington Street, Cambridge CB2 1RP
40 West 20th Street, New York, NY 10011, USA
10 Stamford Road, Oakleigh, Melbourne 3166, Australia

First published 1988
Third printing 1990

Printed in the United States of America

Cover design by Thomas Wharton

Library of Congress Cataloging-in-Publication Data

Chaudron, Craig, 1946–
Second language classrooms.
(Cambridge applied linguistics series)
Bibliography: p.
1. Language and languages – Study and teaching.
2. Second language acquisition I. Title. II. Series.
P53.C43 1988 418'.007 87–6555

British Library Cataloguing in Publication Data

Chaudron, Craig
Second language classrooms : research on
teaching and learning.
1. Language and languages – Study and
teaching
I. Title.
418'.007'1 P51

ISBN 0-521-32775-X hardback
ISBN 0-5 21-33980-4 paperback

For my mother, Eleanor,
and the memory of my father, Cliff,
who introduced me to the world of languages

Contents

Tables and figures

Tables

Figures

Series editors' preface

The Cambridge Applied Linguistics Series (CALS) provides a forum for the best new work in applied linguistics by those in the field who are able to relate theory, research, and teaching practice. Craig Chaudron's book fulfills this criterion admirably.

Classroom-centered research has already contributed a great deal to our understanding of what actually goes on in second language classrooms, as opposed to what we sometimes think goes on or are told should go on. In *Second Language Classrooms: Research on Teaching and Learning*, Chaudron offers a comprehensive overview and synthesis of theory and research on foreign and second language classroom processes. He summarizes the results of numerous studies of teacher and student classroom behaviors and teacher-student interaction, and looks at how such behavior affects language learning. Also included are conclusions drawn from his own work on teacher speech, error correction, and classroom discourse.

Many gaps remain in our knowledge of the relationship between language learning and what goes on in the classroom, and Chaudron therefore offers methodological suggestions for future studies. We hope that readers of this book will be inspired to initiate research that will fill in these gaps and enhance our knowledge of how language is learned.

Michael H. Long
Jack C. Richards
University of Hawaii at Manoa

Preface

This book reviews classroom-based research and attempts to provide confirming or disconfirming evidence for claims about the influence of language instruction and classroom interaction on language learning. This is achieved by comparing studies that describe teachers' and learners' behaviors in classrooms and synthesizing them into generalizations about the processes that take place in second language classrooms. Studies that point to relationships between these behaviors and second language development are also summarized. Classroom teachers, school administrators, teacher trainers, and second language researchers should all find in the review of these relationships useful implications for language teaching, language curriculum development, and further research goals. Theories and claims about language teaching methods, effective curriculum, or the importance of learner characteristics have rarely been based on actual research in language classrooms, despite the integral role that classroom teaching and learning plays in theoretical and practical proposals.

Also, professionals involved in first language pedagogy should find many methods and principles relevant to their educational context, because studies of second language instruction have addressed issues analogous to those in native language educational research, and the goals of the research are quite similar. In second language (L2) research the greater attention to the linguistic phenomena involved can afford some important perspectives for first language (L1) researchers. A linguistic focus has been evident in much L1 classroom research (e.g., Bellack et al. 1966; Cazden, John, and Hymes 1972; Wilkinson 1982), yet L2 researchers have at times maintained greater precision about the nature of the linguistic phenomena and greater caution in interpreting the meaningfulness of classroom events for the participants. In L2 research, the intelligibility and meaning of classroom language for learners is the primary focus of investigation. L1 researchers and teachers should, therefore, also find in this book valuable information and perspectives about classroom teaching and learning.

The survey and discussion in this book is perhaps most relevant to current and future researchers of L2 classroom behaviors and processes, who should benefit from the comparison of methodologies and results of different classroom research, and from the focus on the theoretical foundations for the investigation of classroom processes. It is hoped that the conclusions reached in the book and the directions suggested for future studies will lead researchers to investigate more carefully claims regarding L2 teaching and learning and to adopt new methods and goals in their research.

The author wishes to thank many individuals for their contributions to the development of this book. In particular, Mike Long and Jack Richards have been extraordinarily supportive and understanding throughout; their initial suggestion and encouragement was the impetus for me to write the book. They have both read drafts of all the chapters and provided useful comments. Mike Long has, especially, followed the book through various drafts, always with a calm and helpful prod to proceed. He has significantly influenced the content of the book, providing references and insightful critiques at many points, including comments throughout the final draft manuscript. I have too few ways in which to thank him.

Graham Crookes and Bernie Mohan also read the entire final draft and provided extensive suggestions for improvement in content and style. Their assistance has been most helpful. Several others have read chapters of the book and offered critical comments on style, coverage, and accuracy. I am grateful to Mary McGroarty, Ruth Cathcart, Fred Genesee, Dick Day, and R. Keith Johnson. I appreciate the time they have spent; their expert advice has been an incentive to provide more detail in several crucial areas.

I also appreciate the help that other colleagues and students have given me over many years, although they may not recognize the benefits I have reaped in discussions with them on the issues dealt with here. I thank especially Dick Allwright, Charlie Sato, Claus Faerch, Gabi Kasper, Mike Strong, Kathi Bailey, Maria Fröhlich, Steve Gaies, Nina Spada, Brina Peck, Evelyn Hatch, Leo van Lier, Peter Shaw, Patsy Lightbown, Tere Pica, Cindy Brock, Kathy Rulon, Patsy Duff, J. D. Brown, Sue Gass, and Catherine Snow. I must also mention here my lasting debt to my early mentors in classroom research, especially Merrill Swain, and Patrick Allen and H. H. Stern. Although we have seldom interacted while I was writing this book, their initial confidence in my work and their influence on me has remained with me in countless ways.

It is also fitting to express my appreciation to several of the previously mentioned colleagues, especially Mike Long and Graham Crookes, as well as Ros Mitchell, Yolanda Beh, and John Chow, who helped me obtain important references and materials. And when it comes to references, no one has helped me more through the years, to keep me up on research, psychology, and education, than my brother Doug; I owe him much for everything he has done.

I thank, furthermore, the capable editors of Cambridge University Press for their advice and supportive enthusiasm for this project, especially Peter Donovan, Ellen Shaw, and Sandra Graham.

Finally, I must thank Aileen, for all she has done to urge me on with my work, despite the minimal hours which the demands of such a task left for us to share together. She has indeed been the bright spot that has kept me going.

1 Major issues in second language classroom research

Since the 1960s, there has been an increasing attempt in research on teaching and learning from instruction to relate the major features of teacher and student behavior in classrooms to learning outcomes. There have been extensive investigations into the types and quantities of instructional and noninstructional tasks, the relative amounts of participation by the teacher and students, and the functions and forms of language in interaction. At the same time, various personality, attitudinal, cognitive, and other individual or social factors which are thought to influence observable classroom behaviors have been the object of instructional research. The fundamental goal of most such research has, of course, been to determine which variables best, or more frequently, lead to academic achievement. Careful evaluation of results can lead to well-informed decision making at all levels of educational planning: development of the curriculum, preparation of materials, training of teachers, preference for classroom teaching activities and techniques, decisions about individualization of instruction, and even teacher's modifications of speech in explanations. The range of applications of classroom-based research is broad, and the number of factors and issues studied seems endless. While second language classroom research has tended to lag behind native language research in the topics and methods for investigation, these statements apply equally to both contexts.

In addition to the intrinsic interest that the description of classroom processes has for researchers, probably the ultimate objective of classroom research is to identify those characteristics of classrooms that lead to efficient learning of the instructional content, so that empirically supported L2 teacher training and program development can be implemented. The researcher will not approach this objective with any rigid notion of the principal sources of those characteristics, for there equally as well may be other qualities of the program responsible for learning, such as materials, classroom environment, the teacher, the students, and teaching methods. On the other hand, effective research will be based on well-reasoned theory and synthesis of previous knowledge, so that these sources are not investigated randomly.

In this book second language research on teachers, learners, and the

1

interaction between them will be reviewed, in order to determine the degree to which specific classroom processes or behaviors are sources of positive effects on second language learning. The focus on just these factors does not, however, imply that other environmental or programmatic influences may not contribute to learning, but rather that the accumulating wealth of information on teacher and learner classroom behavior is now substantial enough to warrant detailed study in its own right.[1]

In an outline of requirements of research on teaching effectiveness, Cooley, Leinhardt, and McGrail (1977) include measures of a) student outcomes, b) teaching behavior, and c) other variables, as well as procedures for collecting and analyzing data, and "a model of classroom processes for use in selecting, constructing, and organizing all these measures" (p. 120). Although no explanatory model exists that interrelates all the possible variables involved in L2 classrooms, a general model for the study of classroom teaching is outlined by Dunkin and Biddle (1974:38). This model, shown in Figure 1.1, serves well as an initial guide for the classification of variables and behaviors.

The research reviewed in this book deals primarily with the "process" variables within the "classroom" box in Figure 1.1, that is, research on the nature of teacher and student behavior in real classrooms. To the extent that investigators have related teacher "presage" variables, student characteristics,[2] or program types (which should be included under "context" variables) to classroom processes, this research will also be considered. However, description of the interaction of process variables with one another and analysis of the relationship between process variables and product variables (learning outcomes) are the main focus of the research discussed in the book.

---

1 This accumulation of research is evidenced by the publication in recent years of several books and anthologies of L2 classroom-oriented research, although no review similar to this book has been conducted. See, for example, Trueba, Guthrie and Au (1981), Chamberlain and Llamzon (1982), Seliger and Long (1983), Ellis (1984b), Gass and Madden (1985), Faerch and Kasper (1985a), Kasper (1986), Day (1986), Allwright and Bailey (in press), and van Lier (in press). There have also appeared several review articles and a bibliography on the topic (Allwright 1983; Gaies 1983a; Mitchell 1985; Bailey 1985; Long 1985b), and numerous colloquia and seminars (most notably the annual Colloquium on Classroom Centered Research held at TESOL conventions and the RELC Regional Seminar on Patterns of Classroom Interaction in Southeast Asia, Singapore, 1986).

2 Dunkin and Biddle (1974) include these in "context" variables because of the lack of control teachers have over student characteristics; they take a teacher-focused position with regard to the institution of change in teaching. Also, it should be noted that, while their model and focus was on regular school learning, the research dealt with in this book will extend these factors to child, adolescent, and adult contexts.

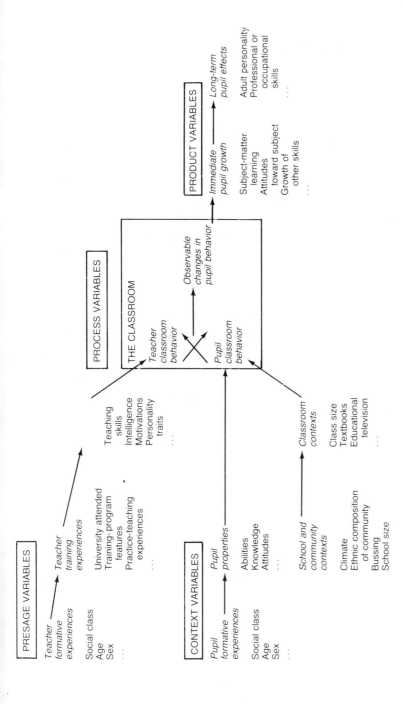

Figure 1.1 A model for the study of classroom teaching. (From: The Study of Teaching by Michael J. Dunkin and Bruce J. Biddle, p. 38. Copyright © 1974 by Holt, Rinehart & Winston, Inc. Reprinted by permission of Holt, Rinehart & Winston, Inc.)

The value of second language instruction

There are, of course, a number of theoretical issues relating to the teaching and learning of second languages, many of which will be brought out in the context of specific research studies and factors. One overriding issue in L2 research concerns the ultimate *value* of second language instruction. Does language instruction help at all? There is little reason to investigate which teaching behaviors might improve L2 learning slightly if, overall, instruction in an L2 is not especially productive. This issue hinges on the degree to which an L2 is acquired through natural development and exposure to it in meaningful, social interaction, compared to the degree to which a structured, formalistic environment (i.e., school instruction) can contribute to acquisition. Since, as most readers of this book will recognize, the average L2 learner is seldom able to engage naturally and extensively in a target language environment, because the learner either lives in another country or is isolated socially or economically from full participation with L2 speakers, the potential value of instructional access to the L2 increases by default. The question of whether L2 instruction has an *absolute* positive effect on acquisition will obviously depend on particular programs and circumstances, but in a synthesis of several studies which compared naturalistic with formal instruction, Long (1983a) argues that the outcomes favor instruction, *all other factors being equal.* In other words, instructional contexts appeared to contribute more positively to acquisition of the L2 than naturalistic exposure, when duration of exposure and other factors (e.g., age) were controlled. However, classroom-based research alone cannot answer the question regarding the absolute value of instruction, since program evaluation is ultimately required.

Yet, in regard to the *relative* effects of instruction on acquisition, the question remains open as to which features of L2 classroom instruction might contribute to different learners' development, or to development of only selected features of L2 performance. That is, some classroom processes may aid the acquisition of certain structures (e.g., vocabulary) without influencing others (syntax). By noting differential effects, classroom-oriented research can guide the teacher, researcher, curriculum developer, or administrator toward principles of effective instruction.

The context of second language instruction

Another major source of theoretical issues in L2 classroom learning concerns the *nature* of instruction that results from different learning contexts. Most broadly, second language instruction occurs in two contexts. In one, the "foreign language" context, relevant to perhaps the majority of L2 learners, the learner acquires the L2 when there is little natural use of the language in the surrounding society (such as English in Japan, French in the United States, Chinese in Tanzania). As a consequence, the L2 is usually treated as equivalent to any school subject, like geography and mathematics, in which terminology, concepts, and rules are taught, homework is written, and tests are taken. Associated with the subject are of course a wide range of attitudes toward the L2 people and culture, derived in part from the learner's out-of-school exposure to, or knowledge about, the target language community.

In the second, the "second language" context, the L2 is not only the content of instruction but the medium of instruction, because of either programmatic decisions (as in "immersion" settings in which the community around the school is still a native language environment) or linguistic necessity (as in most multilingual settings). Especially in the latter case, when *only* the L2 can be used for communication, the social relationships and the curriculum content are conveyed to learners in a cultural and linguistic medium that surpasses their competence to some degree, and there is usually little recourse to L1 sources of interpretation. The learner's task is therefore threefold: first, making sense of instructional tasks posed in the L2, then attaining a sociolinguistic competence to allow greater participation, and finally learning the content itself. Attitudes may again have an influence, but the cognitive demands of communication and socialization into the L2 community are dominant.

As a result, in the second language context, teachers need to anticipate learners' needs for additional assistance in understanding both the instructional processes and the linguistic medium that conveys them. Effectively meeting learners' needs may involve modifications of the language used for management, social relations, and instruction, aside from possible methodological choices concerning materials and learning tasks. This is not to say that a second language context is inherently more difficult to manipulate than a foreign language one, but rather that there are quite different demands on the learner in the two cases. Classroom-oriented research must not only take these differences into consideration when comparing results across the contexts, but it must adopt the secondary goal of understanding the nature of the contextual demands on learners and teachers. In this way, research would derive principles for instructional decision making that are valid across contexts. In the following chapters, similarities and differences between these contexts will be noted when research studies permit comparison.

Major issues

The following discussion briefly outlines four general issues concerning the effectiveness of classroom instruction. Later, each will be defined more thoroughly and the research basis for the major positions on them will be explored.

Learning from instruction

Perhaps the most well-known position concerning the influence of instruction on L2 development is that of Krashen. Krashen (1982:ch. V) offers an extensive analysis of the role of instruction within his framework for interpreting L2 acquisition. He views the effects of instruction as limited, however: the classroom should function to provide the learner with comprehensible target language (TL) input in an affectively supportive climate. Only insofar as the input is comprehensible, at the appropriate level just ahead of the learners' stage of rule development $(i + 1)$, will learners be able to derive support for or disconfirmation of their interlanguage rules. Given affective support, this should be sufficient for learners to progress in the TL. Instruction will especially be valuable when other naturalistic input is not available, as in foreign language instruction contexts, or when learners are at a low level of proficiency and not as likely to obtain sufficient comprehensible input in naturalistic encounters.

In Krashen's view, instruction directed toward conscious learning of TL rules does not substantially contribute to learners' progress. Yet Long (1983a) argues that the advantage instruction has over a naturalistic acquisition context must lie in part in the experience of "treating language as object" and "learning" to control performance on a variety of L2 tasks. Krashen considers conscious learning to be limited to learning to *control* production of easy L2 rules, which still will not guarantee subsequent acquisition of such rules. Long claims, however, that such limited effects would not account for the relative success of more advanced learners in instructional settings over naturalistic acquirers. In his view, more complex rules and metalinguistic awareness would also be obtained through instruction. Many second language acquisition (SLA) researchers have investigated this issue of conscious versus unconscious rule acquisition (see Bialystok 1982 and selections in Davies, Criper, and Howatt 1984 for important summary positions on the topic), but the matter remains unresolved and in need of a precise methodology for distinguishing learners' conscious rule knowledge from unconscious performance. (For a review of research on this last topic, see Chaudron 1983c.) How teachers achieve a focus on language as object, and the ways learners make use of such a focus, have barely been investigated in classroom research (though see Faerch 1985, 1986, and Chapter 6, this volume).

In a review of applications of SLA theory to teaching and syllabus construction, Pienemann (1985, see also Meisel, Clahsen, and Pienemann 1981, and Pienemann 1984) takes an important theoretical position on this question. He proposes that L2 learners' procession through developmental stages is determined by a few fundamental psycholinguistic "processing prerequisites," that is, cognitive operations that are ordered by their complexity. Not all TL rules are affected by these operations, so that some will vary according to affective states in the learner, exposure, and other factors. Nevertheless, that subset of rules which are developmental can be influenced by instruction – not to the extent that stages in development can be surpassed, but in the rapidity with which a learner can develop to the next stage ahead. Those TL forms which are produced by the next stage of processing prerequisites above the learner's current state are amenable to instruction. Pienemann acknowledges that the issue of conscious control by the learner of these rules through formal means is not resolved in current research, so the precise manner in which instruction can influence the learner's development is not clear. This "teachability" hypothesis is discussed by a number of subsequent papers in Hyltenstam and Pienemann (1985), and it will be discussed further in Chapter 6.

Generally speaking, a learning task will usually involve 1) the acquisition of certain fundamental units or elements (e.g., words, facts, rules, concepts) and 2) their integration in functional relationships and applications by means of 3) a certain amount of production, practice, or other mental operations with those elements. (Cf. the information-processing view of L2 acquisition in McLaughlin, Rossman, and McLeod 1983.) This is not to suggest that learning takes place by following these steps in order, nor that these are the only steps involved. With the case of language acquisition as an example, the student must learn to recognize the elements (sounds, morphology, lexis) and to organize them in their syntactic combinations, according to their pragmatic functional applications. If instruction is to make a difference, the TL input (modified or not) must provide the learner with the information necessary for identifying the elements and their combinations and applications. But the learner must also operate on these fundamental aspects in order to incorporate them in a behavioral repertoire. This general view does not presuppose the exact nature of the operations involved, whether they require consciousness, active production, receptive analysis, or any other specific mental activity.

Chaudron (1985b) makes an additional critical point: from the L2 learner's point of view, the recognition of the structures in input and their meanings is not only necessary for the acquisition of the structures in the abstract, but, insofar as the TL is the medium of instruction (as in second language contexts), it is necessary for understanding the *content* of the instruction as information and social interaction. Similarly, learners will realize not only the cognitive need to practice with the language as a learning operation, but also the communicative need to interact and negotiate meaning to achieve successful comprehension.

A brief point is in order concerning the relationship between teaching methods and these theoretical issues. In this book, no preconception or analysis will be made as to programmatic or methodological prescriptions for teaching. As Swaffar, Arens, and Morgan (1982) have demonstrated, teachers of supposedly different methodological persuasions in fact acknowledge quite diverse and overlapping behaviors in classroom practice (cf. discussion in Stern 1983:ch. 20–21, on language teaching methods). Moreover, it will be noted in Chapters 2 and 6 that comparison studies among methods have been highly inconclusive and have rarely involved reliable, controlled observation of the classroom behaviors supposedly accompanying the methods under investigation. For these reasons, the approach here will be to describe behaviors and processes directly on the basis of exploratory or experimental classroom-oriented studies, rather than to assume the occurrence of particular classroom behaviors as consequences of adopted materials or professed methods.

Teacher talk

Theoretical attention to comprehensible input and formal instruction has led to a substantial amount of research on L2 teacher speech, often referred to as "teacher talk." The initial approach of this research has been to describe the features of L2 teacher talk which distinguish it from speech to L2 learners in noninstructional settings. Although the sociolinguistic variability in register for instructional purposes is intrinsically interesting, the main goal of this research has been to determine what makes teacher talk an aid to learning. If input to learners must be comprehensible, what factors make teacher talk in classrooms appropriate for L2 learners' differing proficiency levels? This area of research has generally attempted to explore the nature of classroom speech and, specifically, to describe and quantify the large number of features of teacher speech which might be modified – speech rate, syntax, vocabulary, pragmatic functions, and so on. Studies of these candidates for effective input in the classroom will be reviewed here, yet only a few have been investigated with respect to their effects on learners' development.

Learner behavior

The foregoing issues also lead to research goals concerning learner behavior. Whereas in the study of teacher behavior L2 researchers have tended rather narrowly to investigate teachers' linguistic and pedagogical production, learners have been viewed in a slightly broader perspective. Not only their linguistic behavior but their learning strategies and social interactions with other learners have been the target of research. Just as in the case of teacher talk, research investigates the behaviors manifested by L2 learners in classrooms, and to what extent these are related to L2 learning outcomes.

Also, since teachers are ultimately concerned with structuring the learning environment for learners so as to favor effective outcomes, some research has addressed the question of what factors (e.g., classroom grouping or tasks) facilitate optimum learning behaviors. A further notable issue in this research concerns the degree to which learners are viewed as being in control of their own learning. That is, some researchers have placed great emphasis on finding out whether learners' own initiatives, productivity, and strategies in classroom learning are the source of learning, rather than passive absorption of the teachers' information or precise adherence to the performance of classroom activities.

Interaction in the classroom

A further issue in research concerns the influence of interaction in the classroom on L2 development. Long (1980b, 1981a, 1983b) has supplemented the strict view that comprehensible input leads to acquisition with the additional notion that native speakers' speech to nonnatives is most effective for acquisition when it contains "modified interaction." These interactive features consist of ways of negotiating comprehensibility and meaning. Long suggests, in fact, that interactive modifications are more important for acquisition than modifications of NS speech that only result in simplified TL syntax and morphology.

These NS-oriented factors promoting comprehensibility have consequences for L2 learners' participation. Ellis (1980) speculated that L2 learners obtain more practice in the TL, and are more motivated to engage in further communication when they have greater opportunities to speak (e.g., when native speakers allocate turns to them) and when they achieve successful communication. (Cf. Ellis 1984b, which adds several other features of interactive discourse which he deems to be important.) This point has been underscored in research by Swain (1985). Ellis also emphasizes the benefit of the instructional focus on formal specific elements of the TL.

A further part of the argument favoring interaction hinges on a phenomenon known as "scaffolding," which derives from cognitive psychology and L1 research, and was applied to L2 acquisition by Hatch (1978). In language acquisition studies, scaffolding refers to the provision through conversation of linguistic structures that promote a learner's recognition or production of those structures or associated forms. The import of this concept is that in various conversational or other task-related interaction, the "vertical discourse" – the sequence of turns taken with conversants – aids learners in gradually incorporating portions of sentences, lexical items, reproducing sounds, etc., in meaningful ways rather than in mechanical repetition or lengthy monologues.

As a consequence of these issues, in recent years a much greater role has been attributed to interactive features of classroom behaviors, such as turn-taking, questioning and answering, negotiation of meaning, and feedback, in contrast to a more traditional view of teaching and learning which conceptualizes classroom instruction as the conveyance of information from the knowledgeable teacher to the "empty" and passive learner. Interaction is viewed as significant because it is argued that 1) only through interaction can the learner decompose the TL structures and derive meaning from classroom events, 2) interaction gives learners the opportunities to incorporate TL structures into their own speech (the scaffolding principle), and 3) the meaningfulness for learners of classroom events of any kind, whether thought of as interactive or not, will depend on the extent to which communication has been jointly constructed between the teacher and learners (Allwright 1984; Breen 1985). While the overall meaningfulness of instruction is a difficult construct to observe and evaluate, each characteristic of interaction that is considered to promote L2 development needs to be individually investigated for its contribution to communication and learning.

Methodological problems

The fact that this book is reviewing research on the preceding issues does not guarantee that the research will provide unambiguous answers to them. For economic, social, and sometimes academic reasons (e.g., poor application of research methods), research on L2 classrooms has often been flawed, incomplete in analysis, and contradictory in outcome. These problems require sound research methodology for their solution: adequate sampling of program or class types; random sampling of teachers or students; control of independent or intervening variables (such as age, language proficiency, and educational background of learners); reliable instrumentation (such as observation schedules and measures of

L2 development or attitudes); appropriate, reliable, and complete analysis; and complete reporting.

Weaknesses in these areas often lead to uninterpretable or ungeneralizable results and unjustified claims. In this book, such findings have been qualified when appropriate, although an attempt has still been made to draw from the studies the sometimes important insights they display or the implications they have for further research.

But even in studies conducted with the best designs and under the best of conditions (instrumentation and analysis), the lack of uniformity across studies in theoretical or descriptive constructs makes complete comparison difficult. On numerous occasions in the following pages, findings will be consolidated from studies which, while investigating similar phenomena, have used slightly different terminology and procedures, or have controlled and classified independent variables in different ways. For the sake of such comparisons, in several cases the raw data have been reanalyzed if they were available, for example to derive summary statistics when they were not reported or to recategorize an event in terms of another construct. In many comparative cases, some of the differences have been overlooked for the sake of revealing possible generalizations, while potential qualifications and limitations must be recognized. The purpose throughout is to promote greater consistency in theory, procedures, and analytical constructs, and to point toward further research which would resolve the discrepancies and qualifications.

Overview of the book

In the chapters that follow, the primary research studied is that conducted in L2 classrooms, in simulations of language classrooms, or in semi-instructional, tutoring interactions between teachers or L2 speakers and language learners. Reference to L1 classroom research, and to non-classroom research on L2 learners' interaction with native speakers, is occasionally made as the issues warrant, but no attempt is made to represent the current state of knowledge or the dimensions of the issues involved in the general study of L1 education or of naturalistic L2 acquisition. Likewise, the complex research on the particular forms of L2 developmental sequences, whether universals or TL-specific, will not be a focus of the book, in part because classroom research has not explored these matters, but also because the issues involved are well covered in a variety of other SLA publications (for reviews, see Hatch 1983; Ellis 1985b; Klein 1986; Larsen-Freeman and Long, in press).

Each chapter will treat the issues just outlined in greater detail. Chapter 2 presents the principal studies and concepts that have elaborated the methodology for observing and analyzing classroom instruction and interaction. Chapter 3 surveys research on the linguistic and discourse characteristics of teacher speech to L2 learners. Chapter 4 reviews research on the characteristics of learner behavior – participation and speech. Chapter 5 describes research on teacher-learner interaction. Chapter 6 draws together all of the foregoing research, as well as other studies, to determine the state of knowledge about learning outcomes resulting from teachers' and learners' classroom interaction.

Throughout the book, emphasis will be placed on a critical synthesis and on revealing limitations both of the research findings and of the methodology for classroom-oriented research. The concluding Chapter 7 will point to areas for future research on classroom teaching, outline major implications for curriculum planning and L2 instruction, and suggest ways of achieving greater consistency across classroom research studies.

2 *Classroom research methods*

Methodological approaches to the study of L2 classrooms are extremely varied, reflecting both a great diversity of research questions and purposes, and a range of theoretical perspectives on the conduct of research. In general, these approaches have followed methods adopted by researchers in native language schooling or other sociological and sociolinguistic studies of communicative interaction. But in L2 classrooms communication between teachers and L2 learners becomes a particularly important issue, so L2 methodology has had to evolve new concepts, instruments, and procedures to adequately describe and analyze interaction. The purpose of this chapter is to describe these methods with regard to their capacity to extract and validate generalizations about the social and linguistic processes occurring in L2 classrooms. The specific content of various studies, such as the study of teachers' speech modifications, language choice, feedback on error, student interaction, and other phenomena, will be dealt with more fully in subsequent chapters.

Four traditions in research

Because the study of L2 classrooms has arisen through the influence of researchers from different disciplines (education, sociology, psychology, linguistics, applied linguistics), research developments in each of these areas have separately contributed to procedures for investigation. Although it should be recognized that few researchers adopt only the procedures and analyses of one tradition, at least four traditions are distinguishable: *psychometric, interaction analysis, discourse analysis,* and *ethnographic*.

The first, the psychometric tradition, was applied in early evaluations of L2 instruction (e.g., Scherer and Wertheimer 1964), which followed as much as possible standard educational psychometric procedures, with comparison treatment groups and measurement of outcomes on proficiency tests. These context- and presage-product studies have been followed by process-product studies in this tradition (see Dunkin and Biddle's model in Figure 1.1), which investigated the quantitative relationships between various classroom activities or behaviors and language achievement (e.g., Politzer and Weiss 1969; A. Ramirez and Stromquist 1979).

The second tradition, interaction analysis, developed by the mid-1960s, when the influence of sociological investigations of group processes (e.g., Bales 1950) had led to the development of systems for the observation and analysis of classroom interaction in terms of social meanings and an inferred classroom climate ("direct" or "indirect"; Flanders 1960). This L1 educational research inspired some researchers to adapt such systems and analytical approaches to the L2 classroom (Moskowitz 1967, 1971, 1976; Wragg 1970). Inherent in this approach was, first, an interest in the nature of the dependency of student behaviors on the atmosphere and interaction engendered by the teacher. Second, researchers in this tradition have not pursued quantitative analyses, although measurement of the frequency of specific behaviors implied a quantitative focus (see Mackey's 1978 attempt to mechanize the quantification of interaction). The influence of this tradition, which views interaction as a chain of teacher and student behaviors, each one classifiable into one or another category, is seen in the third tradition.

The discourse analysis tradition arose from a linguistic perspective, an attempt to analyze fully the discourse of classroom interaction in structural-functional linguistic terms (rather than inferred social meanings). Early work by Bellack et al. (1966), which derived from Wittgenstein's (1953) notion of language use as a "game," analyzed classroom interaction as a sequence of "moves," each with its own rules for form and context of use. Four moves were identified in their analysis: "structure," "solicit," "respond," and "react." This approach was adopted for L2 classrooms by Fanselow (1977a, b), whose analytical system includes not only a dimension for pedagogical function, but also dimensions for content, speaker, and others. However, the development in this tradition of a more systematic analysis of the entire discourse of classroom interaction, exemplified for L1 classrooms by Sinclair and Coulthard (1975), has yet to result in comprehensive analytical systems for the L2 classroom. Although this approach has the potential of being applied in a quantitative fashion, its development has largely been confined to different researchers' redefining the appropriate categories used to describe discourse.

The fourth, the ethnographic tradition, arose from sociological and anthropological traditions, and has gained wide acceptance in first language classroom research in the last ten years. L1 research such as that collected in Cazden et al. (1972), Cicourel et al. (1974), Green and Wallat (1981), and Wilkinson (1982) exemplifies this "ethnographic" approach, which attempts to interpret behaviors from the perspective of the participants' different understandings rather than from the observer's or analyst's supposedly "objective" analysis. This almost strictly qualitative tradition is represented in L2 (bilingual) classroom studies by the collection in Trueba et al. (1981).

Each of these four traditions has been elaborated upon or modified by L2 researchers, often with combinations of them being adopted for particular studies. In subsequent sections these principal methodological approaches will be examined more closely, to compare their relative merits and weaknesses. But four general methodological issues are essential preliminaries to understanding the comparative strengths of these approaches. One fundamental issue involves the relationship between the quantitative and qualitative methods which each approach invariably relies on, albeit to differing degrees. A second issue concerns the instrumentation and basic categories of analysis used in classroom observation. The third pertains to the different dimensions used in multidimensional instruments for observation and analysis. The final issue regards the reliability and validity of these instruments and other observations or analysis of classroom behaviors. Following an exposition of these issues, the four approaches will be dealt with in turn.

General methodological issues

Quantitative and qualitative approaches[1]

The psychometric tradition, concerned with product outcomes, is the most "quantitative" in approach, in that its methods and instruments involve numerical measurement and statistical analysis and inference. Although the other approaches are more concerned with qualitative methods — the description of classroom behaviors, classification of processes, and more subjective inferences toward generalizations, they frequently make use of quantitative methods, for example, counting events and correlating them with others. Almost every ethnographic or discourse analytical study refers to the frequency, magnitude, or proportion of occurrences of analytical units observed (e.g., a speech act, or a type of participant structure). Generalizations from these quantifications are subject to the same statistical limitations as those derived from psychometric research. Conversely, however, the quantitative approach of the psychometric tradition is subject to qualitatively motivated limitations. How is this so?

In an article on evaluation research, Reichardt and Cook (1979) argue that quantitative and qualitative research methodologies are mutually dependent. They initially distinguish between the two methodologies as

1 I am indebted to Leo van Lier for comments relevant to this section.

supposed "paradigms" for scientific inquiry (Kuhn 1970). They list the typical contrasting attributes of each: the qualitative paradigm involves naturalistic, "uncontrolled," subjective, process-oriented observation, while a quantitative paradigm is obtrusive, controlled, objective, and product-oriented. They point out that qualitative "participant observation," in which the observer takes an active part in the processes being observed in order better to "understand" the experiences and interpretations of the subjects of study, is not necessarily naturalistic or unobtrusive, and it may be difficult to generalize beyond the case under study. Nonetheless, the qualitative paradigm permits objectivity in the form of interobserver agreement. On the other hand, the theoretical underpinnings of a quantitative approach can bias observations in some possibly unrecognized way, due to a failure to recognize some qualitative relationship or category for analysis. And yet, the quantitative paradigm can maintain a high degree of "face validity" in regard to the naturalness of observations and measurements, even in experimental, controlled conditions. These "paradigms" therefore only constitute different perspectives on the most appropriate methods to adopt for particular research questions. Arguments to this effect have also been stated recently for both education and the discipline of the cognitive sciences in general (Tikunoff and Ward 1977; Miller, Polson, and Kintsch 1984), and for classroom observation procedures in particular (Erickson 1977; Hymes 1977; van Lier 1984).

In other words, when we test hypotheses with a quantitative method, we have derived them from qualitative, conceptual considerations. Before we count, we have to decide what categories to count. Even our determination of a level of significance depends partly on what sort of qualitative effect we expect. That is, the statistical power of a test to be made depends on the degree of difference in effects of a treatment that we want to count as meaningful, as in the case of an attempt to improve students' L2 proficiency by means of a teaching method. We need first to decide how much improvement is to be expected over a specified period of time, or what degree of unexpected improvement would count as an unusual effect. Statistical measures cannot determine this "effect size" independently of our anticipated outcomes. (See Rosenthal 1984 for a practical discussion of "effect size.")

On the other hand, if we argue that qualitative research serves to generate hypotheses, we must be concerned about the replicability of the description and categories that result. Single case studies are rarely sufficient to validate the categories and aspects of behavior that are the target of qualitatively oriented research. As the methodological development of the four traditional approaches is described in the section on the traditions in perspective, the mutual dependency of qualitative and quantitative approaches will be illustrated several times.

Classroom observation and instrumentation

The categories for describing classroom processes developed both from the research need for distinguishing between teaching methods and from the need of teacher trainers for appropriate observation and evaluation instruments. In the space of about 10 years, starting in the middle 1960s, a large number of observation instruments were developed for L2 classrooms, following developments in first language research as documented in Medley and Mitzel (1963), Simon and Boyer (1970), and Rosenshine and Furst (1973). These developments and others are discussed in detail in Long (1980a), from which Table 2.1 is adapted. The last three studies in Table 2.1 are more recent and will be discussed later in this chapter.

In Table 2.1 Long has included only those instruments which were designed to describe or classify all verbal interaction in a classroom, as opposed to some subset of behaviors (e.g., questioning behavior, explanations, feedback). Nonetheless, the range of analytical categories is very great, due partly to the diverse intended purposes of the instruments. Some categories interpret the *social interactive purpose* of behaviors (e.g., Allwright's 1980 turn-taking and turn-giving categories, and Moskowitz's 1970 "jokes," "praises or encourages"); others interpret the *pedagogical function* (e.g., Jarvis's 1968 "classroom management" and "repetition reinforcement," or Fanselow's 1977a "solicit" and "respond"); others describe the *objective behavior* (e.g., Naiman et al.'s 1978 "student hand-raising" and "student callout," or Moskowitz's 1970 "student response – choral"); and still others characterize the *semantic or cognitive content* of behaviors (e.g., Fanselow's 1977a "characterize," or Bialystok, Fröhlich, and Howard's 1978 "specific information").

Many further types of categories are possible to describe the *type and grouping of participants*, the type of *activity, materials and paraphernalia* in the classroom, *discourse or linguistic phenomena*, or whatever the researcher considers relevant. Any single instrument usually will include several different types of categories (often in an unsystematic array), but several (e.g., Fanselow 1977a; Bialystok et al. 1978; and the last three studies) have specifically established dimensions for each particular type. Dimensions of instruments will be discussed in the next section, on dimensions of analysis.

As the columns in Table 2.1 suggest, the different systems can be characterized in various ways. A brief explanation of each of these is in order, but the reader is referred to Rosenshine and Furst (1973), Dunkin and Biddle (1974), and Long (1980a) for detailed discussion.

Recording procedure refers to whether or not the observer codes for the behavior every time it occurs ("category") or only whether or not it occurs in a specific period of time ("sign" – e.g., every three seconds

TABLE 2.1. CLASSIFICATION OF INSTRUMENTS FOR THE ANALYSIS OF
INTERACTION IN SECOND LANGUAGE CLASSROOMS

Authors	Type of recording procedures	Item type	Number of categories[a]	Multiple coding
Allwright (1980)	Category	High	16	Yes
Barkman (1978)	Category	Mixed	61	Yes
Bialystok, Fröhlich, & Howard (1978)	Category	Mixed	47	Yes
Capelle, Jarvella, & Revelle (n.d.)	Category	Low	27	No
	Category	Low	19	No
Carton (1966)	Category	Mixed	42	Yes
Fanselow (1977a)	Category	Low	73	Yes
Freudenstein (1976)	Sign	Mixed	53	Yes
Jarvis (1968)	Sign	Low	24	No
Long et al. (1976)	Category	Mixed	45	Yes
MacFarlane (1975)	Category	Low	17	Yes
McEwen (1976)	Sign	Mixed	36	Yes
Moskowitz (1970)	Sign	Low	10	No
(1976)	Sign	Low	34	Yes
Naiman et al. (1978)	Category	Mixed	60	Yes
Nearhoof (1965)	Sign	Low	10	No
Politzer (1980)	Category	Low	16	No
Riley (1977)	Category	Mixed	7	Yes
Rothfarb (1970)	Sign	Low	17	Yes
Seliger (1977)	Category	Low	7	Yes
Wesche (1977)	Category	Mixed	20	No
Wragg (1970)	Sign	Low	20	No
Allen et al. (1984)	Category	Mixed	83	Yes
Mitchell et al. (1981)	Category	Mixed	45	Yes
Ullmann and Geva (1983)	Category	Mixed	61	Yes
	Rating scale	High	38	No

[a]Entries based on Long's or my count or estimation; this sometimes differs from
figures and claims made in the references cited.
[b]*Source of variables*: 1, *explicit* theoretical or empirical base; 2, *implicit* theoretical or empirical base; 3, modification or synthesis of existing system(s);
4, author-originated categories. (This breakdown follows that suggested by
Rosenshine and Furst 1973.)
[c]Teacher training (TT) and/or research (res.) as stated or implied by author(s).

or every minute). A category system thus has a greater potential to
identify every behavioral event that occurs, while a sign system would
tend to avoid an extra weighting for events which occur very frequently
(i.e. many times within the specified interval) and could enhance the

Real-time coding[a]	Source of variables[b]	Intended purpose[c]	Unit of analysis[d]	Focus: range of behaviors and events sampled[e]
No	2 4	Res.	2	1 2 7 8
No	2 3 4	Res.	2	1 2 3 4 6 8
No	3	Res.	2	1 2 3 6 8
Yes	3 4	Res./TT	1	1 5 6 7
Yes	4	Res./TT	1	1 7
No	1 4	Res./TT	2	1 4 5 6 7 8
No	3 4	Res./TT	2	1 2 3 6 7
No	3 4	TT	1	1 3 5 6 7
No	2	Res.	1	1 3 6 7
No	1 3 4	Res.	2	1 4 5 6 8
Yes	2 3 4	TT	1	1 2 5 6 7
No	1 2 3 4	Res.	1	1 4 5 6 7
Yes	3	TT	1	1 5 6
No	3	TT/res.	1	1 2 5 6
No	2 4	Res.	2	1 2 3 6 7 8
Yes	3 4	TT	1	1 6
No	2 4	Res.	2	1 6
No	2 4	Res.	2	1 8
Yes	3	TT/res.	1	1 5 6
Yes	1 4	Res.	2	1
No	4	Res.	2	1 2 3 4 5 6
Yes	3	TT/res.	1	1 5 6
Yes & no	1 3 4	Res.	2	1 3 4 6 7 8
No	3 4	Res.	2	1 6 7 8
Yes	1 2 3 4	Res.	1	1 3 4 6 7 8
No	1 2 3 4	Res.	1	1 3 4 5 6 7 8

[d]*Unit of analysis*: 1, arbitrary time unit (e.g., 3 sec.); 2, analytical unit (e.g., move, cycle, episode). (This breakdown follows that suggested by Biddle 1967.)
[e]*Focus*: 1, verbal; 2, paralinguistic; 3, nonlinguistic; 4, cognitive; 5, affective; 6, pedagogical; 7, content (e.g., grammar); 8, discourse.
Source: The first section of this table adapted from Long (1980a:4–5). The last three studies were added by Chaudron for this volume.

weighting of relatively rarer events.

Item type refers to the degree of inference required of the observer in making the classification. Researchers would normally prefer low-inference categories, that is, categories whose definitions are clearly enough stated in terms of behavioral characteristics (e.g., student hand-raising or words written on the blackboard) that the observers in a real-time coding situation would reach high levels of agreement, or reliability. Yet high-inference categories, which require judgments about the function or meaning of particular behaviors, are often included in observational systems in order to accumulate information about student strategies, teacher intentions, or classroom climate. Such categories (e.g., "teacher encouragement," "student draws conclusion") require greater efforts in training potential observers or transcript coders to identify them reliably.

Multiple coding refers to the possibility in the instrument to assign more than one code to a given behavioral event. As soon as multiple codes are allowed, the instrument obviously has incorporated multiple dimensions of analysis, with one judgment being made of the pedagogical function of an event, and a second being made of, for example, the language of the event, the addressee, the cognitive content, or the affective value. This is not to say that instruments without multiple coding are in fact unidimensional, since several instruments (e.g., Moskowitz 1970) require coding with mutually exclusive categories that are mixed in terms of the criteria used in making the coding decisions (at times social, pedagogical, or linguistic); such instruments risk being either unreliable (because of increased possibility for inconsistent coding) or invalid (in the completeness of their representation of the classroom events).

Real-time coding refers to the application of the instrument, either for live classroom observation (real-time) or for the analysis of a video- or audiotaped record of the class (not real-time).

Unit of analysis is a crucial aspect of observational instruments, in that the specification of a period of time, or of an analytical linguistic or pedagogical unit, involves basic assumptions about the nature of classroom interaction. For instance, to measure pedagogical events in units of time (e.g., Politzer and Weiss 1969, Nerenz and Knop 1982) assumes that the social-psychological significance of classroom events depends on their duration. This may in fact be true with regard to certain learning tasks (cf. Carroll 1975; Rosenshine 1976; and Swain 1981; who suggest a globally positive relationship between instructional time and learning), yet the salience, effectiveness, or meaningfulness of particular instructional methods or other verbal interaction (e.g., parsing a sentence, playing a game, listening to the teacher) has no intrinsic relationship to the duration of the event. Thus, to adopt temporal units as the basic segmentation of classroom events assumes a model of cognitive processes and learning that has yet to be verified. On the other hand, similar remarks apply to the choice of pedagogical or discourse analytical units of analysis, such as the turn, the speech act, the "move," the "episode," and others that have been adopted in some instruments.

Whatever the selection of units, it is incumbent on the researcher to apply rigorous procedures that would assure reliable and valid units of analysis. This issue will be addressed later in this section.

Dimensions of analysis

A comparison of several of the most recent observation instruments reveals the degree to which quite different aspects of classroom interaction have been considered as research foci. The variety of categories used in the instruments in Table 2.1 suggests a diversity of research foci and analyses, yet when multidimensional instruments, which are intended to be more comprehensively descriptive, differ from one another in the choice of dimensions of analysis, it is evident that more conceptual and empirical research is needed. Note in Table 2.2 the dimensions into which Fanselow (1977a), Mitchell et al. (1981), Ullmann and Geva (1983), and Allen et al. (1984) divide classroom interaction. (In the following, comparison between particular categories within dimensions cannot be considered, although the fact that differences exist in virtually all cases further illustrates the, at best, purpose-specific nature of such dimensions.)

All four instruments concur that the *individuals participating* in the interaction should be identified – definitely the teacher, and with varying degrees of specificity the students as individuals or distinct subgroups. They also agree on the need for an analysis of the *content* or *topic*, although they differ considerably in the description of categories within this dimension. After this encouraging start, the amount of coincident dimensions decreases. Three schemes code for *activity* (usually an open-ended and vaguely defined set of categories within which there is little agreement on types and descriptive criteria), for student *skill use/modality* (i.e., reading, writing, listening, etc.), and for *materials* or *medium* (in which there is also minimal overlap in the sets of categories across instruments). Thereafter, each one includes several dimensions which are specific to its own purposes. Allen et al. (1984, Part B), for instance, appears to be the only instrument to include analyses of verbal interaction below the general pedagogical move, and Fanselow (1977a) is the only one concerned explicitly with the cognitive process involved in a behavior, on his dimension "How mediums are used" (e.g., "attend," "characterize," "present").

What this comparison primarily illustrates is that no one scheme in fact includes all the potentially relevant dimensions of information about classroom interaction, nor could any authors maintain that they had included the complete and mutually exclusive set of categories within any dimension. The first qualification does not invalidate the usefulness of any scheme; dimensions should be chosen that have practical or

TABLE 2.2. DIMENSIONS OF ANALYSIS

Fanselow (1977a)	Mitchell et al. (1981)	Ullmann and Geva (1983)	Allen et al. (1984) Part A	Part B
Who communicates? (i.e., speaker)	Class organization	Participants (who to whom)	Participant organization	
Content	Topic of discourse (open-ended)	Content	Content	
	Type of language activity	Activity	Activity	
	Student involvement (skill use)	Skill focus	Student modality (skill)	
		Language used		Language used
Pedagogical purpose				
				T or S verbal interaction
				Incorporation of T or S speech
Medium		Teacher medium	Materials	
		Teacher involvement		Information gap
How mediums used (cognitive)				

theoretical value for the intended use or research. The second qualification, however, raises more serious questions about the general validity of such schemes: when researchers who investigate the same basic dimensions do not agree on the categories of analysis, not only are their results not comparable, but at least one, if not all, are probably not employing a valid set of observational categories.

This last difficulty, which is shared by L1 classroom research instruments as well (cf. Dunkin and Biddle 1974), is one justification for the use of detailed analyses of discourse and ethnographic methods of research, which are intended to reveal the principles and categories of classroom interaction based on the participants' own interpretations. Applications of such methods will be considered in sections on discourse analysis and the ethnographic approach.

Reliability and validity of research instruments

PRINCIPLES OF RELIABILITY AND VALIDITY

Whether an essentially qualitative or quantitative approach is preferred by a researcher, the research goal is to produce descriptions and interpretations of classroom events, and the relationships between them, that will be identified by others as real and meaningful for teachers, learners, and learning. Researchers are furthermore concerned about the generalizability of their claims. In other words, the methodological goal of the research is validity, or the extent to which the observational apparatus and inferences drawn from it will be meaningful, significant, and applicable to further studies. Moreover, an essential element in the attainment of validity is reliability, one aspect of which includes the consistency with which others agree on the categories and descriptions and the frequencies attributed to them.

L2 classroom researchers in the psychometric, quantitatively oriented tradition have always recognized the need for reliable measurement on tests and the control of variables for internal and external validity (see any standard textbook on psychometrics and research design for these issues: e.g., Nunnally 1978; Kirk 1982), yet they have infrequently confirmed the reliability and validity of their observational measures. Similarly, many researchers adopting a process-oriented or descriptive, qualitative approach have appeared primarily to rely on the vividness and logic of their descriptions and inferences as confirmation of the validity of the descriptions. Yet this can hardly be justified merely by asserting the "interpretive" or subjective nature of the qualitative endeavor. In a discussion supporting the use of qualitative research methods, McCutcheon (1981) argues that the initially subjective, interpretive process involved in qualitative methods inevitably requires *inter*subjective agreement, because the researcher writes for an audience that must recognize the meaningfulness of the description and analysis.

The initial test for a classroom researcher developing a system for analyzing classroom events is to demonstrate the reliability of the categories involved in the system. As Frick and Semmel (1978) explain, there is a variety of methods for checking reliability of classroom observation instruments, whether uni- or multidimensional. The simplest approach is to have several raters or coders apply the system to a predetermined segment of classroom interaction, and then calculate the ratio of items agreed upon to those in disagreement (in pairs or triplets of observers, for example). Since, as was suggested in the section on instruments, the researcher must make decisions about the units of analysis, in addition to multiple dimensions and categories within dimensions, the process is not always so simple. More complex ways of determining reliability are needed (see Frick and Semmel 1978 for detailed discussion), not only for interobserver agreement but also for *intra*observer judgments, and for the use of a system with multiple sets of data.

Once reliability is established, and various procedures and steps must be employed in order to attain it,[2] the validity of the observation instrument or categories is still not assured. Further analyses are necessary to determine validity. Hoge (1985) describes various ways of validating observation instruments for L1 classroom behaviors, namely, a) *construct validity* – comparison with alternative instruments for the same behaviors, b) *criterion-related validity* – comparison with observations of events or behaviors that are related to or predicted by those on the instrument, and c) *treatment validity* – sensitivity of the instrument to "direct intervention efforts" (p. 476).

---

2 The following is an example of a procedure for determining reliability on the coding of transcripts of classroom lessons. This procedure was developed by Chaudron and others at the University of Hawaii for the study of J. D. Ramirez et al. (1986) of elementary bilingual education programs: "Four-page segments of two transcripts were coded according to the guidelines by three coders who reached consensus on the codes. Three- to four-page segments of four additional transcripts were coded separately by two of these coders until 90% agreement was reached, and the remaining differences were used to establish modifications and clarifications of the guidelines, and a standard set of codes for the entire set of training transcripts. The first two transcripts were then discussed in group with all the coders to assure understanding of the guidelines.

"Each coder then independently coded one segment of a transcript at a time, until 85% agreement with the standard codes was reached on a given training transcript. After reaching this criterion of reliability, and discussion of the remaining differences in coding, each coder proceeded to code, to the extent possible, the classroom transcripts that he or she had transcribed" (pp. 39–40).

EXAMPLES OF RELIABILITY AND VALIDITY
IN INSTRUMENTS

The proposers of the different observation or analytical systems have rarely reported reliability estimates in use of the instruments, nor have they performed careful or appropriate validation procedures. Naiman et al. (1978), who conducted one of the more carefully developed classroom observation studies, claim that coders reached high levels of agreement during training with the instruments. They do not report these results further; nor do they report whether reliability was determined during the actual study. A different reliability problem was pointed out by L. Bailey (1975), who observed that in the case of the Flanders interaction analysis system, which Moskowitz's (1970/1976) Foreign Language interaction (FLint) system is based on, the method for determining reliability easily overestimates and in fact obscures the event-by-event agreement between observers, since it is based on total accumulated tallies for the categories, not agreement for each event.

Few, if any, instruments have reported extensive enough use and findings for one to judge their validity. Several efforts have been made, however. Moskowitz (1976) intended to determine criterion-related validity by using a revised version of the FLint system to ascertain differences between 11 high school L2 French and Spanish teachers who were rated excellent by their former pupils, and an equal number of "typical" teachers representing a presumed range of effectiveness. Despite this effort, in which there were statistically significant differences between the groups in several categories, no independent theoretical hypotheses were made as to which categories would be most or least appropriate for excellent teachers, so the ex post facto results cannot be used to validate the meaningfulness of the categories. Given the retrospective nature of the student ratings, this research serves more to generate hypotheses about good teaching than to test them. One would have to use the instrument to group teachers as excellent or not excellent based on the specified categories, then independently evaluate differences in their students' achievement.

In recent years, several classroom research teams have developed observation systems with more explicit concern for establishing reliability and validity (see, e.g., the last three studies in Table 2.1). All of these systems attempt to categorize the entire range of possible events that might occur in an L2 classroom. Additionally, each of them exemplifies a slightly different approach to validation.

Mitchell et al. (1981) developed their instrument to study French as a foreign language (FFL) classes in Scotland in a basic process-product correlational design. They report the procedure employed for estimating interrater reliability in using the instrument to code a sample of recorded lessons. Two researchers trained in the category definitions independently coded the activities as they played them back on the recording, and simple percentage agreement of assigned categories was determined. The procedure with a multidimensional instrument such as this one is necessarily first one of ascertaining agreement on the segmentation of the recordings, then of determining agreement on categories within dimensions. Mitchell et al. do not make explicit how agreement was calculated, except for the segmentation into analytical units (simple percentage of activity topics that were segmented the same by both coders, divided by the total of instances segmented by either of them and thus eligible for agreement).

Evidently, they found agreement of 70% or better to be satisfactory (a rather lenient criterion), but in the agreement on assignment of categories within activity types, they found it necessary to adjust or sometimes eliminate the original definitions and categories in order to resolve conflicts or confusions. After revising on the basis of these reliability trials, they proceeded to use the instrument to code 147 lessons by 17 teachers in six schools over the course of two school terms. The authors admit that it would have been preferable to estimate further reliability with the revised instrument. In principle, coders should attain high criterion levels of reliability with fixed instruments *before* applying the instrument further.

Yet the reliability of Mitchell et al.'s instrument was confirmed somewhat by a double application of the instrument on 13 of the teachers, at both early and late observations during the period. They report rather consistent levels of occurrence of most activities across observation periods. This amounts to a test-retest form of reliability estimation, which is an initial approach to construct validation. To consider this a reliability test assumes, however, that little variation or development would occur in classroom activities over the year. As Stodolsky (1984) notes, however, such stability has not been attested.

Ullmann and Geva (1983) report a case intended to establish construct validation. For their Target Language Observation Scheme (TALOS), they designed two different instruments, one a real-time low-inference category instrument (simple classroom behaviors and events) and the other a high-inference rating scale (judgments about the overall degree of occurrence of similar events), to be completed following a lesson. In addition to reporting high interrater percentage agreement (no figures are given) on pilot coding in elementary French as a second language (FSL) classes, they suggest that comparison of results on the same classrooms using the two coding schemes independently would amount to a reciprocal validation of each, since the same theoretical constructs can be extracted from both.

Allen et al. (1984) developed the Communicative Orientation of Language Teaching (COLT) instrument for a large-scale evaluation of communicative language teaching, with the intention of discriminating among language teaching programs by means of categories on the instrument (i.e., criterion-related validity). The instrument is divided into two parts (see Table 2.2). Part A (on lesson activities) is designed for real-time coding, and Part B (on verbal interaction) for postlesson analysis from tape recordings. Because of the research purposes, the authors are concerned about the validation of the instrument as a measure of degree of communicative language teaching. Although they do not report reliability estimates, claiming that reliability would be tested in later uses, Fröhlich, Spada, and Allen (1985) do report the results of a pilot application of the instrument in 13 traditional FSL, immersion FSL, and English as a second language (ESL) classes, mostly at grade 7 level. They propose that the instrument had validity in ascertaining differences among the programs and classes, as measured by the relative frequency of communicative behaviors and activities observed. The criterion in this case is simply the independent classification of the programs on a communicative teaching continuum.

Their approach is essentially to claim that the different FSL (immersion, extended immersion, and core) and ESL classes are programmatically determined to differ in communicative orientation, and thus, when the instrument indeed finds the frequency of communicative categories varying according to the independent ranking, it is thereby validated. In order to demonstrate this validation beyond a category-by-category analysis of the correlation with the predicted order across programs, Fröhlich et al. calculated a simplified score based on observed frequencies in five selected categories (amount of group work, focus on meaning, topic control, use of extended text, and use of semi- and nonpedagogical materials) that are presumed to characterize the degree of communicative activity. This rough metric produced an ordering (a "communicative continuum") that conformed to the expected ranking. Although this appears to be a way of simplifying the comparison of a complex system of categories with a simple scale of program type, there are obvious problems with the procedure, aside from the uncertainty of independent classification of the programs into communicative orientation, or the arbitrariness of selection of the categories for the discrimination test. For one, in principle there seems to be no reason to assign equal weighting to each of the five categories selected; the simplifying calculation resulted in little variation in the scores among programs on three of the five categories. Also, the total derived values for the four programs (6, 7, 10, and 12) resulted more in a two-way split among them than in a discrimination among all four.

The problem therefore remains as to how researchers can validate their complex systems of categories. The L2 research discussed here does not go far enough to establish confidence in the use of entire instruments, nor even in the individual categories used in observation. Each researcher or team chooses to adopt slightly different dimensions and categories, depending on the purposes or theoretical orientation of the study, which leads to results that are difficult if not impossible to compare across studies. The solution resides, in part at least, in a careful development of research on specific sorts of classroom behaviors that would validate their meaningfulness for L2 learning, and in the construction of an empirically and conceptually grounded theory of interaction and language learning in L2 classrooms.

The traditions in perspective

A closer examination of the four traditions outlined in the first section of this chapter is in order. In addition to a more detailed history and exemplification of the techniques and descriptive apparatus of each approach, the ways in which each tradition succeeds or fails in developing understanding and generalizations about L2 classrooms will be considered.

The psychometric approach

The most traditional approach to the study of L2 classrooms involves comparison of the effects of specific instructional programs or methods on student learning outcomes, as measured by standardized proficiency tests or instruction-related achievement tests. This program (context)-product approach was taken by most language education researchers in the post-World War II period until the 1970s (Agard and Dunkel 1948; Scherer and Wertheimer 1964; Smith 1970; and see research review in Smith and in Levin 1972, as well as an overview of design issues in Beretta, in press).

The common method in such comparative evaluation research involves a classification of school curriculum or classroom instructional methodology as being of one or another type. For example, in the case of Scherer and Wertheimer's study of college-level German as a foreign language instruction (1964), the comparison was between the traditional "multiple approach method" (a grammar-translation method emphasizing all language skills) and the (at the time) innovative audiolingual approach (emphasizing listening and speaking skills in dialogue practice). The progress of one cohort of students following each method (in several classes each) was evaluated at several times in a two-year period. Statistical tests of differences between language test results for the two groups (*t*-tests) revealed that each method produced significantly positive effects, in either year one or year two, in precisely the skills given most emphasis by the method (i.e., reading and translation for the traditional, listening and speaking for the experimental).

In a study encompassing many schools in a large school district, Smith (1970) addressed a similar issue, namely, the relative effects of grammar-translation, audiolingual ("functional skills"), and "functional skills + grammar" instructional methods in French and German high school programs. The complex results have proved difficult to interpret, if not entirely inconclusive (see debate in the *Foreign Language Annals* 3/2, 1969, and the *Modern Language Journal* 53/6, 1969). As Krashen (1982) has pointed out, the statistically significant differences between comparison groups in such studies typically favor specific groups only on specific skill measures, yet these differences tend to disappear over time. Moreover, while significant in a statistical sense, the quantitative results do not suggest any practically relevant differences in terms of learning (that is, the effect size is pedagogically trivial).

More recently, international interest in the differential effects of programs in bilingual education and traditional second language instruction, or even "submersion" in the target language, has also led researchers to adopt a quantitative program-product approach (see reviews in Trueba 1979; Baker and de Kanter 1981; Swain and Lapkin 1982; and Genesee 1985; see also Burstall et al. 1974, a study of program differences between early and late introduction of traditional L2 instruction). These studies have typically compared classifications of curricular plans, rather than instructional methodologies. The results of such school comparisons are also difficult to interpret, to the extent that different schools and districts are involved, since the identification of a particular program type (e.g., transitional bilingual, immersion, full bilingual, pull-out ESL, and so on) across schools or districts is usually confounded with other factors, such as social class differences, community support, and the particular implementation at each site. J. D. Ramirez et al. (1986) is a longitudinal study which is attempting to control these factors: the primary differences between the three instructional programs studied appears to be in the distribution of language use by teachers and students (see further discussion in Chapter 3). It has typically been the case, as Baker and de Kanter (1981) illustrate, that findings are often mixed for a given program type, although it should be noted that there are relatively clear trends showing average or better-than-average performance of students in the various innovative bilingual programs over the long run.

The concern at this point is not with the specific outcomes of the methods or programs involved in such comparisons. The question is, how do we know that what actually happens in a program matches its official description? Is a grammar-translation program actually doing grammar translation and not functional skills? Unless care is taken to validate the distinctions made in the classification by method/program, any results in favor of a given type are meaningless. This is to say that both a context-process and a process-product component are essential to the design of such research. Few comparative evaluation researchers have systematically described the classroom processes in the different control and experimental classes. Many, if not most, have recognized the need for this control over process, but they have usually only managed to ensure appropriate implementation of the program/method by occasional visits, specification of materials, pre-training of instructors, teachers' self-reports, and so on. Yet these procedures have regrettably not ensured that the classroom processes across methods or programs differ from one another or are consistent within each type. In a review of methods comparison studies, Beretta (in press) points out that virtually all of them fail to include classroom observation as a component of the evaluation, and the one he cites which did (namely, Smith 1970) used different observation scales for each method. (Ramirez et al. 1986 is a further exception, for they used the same analytical system for all programs.) Therefore, because of uncertainty about qualitative distinctions, we remain unenlightened about the precise quantitative effects of types of instruction on learning outcomes.

Recognizing this weakness in comparison studies, some researchers in the late 1960s and early 1970s began to investigate quantitative relationships between more specifically defined classroom processes and learning outcomes (Politzer and Weiss 1969; Politzer 1970; Naiman et al. 1978; McDonald, Stone, and Yates 1977; A. Ramirez and Stromquist 1979). These studies are usually limited by their not having developed comprehensive validated categories of instructional processes, or by their failing to establish theoretical links between the processes observed and outcomes; they have tended to be exploratory, hypothesis-generating studies using correlational inferential statistics. Such problems have plagued L1 classroom research for some time (Adams 1972; Dunkin and Biddle 1974). Several of these process-product studies will be referred to in the next sections, as well as in Chapter 6, but one will be used to illustrate the methodology here.

Politzer and Weiss (1969; and cf. Politzer 1970) studied high school FFL classes conducted with audiolingual materials. They had raters observe videotape samples of 17 teachers and score each on several process variables (six drill types, and time and frequency of each type, as well as four other categories: reference to book, use of visual aids, student-student interaction, and variation of structures practiced). They then calculated zero-order correlation coefficients between the frequency of the behaviors and students' achievement at the end of their first semester.

The researchers report high interrater reliability in assigning ratings, and the categories observed are recognizable as classroom behaviors (i.e., they have face validity); on the other hand, there is no theoretical justification for the choice of these particular categories instead of any others, so that whatever behaviors show significant correlations with the criterion test outcomes, there are few theoretical grounds for interpreting a direct relationship between the processes and learning products. They might show a correlation, but the observed processes could in fact be results, or composites, of other unobserved variables.

In addition, Politzer (1970) admits that such ex post facto correlation between achievement and measures of duration or frequency of specific classroom activities could tend to conceal true effective or ineffective relationships between the activities and learning, due to coincidental over- or underuse of the activities in the classrooms studied. These teachers were not being explicitly directed to follow theoretically motivated applications of the activities. Without better control over teachers' relative emphasis placed on different activities, few causal inferences can be drawn about the observed classes. There is neither construct, criterion-related, nor treatment validation. Barring an improvement in design and data collection, one quantitative solution to this problem is to apply more sophisticated multiple correlation or factor analytical procedures, which can evaluate the differential influence of each activity independent of the effects of the others. This approach was taken by McDonald et al. (1977), whose study will be discussed in Chapter 6.

The interaction analysis approach

For the purpose of illustration, several representative instruments for observation and analysis will be compared here from among those cited in Table 2.1. Of the earlier instruments for observation of classroom interaction, the most well known was that of Moskowitz (1968, 1970, 1971), shown in Table 2.3. This FLint instrument was derived from Bales's (1950) work on group processes and Flanders's (1960/1970) adaptation of this for classrooms. Moskowitz's adaptation for L2 classrooms involved the separate simultaneous coding for language of each behavior (1970), and later, categories for drill and feedback behaviors (1976) and the like. This system was designed for real-time coding in three-second intervals, where in each interval the observer would place a tally in a grid of columns and rows both representing the same categories. The tally represents the paired sequence of behaviors just observed, with the first behavior category determining the row and the next behavior the column of the tally. The second behavior is then paired with the following one in a new row and column tally.

Two multidimensional systems (see Table 2.2) for observing interaction are also shown in the following figures in their fuller form. One

TABLE 2.3.   THE FLINT SYSTEM

Teacher talk — *Indirect influence*	1.	*Deals with feelings:* In a nonthreatening way, accepting, discussing, referring to, or communicating understanding of past, present, or future feelings of students.
	2.	*Praises or encourages:* Praising, complimenting, telling students why what they have said or done is valued. Encouraging students to continue, trying to give them confidence. Confirming answers are correct.
	2a.	*Jokes:* Intentional joking, kidding, making puns, attempting to be humorous, providing the joking is not at anyone's expense. Unintentional humor is not included in this category.
	3.	*Uses ideas of students:* Clarifying, using, interpreting, summarizing the ideas of students. The ideas must be rephrased by the teacher but still recognized as being student contributions.
	3a.	*Repeats student response verbatim:* Repeating the exact words of students after they participate.
	4.	*Asks questions:* Asking questions to which an answer is anticipated. Rhetorical questions are *not* included in this category.
Direct influence	5.	*Gives information:* Giving information, facts, own opinion or ideas, lecturing, or asking rhetorical questions.
	5a.	*Corrects without rejection:* Telling students who have made a mistake the correct response without using words or intonations which communicate criticism.
	6.	*Gives directions:* Giving directions, requests, or commands which students are expected to follow.
	6a.	*Directs pattern drills:* Giving statements which students are expected to repeat exactly, to make substitutions in (i.e., substitution drills), or to change from one form to another (i.e., transformation drills).
	7.	*Criticizes student behavior:* Rejecting the behavior of students; trying to change the nonacceptable behavior; communicating anger, displeasure, annoyance, dissatisfaction with what students are doing.
	7a.	*Criticizes student response:* Telling the student his response is not correct or acceptable and communicating by words or intonation criticism, displeasure, annoyance, rejection.
Student talk	8.	*Student response, specific:* Responding to the teacher within a specific and limited range of available or previously shaped answers. Reading aloud.
	8a.	*Student response, choral:* Choral response by the total class or part of the class.
	9.	*Student response, open-ended or student-initiated:* Responding to the teacher with students' own ideas, opinions, reactions, feelings. Giving one from among many possible answers which have been previously shaped but from which students must now make a selection. Initiating the participation.

TABLE 2.3.   *(continued)*

10.	*Silence:* Pauses in the interaction. Periods of quiet during which there is no verbal interaction.
10a.	*Silence-AV:* Silence in the interaction during which a piece of audio-visual equipment, e.g., a tape recorder, filmstrip projector, record player, etc., is being used to communicate.
11.	*Confusion, work-oriented:* More than one person at a time talking, so the interaction cannot be recorded. Students calling out excitedly, eager to participate or respond, concerned with task at hand.
11a.	*Confusion, non-work-oriented:* More than one person at a time talking, so the interaction cannot be recorded. Students out-of-order, not behaving as the teacher wishes, not concerned with task at hand.
12.	*Laughter:* Laughing, giggling by the class, individuals, and/or the teacher.
e.	*Uses English:* Use of English (the native language) by the teacher or the students. This category is always combined with one of the 15 categories from 1 to 9.
n.	*Nonverbal:* Nonverbal gestures or facial expressions by the teacher or the student which communicate without the use of words. This category is always combined with one of the categories of teacher or pupil behavior.

Source: Reprinted with permission from G. Moskowitz, "Interaction analysis: a new modern language for supervisors," *Foreign Language Annals* 5: 213 (1971).

is Fanselow's (1977a) system for either live observation or analysis from a recording, which was discussed earlier and is shown in Figure 2.1. This Foci for Observing Communications Used in Settings (FOCUS) instrument illustrates the use of different analytical dimensions for multiple coding. The unit of analysis, instead of a temporal judgment, is the pedagogical discourse "move," with the categories of the pedagogical purpose dimension (structuring, soliciting, responding, reacting) constituting the major criteria for segmenting the classroom interaction. Fanselow adopted these four categories directly from the L1 classroom research of Bellack et al. (1966), but he entirely modified their instructional content dimensions and added the "medium" and "use of medium" dimensions.

Another system is that developed by Naiman et al. (1978) for real-time observation, shown in Figure 2.2. This instrument is similar to that of Fanselow, in that it maintains several dimensions (pedagogical discourse, activity, mode, subject matter, and clues), but it breaks down in

1. Who communicates?

2. What is the pedagogical purpose of the communication?*

3. What mediums are used to communicate content?

4. How are the mediums used to communicate areas of content?**

5. What areas of content are communicated?**

	to structure	linguistic	1 attend	language systems
		aural		contextual
		visual	2 characterize	grammatical
				literary
			21 differentiate	meaning
		ideogram		
			22 evaluate	
		transcribed		mechanics of writing
		written	23 examine	
			24 illustrate	sound
				segmental
				supra-seg.
		other	25 label	
	to solicit		3 present	speech production
		nonlinguistic		
		aural	31 call words	unclassified
teacher			32 change medium	
		visual		life
			33 question	
individual student				

				formula
	real	34 state		imagination
	representational	4 relate		personal
	schematic	41 explain		public
to respond	symbolic	42 interpret		skills
	other			social issues
group of students	para-linguistic	5 re-present		procedure
	aural	51 combine		administration
	visual	52 imitate		cl. social behav.
	real	53 paraphrase		teaching dir.
to react	symbolic	54 sub and change		tchg. rationale
	other	55 sub no change		subject matter
class		56 transform		

*These four pedagogical purposes are from Bellack.
**The uses and areas of content are presented alphabetically.

Figure 2.1 Five characteristics of communication in settings. (From "Beyond 'Rashomon,'" by John F. Fanselow, 1977, TESOL Quarterly 11, pp. 34–35. © TESOL 1977. Reprinted by permission.)

A. ELICITATIVE
1. Elicits specific information (+ clues)
2. Elicits general information (+ clues)
3. Elicits clarification
4. Elicits elaboration
5. Elicits repetition of preceding statement (or asking the student to "speak up")
6. Elicits recommencement of previous response
7. Elicits confirmation of comprehension (or asking if there are any questions)
8. Elicits a complete response
9. Elicits correction
10. Elicits other activities (+ activities)

B. RESPONSIVE
1. Gives a complete response
2. Gives a partial response
3. Gives no response (or says "I don't know")
4. Continues responding
5. Questions or comments on preceding statements, responses, etc.

Aspects of Responses
(a) + repetition (/partial repetition)
(b) with self-correction (b with help)
(c) + clarification
(d) + elaboration
(e) with circumlocution
(f) callouts
(g) not volunteering a response
(h) with hesitation (initial, medial)

C. EVALUATIVE
1. Accepts response
2. Partially accepts response
3. Rejects response
4. Gives no feedback
5. Reacts to behavior
Aspects of Evaluation
(a) + repetition (/partial repetition)
(b) + correction
   (1) explicit
   (2) implicit
   (3) localization of incorrectness
   (4) indication of incorrectness

(c) + clarification
(d) + elaboration
(e) + providing the answer
    (/partially providing)

CLUES
EM   emphasis clue
GR   grammar clue
IL   intralingual clue
EL   extralingual clue
CR   crosslingual clue

ACTIVITIES
R   reading
WR   writing
DR   drill
RT   rote
XR   exercises
MM   memorized material
RO   role playing
MC   mutual correction
DC   declension

MODE (free-speaking assumed)

Oral
R   reading
TR   tape recorder

Visual
BB   blackboard
PM   printed matter
G   gestures
P   pictorial

SUBJECT MATTER
1. Phonology
2. Syntax
3. Lexicon
4. Homework, etc.

TONE OF EVALUATION

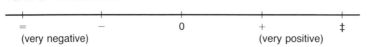

=   −   0   +   ‡
(very negative)   (very positive)

Figure 2.2 Coding categories and additional coding symbols. (Reprinted with permission from The Good Language Learner, *pp. 34–35, by N. Naiman et al., © 1978 OISE Press, The Ontario Institute for Studies in Education, Toronto.)*

OTHER SYMBOLS   *Meaning*
↑   answering with rising intonation
E   use of English (native language)
↘ E   reaction to an English insertion
→L2   asking for an equivalent in the second language
⌐┐   interruption

ELICITATIVE | RESPONSIVE | EVALUATIVE

the question has been asked before

the teacher turns to someone else to ask the same question

= = =
1, or 2, 3 etc.   request for the identical information

Figure 2.2 (cont.)

more detail the pedagogical function of the linguistic units being analyzed (clarification, elaboration, repetition, etc.). However, the unit of analysis is, like Fanselow's, a pedagogical "move" (elicitative, responsive, evaluative). With the simultaneous subcodes for evaluation and clues, Naiman et al. were especially interested in the sort of information a teacher might provide when giving feedback following learners' errors or lack of response.

Several points deserve mention with regard to the Moskowitz, Fanselow, and Naiman et al. systems. An immediately obvious point in comparing them is that the latter two allow analysis of the interactive structure of discourse beyond a pairwise linking. This difference alone reveals an intrinsic weakness of a FLint type of interaction analysis: it can consider no units of interaction besides one behavior and its immediate predecessor or follower. The essence of Fanselow's and Naiman et al.'s instruments, on the other hand, is to consider pedagogical events as, at minimum, a sequence of moves of some sort, the most typical in the classroom being the well-known "teaching cycle" − solicit (elicit)/respond/react (evaluate).[3] A simple example should help to illustrate this point:

Teacher: What part of speech is *from*?   [Solicit]
Student: A preposition.   [Respond]
Teacher: (shakes student's hand)   [React]

(Fanselow 1977a:38)

3 Note that Naiman et al. (1978) lack a "structure" category, principally because they were investigating student learning characteristics and their dependency on teachers' elicitation or evaluative behaviors.

Whereas Fanselow's system, coding this directly or from an audio- or videotaped recording (and/or transcript), will account for the complete sequence of three moves, at least two tallies would appear in Moskowitz's instrument, representing the solicit/respond ("asks questions/student response, specific") and the respond/react ("student response, specific/praises") separately.

A second point to note about these systems is that, in fact, the unit of analysis by which the classroom events are segmented is not well specified in the Fanselow and Naiman et al. category systems. (The three-second unit in Moskowitz's scheme obviously obscures the highly different behavioral units in which the various coded events would occur.) The move in Fanselow's case, and the various teacher eliciting and evaluating, or student responding, actions in Naiman et al.'s scheme, do not specify in what way the discourse is to be segmented. Consider a short sample of classroom discourse from a beginner's ESL class in secondary school (from unpublished data collected by the author) to see what their approaches involve.

1   Teacher: The plural for number five, Lisa.
2   Lisa: What is this—
3   Teacher: Plural!
4   Lisa: What are these. These are books.
5   Teacher: Very good! Very good!
6   All right, if I said, uh, this is a man.
7   What would be the plural?
8   Student: These are men. M E N.
9   Teacher: Good! Good memory!

One might expect each categorical decision to be made primarily on the basis of some observable change in pedagogical function or behavior, as in the switch from praise feedback to the next structuring move, in lines 5 and 6. But such a switch might occur at a variety of points in a participant's speech: at the end of a tone group (indicated by the period in line 6), after a word within a tone group (possibly after the "right" in line 6), after a "sentence" (the graphic representation of a propositionally complete tone group), or a sequence of sentences (as in line 5). The unit of analysis should preferably be determined before the decision of pedagogical function. However, there is an implied segmentation, in examples provided by these researchers, of an independent utterance-boundary segmentation, which is made on the basis either of a speaker turn or of a "sentence" final intonation (see further discussion on discourse analysis which follows). The researcher is then faced with the decision of whether or not to assign one code to *each* turn or other segment (e.g., each "Very good" in line 5 would count as a separate praise), regardless of whether or not a sequence of those segments in fact incorporates a change in function. Quantitative analysis based on such observations thus risks being misrepresentative of the frequency of types of event, in the same way as does the temporally based analysis of Politzer (1970).

A third point about these systems relates to the interpretive complexity of deciding among categories. Each decision must be made on the basis of either the nonverbal or linguistic behavior alone, or the surrounding discourse (i.e., the extent of low or high inference involved). Except in the rare case of fixed linguistic forms with one function, it is a crucial fact of any analysis of discourse that the analysis must *interpret* the meaning of a given segment in terms of its context. Thus, interpretation of any category involving "repeats," "comments on preceding state-ments," "elicits," "elaborates," "paraphrases," "partial response," among many others, relies on the contingent relationships between the current and the preceding or upcoming discourse. Although many verbal behaviors can be quickly and confidently identified as questions (one kind of elicit/solicit), evaluative reactions, or provision of information, there are frequently finer nuances of meaning and tacit rules of discourse implicit in even the simplest expression, converting a question into a (rhetorical) structuring-informational event ("So what can we do about this?"), an evaluation into an implied elicitation ("Not quite . . . "), an informational utterance into an evaluation ("The problem you're having has to do with the past tense"). This fact then requires that the analysis take account not only of the immediate context but the entire proceedings of a lesson. The history of the teacher-student relationships, develop-ments in the lesson content, or the teacher's explicit or implicit expec-tations for student responsiveness can influence the interpretation of virtually any expression (see Edmondson 1980, 1985, on related points). Nevertheless, this context dependency does not invalidate the possibility of applying systems such as those discussed here, although it does limit the final power of the analysis to describe and explain fully what took place in a given situation.

A fourth point follows logically from the preceding ones. At least one condition for observational instruments to be reliable in application and validly related to the events they describe is that the behaviors within any single dimension must be classified with an exhaustive yet mutually exclusive set of categories (called a "facet"), as argued by Dunkin and Biddle (1974:72–74). This ensures that all the behaviors observed are in fact classified and that none is ambiguously in more than one category. If this were not the case, then any quantified results based on the system would also be ambiguous or misrepresentative of the events in some way. A faceted system does not ensure, however, that the categories themselves are the most meaningful (i.e., valid) ones for the purposes of research. To take an obvious though unlikely example, classifying all events in terms of laughter or nonlaughter will not be helpful in research on content learning.

As was shown earlier in the section on reliability and validity, these observational instruments have not been subjected to thorough validation, in the sense that the coded events are shown to have consistent relationships with actual teaching and learning behaviors or outcomes. The derivation of categories for most instruments has tended to be rather idiosyncratic to each researcher and research purpose, rarely based on systematic theoretical argumentation or empirical tests of categories. The result has been, as with L1 classroom research (cf. Adams 1972), a proliferation of terms and categories, much in need of empirical validation.

The discourse analysis approach

The third approach to classroom research, discourse analysis, followed from the evolution in descriptive linguistics of analytical procedures for the description of suprasentential structures (see van Dijk 1972, 1977, 1985; Grimes 1975; Dressler 1978), as well as from ethnographic and sociolinguistic investigations into the structure of interaction (Hymes 1962, 1964; Gumperz and Hymes 1972; and see the following section on ethnographic approaches). The L1 classroom research of Bellack et al. (1966) is the primary early example of this tradition in education, but these researchers credited no particular theoretical foundations other than the work of Wittgenstein (1953).

A major step was made in the discourse analysis of L1 classrooms with the research of Sinclair and Coulthard (1975) on British elementary school classrooms with minority children. They incorporated both the linguistic and sociolinguistic traditions in their conception of classroom interaction as a hierarchically structured system of "ranks," analogous to the rank scale approach to sentential linguistic description (see Halliday 1961).[4] In their system, shown in Figure 2.3, the analytical level of discourse falls in between that of the linguistic level of sentential analysis and the social/pedagogical level of programs and courses. The discourse level is comprised of five ranks (lesson, transaction, exchange, move, act), each of which constitutes the elements of the rank above, according to rank-specific structural rules.

In this scheme, then, the pedagogical "move" seen before in Bellack

---

4 Malcolm's (1986a) observational system is an interesting combination of a Hallidayan perspective with a partly discourse-analytical, partly interaction-analysis component.

et al.'s (1966) and Fanselow's (1977a) schemes in fact consists of various structures, which are realized by "acts," each act having a specific discourse function (see "classes of act"). For example, an "opening" move (in Rank IV) consists of a "head" act, either elicitation, directive, informative, or check, and several possible adjunct acts, such as markers, prompts, and nominations. These acts resemble the concept of "speech act" (Searle 1969), a major unit of pragmatic analysis of language in use. Acts thus constitute the elements of each of the five types of move, just as structured sequences of move constitute either "boundary exchanges" or "teaching exchanges," and so on up the ranks.

Sinclair and Coulthard developed this system with a team of researchers on the basis of observation and a flexible application of basic categories, allowing modifications as the data presented new contrasts and acts for analysis. (They do not describe the full data sample nor the many steps in the derivation of their system.) They argue that an adequate descriptive system of this sort must satisfy the following four criteria:

A. The descriptive apparatus must be finite...
B. The symbols or terms... should be precisely relatable to their exponents in the data...
C. ...the descriptive system should be comprehensive...
D. There must be at least one impossible combination of symbols...

(1975:15–16)

Their segmentation of the classroom discourse into act units and higher ranks follows from considerations of grammar, of the situation-dependent function and meaning, and of the "tactical" placement (according to the expected discourse structure) of any utterance or portion of an utterance.[5]

As with interaction analysis, such discourse analytical procedures may

---

5 Sinclair and Coulthard use a definition of "utterance" that coincides with the bounding of a speaker's turn by the speech of another speaker. They do not fully address the complex problem of segmentation, however. While many discourse analysts appear to adopt the same principle for segmenting into utterances, this and other terms have not been fully conventionalized, so that one also finds the term "utterance" used to refer to segments of speech bounded by pauses, breaths, or final intonation contours (Scollon 1974). Scollon and Scollon (1979:75–80, 146), however, avoid such a clear-cut usage, considering these criteria as evidence only of clause boundaries. Stubbs (1983) and G. Brown and Yule (1983) tend to avoid an explicit commitment to an independent means of segmenting discourse. It would therefore seem that analysts might select whatever physical (breaths, pauses, interruptions) or functional (semantic meanings or pragmatic force) criteria that appear useful to segment the discourse. Such procedures risk being circular, however, if the categorization of acts is also made in functional terms. As will be seen in Table 2.4, a preferred definition of utterance starts with the physical intonation contour and considers secondary features, such as other speakers or pauses, as criterial if they occur.

Figure 2.3. Levels and ranks and the system of analysis. (Reprinted with permission from Towards an Analysis of Discourse, pp. 24–27, by J. McH. Sinclair and Malcolm Coulthard. London: Oxford University Press, 1975.)

Nonlinguistic Organization	DISCOURSE	Grammar
course period topic	LESSON TRANSACTION EXCHANGE MOVE ACT	sentence clause group word morpheme

Rank I: Lesson

Elements of structure	Structures	Classes
	An unordered series of transactions	

Rank II: Transaction

Elements of structure	Structures	Classes of exchange
Preliminary (P) Medial (M) Terminal (T)	PM (M^2 ... M^n) (T)	P, T: Boundary (II.1) M: Teaching (II.2)

Rank III: Exchange (Boundary)

Elements of structure	Structures	Classes of move
Frame (Fr) Focus (Fo)	(Fr) (Fo)	Fr: Framing (III.1) Fo: Focusing (III.2)

Rank III: Exchange (Teaching)

Elements of structure	Structures	Classes of move
Initiation (I) Response (R) Feedback (F)	I (R) (F)	I: Opening (III.3) R: Answering (III.4) F: Follow-up (III.5)

Rank IV: Move (Opening)

Elements of structure	Structures	Classes of act
signal(s) pre-head (pre-h) head (h) post-head (post-h) select (sel)	(s) (pre-h) h (post-h) (sel) (sel) (pre-h) h	s: marker (IV.1) pre-h: starter (IV.2) h: system operating at h; choice of elicitation, directive, informative, check (IV.3) post-h: system operating at post-h; choice from prompt and clue (IV.4) sel: ((cue) bid) nomination (IV.5)

Rank IV: Move (Answering)

Elements of structure	Structures	Classes of act
pre-head (pre-h) head (h) post-head (post-h)	(pre-h) h (post-h)	pre-h: acknowledge (IV.6) h: system operating at h; choice of reply, react, acknowledge (IV.7) post-h: comment (IV.8)

Rank IV: Move (Follow-up)

Elements of structure	Structures	Classes of act
pre-head (pre-h) head (h) post-head (post-h)	(pre-h) (h) (post-h)	pre-h: accept (IV.9) h: evaluate (IV.10) post-h: comment (IV.8)

Rank IV: Move (Framing)

Elements of structure	Structures	Classes of act
head (h) qualifier (q)	hq	h: marker (IV.1) q: silent stress (IV.11)

Rank IV: Move (Focusing)

Elements of structure	Structures	Classes of act
signal(s) pre-head (pre-h) head (h) post-head (post-h)	(s) (pre-h) h (post-h)	s: marker (IV.1) pre-h: starter (IV.2) h: system at h; choice from metastatement or conclusion (IV.12) post-h: comment (IV.8)

or may not result in low-inference criteria for classifying classroom speech. There has yet to be a demonstration of the reliability or validity of Sinclair and Coulthard's system. Still, greater analytical power at higher levels of organization (e.g., the exchange or transaction) is permitted by a hierarchical model. Furthermore, a more theoretically sound relationship between levels obtains than was seen with the separate dimensions of interaction analysis.

Second language classroom researchers have not employed such a comprehensive discourse analytical scheme in their studies but, as will be seen in later chapters, have usually limited themselves to specific areas of discourse (e.g., Chaudron's 1977a analysis of teacher feedback, or Tsui 1985, both working within the general framework of Sinclair and Coulthard's system). Nonetheless, a variety of discourse analytical units with identifiable linguistic structure or serving specific functions have been adopted for these narrower analyses. Some of these are listed and briefly defined in Table 2.4, along with several structural terms that have been used for comparative analysis. (As a number of terms in current use are identical to Sinclair and Coulthard's, their acts and moves will not be repeated here.) These terms will be discussed more fully in later chapters, so references will not be cited here.

In addition to these discourse units, there are many further functions of language in the L2 classroom which might be considered pertinent to particular research goals. Cathcart (1983) shows, for instance, that Sinclair and Coulthard's "informative" is not adequate to distinguish the possible functions of language in interaction (in her case evidenced in these example quotes by children):

announce: "He's gonna do it."
initiate: "Guess what?"
express opinion: "I like boys."
express internal state: "I feel sick."

These and other distinctions could be made for the various internal structure and functions of other acts, such as teachers' or students' directives, evaluates, comments, and replies.

The analysis of the verbal discourse of classroom interaction must of course be viewed as embedded in the social and cognitive operations which take place in the instructional period or lesson. For this reason, various aspects of the interaction that were considered in the section on dimensions (e.g., participant organization, nonverbal and material aspects) would have to be included for the sake of a comprehensive analysis of the classroom interaction. Discourse analysis has contributed to a growth in awareness of the internal formal structure and functional purpose of the verbal classroom interaction. Yet research on specific types of discourse phenomena in the classroom has drawn much of its inspiration from the ethnographic tradition.

TABLE 2.4. ANALYTICAL UNITS EMPLOYED IN L2 DISCOURSE ANALYSIS

STRUCTURAL UNITS

utterance: a string of speech by one speaker under a single intonation contour, and preceded and followed by another speaker's speech, or a pause of more than *x* seconds

turn: any speaker's sequence of utterances bounded by another speaker's speech

T-unit: any syntactic main clause and its associated subordinate clauses

communication unit: an independent grammatical predication; the same as a T-unit, except that in oral language, elliptical answers to questions also constitute complete predications

fragment: any utterance which does not constitute a completed proposition (i.e., with explicit subject and verb)

FUNCTIONAL UNITS

repetition: an exact repeating of a previous string of speech (either partial or full, and either a self- or other-repetition)

expansion: a partial or full repetition which modifies some portion of a previous string of speech by adding syntactic or semantic information

clarification request: a request for further information from an interlocutor about a previous utterance

comprehension check: the speaker's query of the interlocutor(s) as to whether or not they have understood the previous speaker utterance(s)

confirmation check: the speaker's query as to whether or not the speaker's (expressed) understanding of the interlocutor's meaning is correct

repair: an attempt by a speaker to alter or rectify a previous utterance which was in some way lacking in clarity or correctness (either self- or other-directed);

model: a type of prompt by a speaker (usually a teacher) intended to elicit an exact imitation or to serve as an exemplary response to an elicitation

The ethnographic approach

The ethnographic approach is generally identified as a qualitative, process-oriented approach to the study of interaction. It has developed in various ways in research on L1 classrooms, but it has not been extensively employed in L2 classrooms, in part because it requires highly trained observers, and because it demands a great deal of time and commitment of research personnel. (For descriptions, examples, and some summary results of this approach in L1 classrooms see Barnes, Britton, and Rosen 1969; Cazden et al. 1972; Stubbs and Delamont 1976; Tikunoff and Ward 1977; Wilson 1977; Heltoft and Paaby 1978: Chaudron 1980; Green and Wallat 1981; Hymes 1981; Wilkinson 1982; Green 1983; and Cazden 1986; for discussion and some exemplification of this approach with respect to L2 classrooms see Cazden et al. 1980;

Long 1980a; Trueba et al. 1981; Trueba and Wright 1981; van Lier 1982, in press; and Rudes, Goldsamt, and Cervenka 1983.)

The procedures for conducting ethnographic research involve considerable training, continuous record keeping, extensive participatory involvement of the researcher in the classroom, and careful interpretation of the usually multifaceted data (for description of such procedures see Wilson 1977; Mehan 1979; and Levine et al. 1983). The result of such an investigation is usually a detailed description of the research site, and an account of the principles or rules of interaction that guide the participants to produce their actions and meanings and to interpret the actions and utterances of others.

The typical approach of L2 researchers has, however, notably not been to provide a complete ethnography of the classrooms they have observed, but instead to provide certain details or analyses of specific areas of interaction, which were observed and analyzed following qualitative and interpretive procedures. Examples of areas delimited by such studies are: teacher awareness of student performance (Carrasco 1981), turn-taking and repair (van Lier 1982), and teacher management of turns (Enright 1984). Although these studies do not fulfill the broadest expectations of ethnography, namely, an exhaustive treatment of the rules for interaction in general, their adoption of ethnographic methodology is intended to reveal the underlying social norms for interpreting the specific interactive events. Insofar as the categories of analysis are derived from the teachers' and learners' own perceptions, they have the potential of being much more psychologically valid than externally imposed constructs.

An especially interesting area in L2 research that has employed some ethnographic techniques is that known as "diary studies" (Schumann and Schumann 1977; Schumann 1980; K. Bailey 1980, 1983; K. Bailey and Ochsner 1983; C. Brown 1985). Diary studies usually involve the researcher-as-learner 1) recording events in a language classroom or language learning context, 2) preferably reflecting on the diary entries soon afterward, in order to add appropriate interpretations before they are forgotten, and then 3) compiling and summarizing key elements. This procedure epitomizes the more subjective aspects of ethnographic methods, yet to the extent that the researcher brings independent theory and research to bear on interpretation, or elicits judgments on the recorded events from other experts and participants, the data and interpretations can fulfill most of the requirements of valid research. C. Brown (1985), illustrating the extent to which diary studies differ from ethnographic participant observation, argues that the former can result in more valid insights. K. Bailey (1983) also illustrates the depth of insight available in her own diary analysis of anxiety in an FFL class.

One large-scale study of bilingual instruction involved longitudinal participant observation (see Wong-Fillmore 1982), although it was also not an exhaustive ethnographic study. While the study has led to several reports of specific qualitative aspects (e.g., functions of language use – Cathcart 1983, 1986a, b; students' choice of social interactant – Strong 1983, 1984; and teacher structuring of input – Wong-Fillmore 1985), at the same time, quantitative analyses of frequency of interactions, student personality, language use, and achievement outcomes have been obtained (Cathcart, Strong and Wong-Fillmore 1979; Strong 1983, 1984, 1986; Cathcart 1986b). The quantitative data in Strong's studies (1983, 1984) in fact constitute the critical data on which he tests his hypothesis regarding the influence of choice of interactant on language progress; nevertheless, the qualitative analysis of different interaction patterns provided the basis on which the data were quantified.

A final example of ethnographic research is an exhaustive analysis of engineering lecture discourse (Shaw 1983), which, although conducted in L1 university classrooms with native speaker lecturers, was motivated by concerns for the comprehension of such lectures by L2 learners in the classes. The implications apply equally to training L2 learners to comprehend scientific discourse, as well as to training native and non-native-speaking lecturers and tutors to present clearer lectures. The methodology was extremely time-consuming. Shaw attended one lecture course for an entire semester (longitudinal) and 17 courses for a sequence of several sessions each (cross-sectional). Most of the latter were audio-recorded, and Shaw took a variety of notes on contextual events. Table 2.5 displays the sequence of research activities in this study.

Note that Shaw collected all of his data before generating hypotheses, a practice typical of true ethnographic studies, although all researchers will of course apply some preconceived perspectives and suppositions in the course of their data collection and transcription. The effort of ethnographers is to become as aware as possible of their own preconceptions. Shaw's ensuing detailed analysis of the discourse of science lectures resembles the sort of discourse analysis model seen in the previous section (although Shaw does not adopt a rank-scale system), and it allows him to draw a variety of conclusions, especially on the qualitative distinctiveness of engineering lectures compared with a traditional conception of lectures in the humanities.

Most researchers adopting qualitative or ethnographic techniques have recognized the need to continue their analysis with some quantification of events, whether frequency of turns or other units of participation (Allwright 1980; Enright 1984), amount of language of a certain function produced (Cathcart et al. 1979), duration of activities (Mohatt and Erickson 1981), or other quantitative analyses. The value of the

TABLE 2.5. SUMMARY OF RESEARCH SEQUENCE

Stage in research sequence	Research outcome	Research activity	
		Off-site	On-site
I	Conditions and limits of study established; sites selected	Literature reviewed	Pilot study (ethnography and audio recording)
II			Longitudinal ethnography begins
III	Class for audio taping selected	Initial professor interviews	Cross-sectional ethnography begins
IV			Audio recording Videotape recording
V	"General picture" emerges	Transcription begins Professors debriefed	Cross-sectional ethnography ends
VI	Hypotheses generated from transcript review	Fieldnotes completed and reviewed	Longitudinal ethnography ends
VII	Data matched against hypotheses generated in VI	Transcripts complete Transcripts reviewed and analyzed	
VIII	"General model" emerges	Final data analysis (integrated analysis)	

Source: Reprinted with permission from Peter Ambler Shaw, "The language of engineering professors: a discourse and registral analysis of a speech event," p. 140, Ph.D. dissertation, University of Southern California, Los Angeles.

qualitative insights lies in their power to alter perspectives on the variables of interest and to aid in the development of theoretical constructs or relationships.

Process-oriented qualitative researchers explore the intersubjective and context-dependent nature of classroom events as they occur, noting the regularities and idiosyncrasies in the events. In order for researchers to derive the implicit rules governing the participants' behavior, however, regularity of particular events or sequences in the discourse must be observed. This regularity then will support reliable claims about rules of interaction. It also allows for counting and other quantitative analyses;

the ultimate need for generality and for comparisons across classroom contexts inevitably requires such quantification of events. Regrettably, too few researchers with an ethnographic orientation have provided the validation necessary for generalization to other contexts. On the other hand, a danger exists for researchers to attribute too great a meaning to the numerical values alone and not question the inherent variability that a summary frequency, a percentage, or a mean tends to obscure.

Conclusion

In the survey of L2 classroom research that follows, the reader will recognize a continuous give-and-take between the successes and failures of quantitative or qualitative approaches to portray and explain adequately the processes and products of classroom interaction. Teachers' and learners' speech has been analyzed in quantitative terms, such as words or clauses per T-unit, words per turn, proportion of turns taken, proportion of types of questions, frequency of comprehension checks and repetitions, types of repair, and so on, all with regard to their influence on the process or product of interaction. These analyses have inevitably raised further questions of descriptive and explanatory power which cannot be resolved on the basis of current research, but which instead require the development of more comprehensive models, or a theory of classroom interaction and its effect on learning, in addition to more rigorous observational procedures and validation of the methodology and concepts used.

The usefulness to researchers of particular observational instruments or research approaches as described in this chapter will depend almost entirely on the purposes of the research and the limits of generalizability and descriptive validity that the researcher chooses to strive for. The next chapters will illustrate how much more broadly those limits should probably be set for future research to contribute to our knowledge of L2 classroom interaction processes and products.

3 *Teacher talk in second language classrooms*

This chapter reviews research that has investigated second language classrooms in terms of teachers' language use in the classroom, especially the characteristic features that differentiate speech to nonnative speakers from that to native speakers. It will be seen that teacher speech displays a variety of structural modifications depending on the nature of the task and the competence of the student or listener. As was pointed out in Chapter 1, these may be important modifications, to the extent that they would enhance learners' comprehension and consequent ability to process the TL grammar and lexis. Research on the effects for learners will be addressed in Chapter 6.

In addition to studies of teachers' modifications, the general nature of teacher speech in classrooms is explored, especially phenomena which could influence the opportunities that learners have to participate or to assimilate instructional content. In particular, this discussion considers 1) the amount of teacher talk as compared with student speech in classrooms, 2) the distribution of teacher talk in terms of pedagogical and functional moves or acts, and 3) the nature of teachers' explanations. Other teacher acts which are more interactive, that is, functionally related to the preceding and following student behaviors (questions, feedback), will be discussed in Chapter 5.

Amount and types of teacher talk

Research in first language classrooms has established that teachers tend to do most of the talking (about 60% of the moves), mostly as soliciting and reacting moves (cf. Bellack et al. 1966 and Dunkin and Biddle 1974). The proportions of soliciting, responding, reacting, and structuring moves is about 30/30/30/10, with students uttering most of the responding moves. These proportions reflect of course only general averages, for there is great inter- and intrateacher variability, as well as variability depending on class content, size of class or learner group, and so on. In L2 classrooms, the research tends to support the conclusion from L1 research. Teachers dominate classroom speech. This section will first summarize the overall amount of teacher talk found in observational studies, then explore the functional distribution of this speech in terms of type of teacher moves or acts.

Legarreta (1977) investigated five bilingual education kindergarten classrooms representing two program types ("Concurrent Translation" and "Alternate Days"), using time intervals in an adaptation of Flanders' observational system (see Chapter 2) to code segments of teacher talk and student talk. She found the students accounting for only 11% to 30% of the total talk (including instances of both choral and individual speech), so that the teachers and teacher aides together accounted for 70% to 89%, with a median of 77%. These rather high proportions of teacher talk may be due to the particular teachers or programs studied, to the type of segmentation of talk adopted (which Legarreta does not elaborate on – these were presumably three-second or longer intervals and thus may have omitted frequent student short responses), or to the fact that only one day was sampled per class. In contrast, a study by Enright (1984) in two bilingual kindergarten classes similar in context to those in Legarreta's study found the teachers and aides speaking noticeably less. Here, the range for a variety of small group and whole class activities was between 42.9% and 84.9%, with a median of 64.5% (with little apparent difference in distribution of talk across type of activity organization). Enright counted numbers of "speech acts" (utterances and parts of utterances with distinct meanings), a narrower analysis of instances of speech than Legarreta's, and this may increase the possibilities for accounting for student participation.

A proportion for teacher talk similar to Enright's was observed in a comparison between one grade 6 French immersion class and one grade 6 "core" French (FSL) class in Canada (Bialystok, Fröhlich and Howard 1978), where the number of teacher and student moves (as in Bellack et al.'s 1966 scheme) were counted: 68.8% of the moves were by the French immersion teacher, and 61.3% by the core French teacher, although there were considerably different distributions by specific function of move. Finally, J. D. Ramirez et al.'s (1986) study of 72 kindergarten through grade 3 classes (L1 Spanish children in English immersion, and early-exit and late-exit transitional bilingual education classes) found teachers' proportion of utterances (coded from transcripts, see definition in Table 2.4) to all teacher and student utterances falling within a 60%–80% range, with the average at 70%. This finding held across program type and grade levels, with the exception of teachers' use of Spanish in kindergarten and grade 1 English immersion classes, where the teachers accounted for only 42% to 47% of talk in Spanish. Notwithstanding Legarreta's slightly higher values, and some variability in Ramirez et al.'s findings, these results confirm the standard first language finding of about two-thirds of classroom speech being attributable to the teacher.

Functional distribution of teacher talk

Perhaps of greater interest to classroom researchers is the question of *how* teacher talk is distributed; that is, how does it differ in function, and to what extent is the teacher's speech directed to individuals as opposed to groups of learners? The first part of this question is considered here, while the second, more related to the *interactive* aspects of the classroom, will be dealt with in Chapter 5.

It is evident from the diversity of observational instruments in Chapter 2 that studies describing the functions of teacher talk in L2 classrooms would vary greatly, depending on the particular instrument or theoretical framework selected. The presumed effect of differences in function of teacher talk is that learners are thereby engaged in learning tasks in different ways. That is, if teachers devote large amounts of time to explanations or management instructions, learners have less opportunity to produce the target language, and contrariwise, if teachers spend much time in drills or drill-like questioning, learners may thus have less opportunity to evaluate input or produce creative language. Whether any one function is deemed better than another will depend either on the researcher's theoretical assumptions about language learning or on observations of differences in learning following specific teaching practices, issues which will be considered in Chapters 5 and 6.

A complete survey of research findings for differences in teacher functions is beyond the scope of this book, but representative studies will serve to illustrate the variability among teachers and programs. Included here are only studies which attempted to analyze all teacher behaviors in the classroom interaction.

Shapiro (1979) reported a study of seven Spanish-English elementary classrooms (grades 2–6) in New York City, using Fanselow's (1977a) FOCUS instrument (see Figure 2.1) for observations at the beginning and end of the school year. During the year the teachers participated in a training program in which they were familiarized with the instrument and, along with other guidance, were encouraged to vary their use of questions and to promote student-initiated contributions and solicits. In terms of types of move, the teachers produced around 90% or more of the structuring or soliciting moves (with the range among teachers between 70% and 100%), 70% of reacting moves (range 33.5%–97%), and 5% of responding moves (range 0%–12%). Soliciting moves accounted for about 60% of the total teacher moves, reacting moves 30%, structuring moves about 5%, and responding moves also about 5%.

Bialystok et al. (1978) also coded for these four move types in their comparison of grade 6 core and immersion French. In the core French class, they also found the teacher dominating the structuring ("initiate" – 100%), soliciting (100%), and reacting moves (88.9%), while contributing virtually no (0.6%) responding moves. The authors do not provide the raw data from which to calculate the differential weighting of teacher moves, but it appears that teacher soliciting and responding moves were less frequent (about 42% and 0.2%), and reacting moves were more frequent (49%), in the core French than in Shapiro's classes. "Initiates" accounted for 8% of total teacher moves. As evidence for difference possibly attributable to program type, however, the immersion class showed a markedly reduced proportion of teacher solicits to student solicits (57.8%) and an increased proportion of responding moves (22.6%). Relative to other teacher moves, however, initiates/structures were more frequent than in the core French (about 33%).

Unlike Shapiro's findings with classes which were comparable, Hernandez (1983) found a similar pattern to that of Bialystok et al.'s core French class, in a study of eight Spanish-English bilingual classes, grades 1–3, in California. Of total moves, the teachers dominated with 46% opening moves (using Sinclair and Coulthard's 1975 category – see Figure 2.3, which roughly includes the soliciting and structuring moves of Fanselow's 1977a system), 16% follow-up moves (reacting), and left most of the remaining 39% responding moves to the students. This result appears to put the learner in a more active role than the L1 pattern noted above, although the measure of moves may not reveal the actual amount of speech produced by the participants (a single move may comprise one word or a complex sentence or more in either the Sinclair and Coulthard type of system or that of Fanselow).

The pattern in these classes in second language contexts is corroborated by Tsui's (1985) study in English language classes in Hong Kong (a virtual second language context), where the teacher's dominance was even greater (more than 80% of all speech, including about 60% of responding moves).

These and other researchers have also been interested in the specific functions served by general pedagogical moves. As seen in Chapter 2, however, it is rather difficult to compare such categorization across studies that employ different analytical systems. Thus, while Shapiro (1979) analyzes in terms of the FOCUS system "task" areas (where the dominant task – about 60% – is "present"), Bialystok et al. (1979) analyze in terms of functions adopted from Naiman et al.'s system (1978; see also Figure 2.2, Chapter 2), where the several functions account each for between 10% and 18% of the total moves (the most prevalent are "complete response" and "specific information"). By comparison, Milk (1982) used an adaptation of Sinclair and Coulthard's scheme in counting the functions of teacher utterances in a grade 12 bilingual education civics classroom. Of eight types identified, the dominant ones were "elicitation" (23%), "informatives" (22%), "reply" (19%), and "follow-up" (about 14%).

J. D. Ramirez et al. (1986; see previous discussion on amount of teacher talk) analyzed the pedagogical functions of explaining, commanding, questioning, modeling, feedback, and others. They found an order of dominance that was roughly consistent across program and grade levels, although commands were significantly different across program types (early-exit transitional bilingual teachers were low in use of commands). The medians across all programs and teachers were: explaining, 23.7%; questioning, 17.6%; commands, 15.8%.

Other researchers have preferred to analyze in terms of other principal categories of teacher behaviors which are not based on an exhaustive discourse analytical segmentation. For example, Mitchell et al.'s (1981) analysis of secondary French as a foreign language classes in Scotland used "activity" as a unit of segmentation, with types of activity identified as "translation," "L1," "real FL," "transposition," "presentation," "imitation," "compound," and "drill/exercise." This last type was by far the dominant one – 34.6% of all activities. Fröhlich et al. (1985) analyze in terms of several of their communicatively oriented dimensions, which do not, however, appear to be mutually exclusive. Thus, in their case the only possible comparison is on each category at a time, across the different program types they studied.

Regrettably, much classroom research has neglected to fully report raw data with exclusive categories, so that few adequately rigorous contrasts can be made across teacher behaviors. While the evident pattern is that teacher speech dominates the classroom, there is a suggestion in these studies that there is both variability among teachers, and possibly equally great variability among program types or among particular classroom organizational patterns. Some of this variability is discussed in the next section as modifications of discourse, and some will be dealt with in Chapter 5.

Modifications in teacher speech

One of the principal questions addressed by research on L2 teacher speech is whether or not teachers adjust their speech to nonnative speakers in quantifiable ways. Theoretically, there is the concern that L2 teacher speech in classrooms may represent a distinct sociolinguistic register, different from either that of L1 speech in classrooms or NS speech to NNSs in noneducational contexts (commonly referred to as

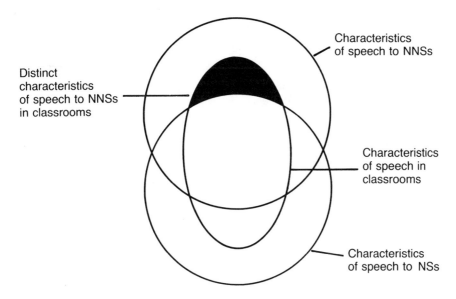

Figure 3.1   Relationships between speech to natives and nonnatives in and outside classrooms

"foreigner talk"; see Clyne 1981 and Freed 1980, 1981). It is of interest to find characteristics of teachers' speech to NNSs that are peculiar to the classroom. This distinction is represented in Figure 3.1, which illustrates hypothetical relationships between the nature of speech to natives and nonnatives, both in and outside classrooms. While speech to nonnatives and speech to natives share many characteristics, each type has hypothetically distinct features. Similarly, features of speech in classrooms are a subset of features of general speech, so that hypothetically, there is a subset of characteristics of speech to NNSs in classrooms that is distinct from other speech (i.e., the shaded area in Figure 3.1).

It will be seen in the following, however, that on various comparisons, teacher talk in L2 classrooms differs from speech in other contexts, but the differences are not systematic, nor are they qualitatively distinct enough to constitute a special sociolinguistic domain, as has been argued for the case of foreigner talk. Rather, it appears that the adjustments in teacher speech to nonnative-speaking learners serve the temporary purpose of maintaining communication – clarifying information and eliciting learners' responses – and do not identify the interaction as an entirely different social situation. This is an important finding, which indicates that if teachers' efforts to modify their classroom speech have any effect on L2 learners, it is more likely that the effects contribute to comprehension and learning than that they mark the

TABLE 3.1. STUDIES OF TEACHER TALK WITH MORE THAN ONE INDEPENDENT
FACTOR

Study	Class levels(s)	Real/ simulated	L1	L2	Teacher (N)
Gaies (1977b)	Adult preacademic university at 4 levels	Real	Mixed	English	6
Mizon (1981)	Primary	Real	Kannada	English	1
Downes (1981)	Adult preacademic university at 3 levels	Real	Mixed	English	10 (?)
Long & Sato (1983)	Adult preacademic university (beginners)	Real	Mixed	English	6
Milk (1985)	Adult community classes at 3 levels	Real	Spanish	English	14 NNSs
Pica & Long (1986)	Adult preacademic university & community conversation classes	Real	Mixed	English	10
Håkansson (1986)	Adult community conversation classes; beginners at 3 times	Real	Mixed	Swedish	6

Comparison group(s)	Phonological differences	Lexical differences	Syntactic differences	Discourse differences
Same teachers in NS discussions			*Fewer subordinate clauses per T-unit *Fewer words per clause	
Similar lesson in L1 English (British class)		Less variety of content and function words Proper nouns dominant	Shorter mean length of utterance Higher proportion of simple present tense *Higher proportion of interrogatives & declaratives	
15 foreigner talk NS-NNS service encounters (separate NS group)	More exaggerated articulation Extended pauses		No omissions of definite article More contracted forms	More correction
NS-NNS conversation in pairs (separate NS group)			*More present tense marking than non-present (within teacher) *More present tense marking (classroom over conversations) More statements than imperatives Fewer questions	
Same teachers in interview with NS			*Shorter T-units *Fewer complex T-units per total T-units	
NS-NNS conversations in pairs (separate NS group)				
NSs informal discussions (separate group)	Increase in rate of speech over time		Higher proportion of well-formed sentences Fewer words per sentence Fewer subordinate clauses per 100 well-formed sentences More sentence fragments	

TABLE 3.1. (*continued*)

Study	Class levels(s)	Real/ simulated	L1	L2	Teacher (N)
Håkansson (*continued*)					
Ishiguro (1986)	College at 3 levels	Real	Japanese	English	9 NSs 9 NNSs
Mannon (1986)	University	Real	Mixed	English	1

*Indicates significant differences favoring observed group over comparison; other differences are only relevant trends noted by authors.

classroom events as unusual or stigmatized (see discussion of this question in Chaudron 1983a).

In Tables 3.1 to 3.4, the major aspects of the design of studies on teacher modifications are tabulated, and the different linguistic features of teachers' speech are divided into the areas of phonology (including speech rate, pauses, and prosody), lexis, syntax, and discourse. Each area will be examined separately. Those characteristics that studies identified as notable in L2 teacher speech, in comparison with other contexts, are tabulated here. The direction of effect is assumed to be in favor of the main group against the comparison. Whenever statistical tests were performed on the quantified results and significance was found, the result is asterisked. It is always preferable for researchers to attempt such statistical inferences; nevertheless, in several of the studies reviewed here, statistical analyses are restricted or precluded by a) narrower research goals, b) methodological weaknesses, such as the lack of equivalence of measures across conditions, c) differences in the comparison groups, d) limited samples, or e) the nonquantifiable nature of some features.

Table 3.1 lists several studies which compared teachers' classroom speech to L2 learners, with measures of instruction to NSs or conversations outside classrooms with NSs or NNSs. These studies thus have uncontrolled variability on more than one independent factor, usually

Comparison group(s)	Phonological differences	Lexical differences	Syntactic differences	Discourse differences
			Increase in variability of sentence length over time Some ungrammatical fragments More canonical word order	
Same teachers in discussions (with NSs)			Shorter utterances in wpm (monologues)	
Same teacher to NS content students	Slower rate of speech Less reduction *Fewer contractions		*Shorter T-units	More 1st-person reference *More self-repetitions

including a simultaneous change in two or more of either the competence of the interlocutor (NS vs. NNS), the task (instruction or conversation), or the comparison speaker(s). Consequently, there is potential for confounding of the independent variables, and it becomes more difficult to accept these comparisons as confidently as those of several of the studies in Tables 3.2 to 3.4, which controlled for the relevant independent factors. However, insofar as large enough groups of comparable NS subjects are included (as in the case of Downes 1981, and Pica and Long 1986, for example), the comparisons are strengthened.

Table 3.2 summarizes several studies which compared the same task for either different NSs speaking to NNSs, or the same NSs' speech to NNSs and NSs, thus controlling for all but one factor. In these cases, the variable of interest was either a) the degree of teacher training and experience of the NS, and its influence on ability to adjust to NNSs, b) the ability of the same individual to adjust differentially to native- and nonnative-speaking listeners, or c) differences in adjustments by NSs and NNSs.

Table 3.3 shows four studies which compared the same teachers' speech to nonnative groups of different proficiency levels.

In order to interpret the findings from these reports, the types and ranges of each feature will be compared across the studies, whenever observed frequencies are reported on comparable measures. One is then no longer entirely confined to comparisons within each study and can thus achieve a more general description of teacher discourse in L2 classrooms.

TABLE 3.2. STUDIES OF TEACHER TALK WITH ONE INDEPENDENT FACTOR

Study	Class levels(s)	Real/ simulated	L1	L2	Teacher (N)
Henzl (1973)	Adult university (inter- mediate?), 4 levels	Simulated (storytelling)	English	Czech	8 non- teachers
Steyaert (1977)	Adult preacademic university	Simulated (storytelling)	Mixed	English	6
Bialystok et al. (1978)	Grade 6, French im- mersion and core French	Real	English	French	2
Henzl (1979)	Secondary and univer- sity, beginning and advanced	Simulated (storytelling)	Mixed English English	English German Czech	3 3 5
Chaudron (1979, 1982)	Secondary and univer- sity; beginning, inter- mediate, & advanced Content classes	Real	Mixed	English	3

Comparison group(s)	Phonological differences	Lexical differences	Syntactic differences	Discourse differences
Same subjects with same task to NSs	More standard literary pronunciation Louder & slower More pauses Less vowel redundancy Fewer consonant cluster reductions	More basic vocabulary Stylistically neutral Less colloquial Fewer indefinite pronouns More concrete & proper nouns	Fewer words per sentence Fewer subordinate clauses More complete, well-formed sentences Less inflectional complexity Fewer past-tense verbs	
Same tasks to NSs			Fewer words per minute	
Between program types (immersion compared with core French)				Fewer functions per time unit More verbalization per function More administrative direction More reading Less repetition Fewer "accept" acts More teacher-initiated moves Fewer teacher responses
Same task to NSs Same task to NSs Same task to NSs			Fewer words per sentence One-half to one-third slower Fewer subordinate clauses Less diversity in case roles More present tense, indicative active verbs (to beginners) No conditionals, passives Literary morphology (in Czech)	
Same teachers to NS classes			Fewer clauses per communication unit	

TABLE 3.2. (*continued*)

Study	Class levels(s)	Real/ simulated	L1	L2	Teacher (N)
Dahl (1981)	Adult university at 3 levels	Simulated (picture description)	Arabic	English	6
Schinke-Llano (1983)	High school NS classes with some L2	Real	Spanish	English	12
Kliefgen (1985)	Kindergarten L2 and NS children at 3 times	Real	Mixed	English	1
Wesche & Ready (1985)	University psychology for NNSs	Real	French	English	1
			English	French	1
Early (1985)	High school ESL social studies, under- and upper classes	Real	Mixed	English	5
Ellis (1985a)	Secondary beginners	Real	Punjabi	English	1
Pica & Long (1986)	Adult preacademic university & community conversation classes	Real	Mixed	English	6

Comparison group(s)	Phonological differences	Lexical differences	Syntactic differences	Discourse differences
6 nonteachers on same task to same listeners				Fewer explicit request forms
Teachers' speech to NS students in same classes				Less directed interaction More managerial & fewer instructional interactions (high variability between teachers)
Teacher speech to NS children in same class		Greater token/ type ratio	Some ungrammatical speech Increase in length of utterances over time	More functions were: information exchange, action directives, clarifications
Same professor with NSs	*For English L2:* *Slower speech *More long pauses *More total pause time		*For English L2:* Avoidance of conditional *More tensed verbs *Fewer non-present tense *be* *Fewer words per T-unit	*For English L2:* More words in self-repetitions More imperatives
Same professor with NSs	*For French L2:* *More filled pauses			*For French L2* More words in self-repetitions
10 classes in NS social studies				*Proportionately more imperatives, fewer statements *More conversational frames
Same teacher over time				*Fewer self-repetitions
a) 6 inexperienced teacher trainees (some within teacher)			a) Equal length of utterance Equal S-nodes per T-unit *Different proportion of questions/ statements/ imperatives	

TABLE 3.2. *(continued)*

Study	Class levels(s)	Real/ simulated	L1	L2	Teacher (N)
Pica & Long *(continued)*					

*Indicates significant difference favoring observed group over comparison; other differences are only relevant trends noted by authors.

TABLE 3.3. STUDIES COMPARING CLASSROOM TEACHER TALK ACROSS PROFICIENCY LEVELS

Study	Class levels(s)	Real/ simulated	L1	L2	Teacher (N)
Gaies (1977b)	Adult preacademic university at 4 levels	Real	Mixed	English	6
Chaudron (1979)	Secondary and university; beginning, intermediate, & advanced Content classes	Real	Mixed	English	3
Milk (1985)	Adult community classes at 3 levels	Real	Spanish	English	14 NNSs
Ishiguro (1986)	College at 3 levels	Real	Japanese	English	9 NSs 9 NNSs

*Indicates significant differences among proficiency levels; trends suggest reduction in complexity for lower levels (see text and Table 3.6 for details).

Modifications of speech rate, prosody, phonology

RATE OF SPEECH

Henzl (1973, 1979), Håkansson (1986), Steyaert (1977), Dahl (1981), Wesche and Ready (1985), Ishiguro (1986), and Mannon (1986) all found teachers' speech to second language learners to be slower, in comparison with other contexts and conditions. Three of these studies

Comparison group(s)	Phonological differences	Lexical differences	Syntactic differences	Discourse differences
b) 2 experienced teachers unfamiliar with classes (visiting)			*Fewer dysfluencies b) Equal length of utterance Equal S-nodes per T-unit *Equal dysfluencies	

Comparison group(s)	Syntactic differences
Same and different teachers across proficiencies	*Fewer subordinate clauses per T-unit *Fewer adjective, adverb, noun clauses (ANOVA across all levels)
Same and different teachers across proficiencies	Fewer clauses per communication unit Fewer adjective clauses per 100 communication units
Same and different teachers across proficiencies	No differences in length of utterance
Same and different teachers across proficiencies	No differences in length of utterance

found the differences to be significant. The overall means from these studies are shown in Table 3.4.[1]

Steyaert (1977) adopted an elicitation procedure used by Henzl

---

1 In this and subsequent tables, means have been calculated by averaging the figures given by the different researchers for individuals or for group means. These calculations are indicated by a dagger. While this method does not provide a true mean (because of unequal weightings of units per group or feature, or some other variability that is not evident in the data reported), there was nonetheless no other way to make adequate comparisons across studies, and the procedure should not result in gross distortions of the relative magnitudes. It is unfortunate that the original researchers neglected to calculate these means themselves, since they did have the original raw data.

TABLE 3.4. MODIFICATIONS IN RATE OF SPEECH

Study	Task/Measure	Speakers[a]		Addressees[b]			
				Native speakers	Advanced NNSs	Intermediate NNSs	Beginning NNSs
Steyaert (1977)	Storytelling	Teachers	(N = 6)				
		Story 1		160.68		152.28	
		Story 2		164.13		150.65*	
Dahl (1981)	One-way description	Nonteachers	(N = 6)	153†	139†	148†	112†
		Teachers	(N = 6)	154†	146†	136†	110†
Henzl (1973)	Storytelling in Czech	Nonteachers	(N = 8)	127†		86.4†	
Henzl (1979)	Storytelling	Teachers					
		Czech	(N = 5)	118.2†	78†		54.1†
		English	(N = 3)	203.8†	152.4†		107.6†
		German	(N = 3)	137.6†	126.7†		99.5†
Wesche & Ready (1985)	Classroom Instruction	Teachers					
		English	(N = 1)	134.5†	90.1†		
		French	(N = 1)	80.3†	77.7†		
Håkansson (1986)	Classroom instruction	Teachers					
		Time 1	(N = 6)				79
		Time 2	(N = 6)				114
		Time 3	(N = 2)				125

	Classroom instruction (monologues) (NS addressees in discussions)	Teachers					
Ishiguro (1986)		NS	(N = 9)	137.88*	111.49**	106.73	97.53
		NNS	(N = 9)	103.8	85.55	86.49	86.33
Mannon (1986)	Classroom lecture	Teacher (content)	(N = 1)	122.97		112.26	

[a] All ESL teachers except when noted.
[b] All figures in words per minute (wpm).
* Differences between NNS and comparison NS significant.
† Means calculated from tabled figures.
** Advanced significantly different from beginners.
Source: Adapted from Chaudron (1985b:220).

(1973), to be described later. Her six practicing teachers had a mean rate of speech of 150.65 words per minute (wpm) when telling a story to intermediate ESL students, and 164.13 wpm to NSs on the second telling of the story. This was a significant difference. The rates on the first story were closer by about 6 wpm and did not show significance. Given these values, it is likely that the usually larger differences in wpm in the other studies are not due to chance, although the intersubject and intrasubject variability often appears high.[2]

Dahl's (1981) subjects were six ESL teachers and six graduate student NSs without experience in teaching. They were given a description task to present to assumed audiences of NSs and to advanced, intermediate, and beginning learners. Tape recordings of the intended listeners' speech were played to the subjects in order to prime them about the listeners' proficiency, and therefore, the appropriate level of address. While the range in mean rates for all the NS subjects was about the same in addressing the NSs, the advanced, and the intermediate learners, it appeared to shift downward for the intended beginning listener (from 134–161 to 107–120 wpm). Analysis of variance shows this tendency to be significant for both the teachers and the graduate student NSs. However, the task used in this study may well account for the results obtained. It can be argued that the lack of differences for most of the subjects was due in part to the lack of feedback available to them as they spoke. In addition, it is conceivable that only the tape of the lowest-level NNS was noticeably foreign enough to trigger consistent modifications in these native speakers. This methodological weakness limits the discriminating power of several of Dahl's measures.

Henzl's two studies (1973, 1979) also evidence great intersubject variability. However, these investigations show consistent intrasubject tendencies to simplify when telling stories to less proficient listeners. In her studies, native speakers of the TL were given two picture sequences, which they were to tell as stories to L2 classroom groups as well as to listener groups who were also NSs. Unlike Dahl's study (1981), all the listeners were present, although in the 1973 study there was apparently little interaction between them and the listeners before the first storytelling. Also, this earlier study had only Czech speakers without teaching experience, while the 1979 study involved storytelling by teachers in three different TLs – Czech, German, and English – with L2 class groups at two learner levels in their regular educational institutions. Thus, the findings of the later study not only provide a more realistic range of results, but the teachers' probable familiarity with the two levels of learner competence would lead to more authentic adjustments in speech to the nonnative-speaking listeners. In both studies, only 1 subject

2 Calculation of statistical differences is omitted, owing to uncertainties about the exact conditions of sampling and identification of the subjects in these studies; the statistical claims made are those of the original authors unless otherwise noted.

out of 19 (German subject number 10, 1979, p. 163) spoke noticeably faster to NSs than to NSs.

In studies of real instructional classroom speech, the pattern is similar, although not as clear. Håkansson (1986) found that Swedish as a second language teachers observed at five-week intervals increased their rate of speech (from 79 to 125 wpm). No comparison is available with Swedish NSs outside classrooms, however. Downes (1981) compared teachers in their classrooms with two levels of learner. She did not quantify rate of speech, but she reports that fewer of the teachers (from 100% to 50%) spoke slowly with advanced learners. Wesche and Ready (1985) studied two "sheltered" university psychology classes that were conducted in the students' second language, either French or English. In comparing the professors' rate of speech during identical psychology lectures to nonnative-speaking and native-speaking students, Wesche and Ready found that the English professor, but not the French, used significantly slower speech to NNSs than to NSs. It is impossible to determine whether this is an artifact of a) variability within the professors observed, b) French versus English language-specific norms for speech rate (note the differences in speech rate across languages in Henzl 1979, Table 3.4), or c) the instructional context. Mannon (1986) observed a linguistics professor presenting the same lecture to her regular (NS) class, and to a low-intermediate academic-oriented ESL class. In this case, both the listeners' language proficiency and content knowledge could be factors influencing the slower rate of speech to NNSs.

Finally, Ishiguro (1986) compared the English speech to three levels of EFL learners in Japan of nine NNS and NS teachers. Ishiguro also examined the teachers' speech in teacher group discussion. Analysis of variance resulted in significant differences across levels for the NS teachers, but not for NNSs. Post hoc analyses revealed that NS teacher speech among teacher peers was significantly faster than their speech to learners, and speech to advanced learners was faster than that to beginners.

What is most interesting about these studies is that the absolute values of teachers' and nonteachers' speech to beginning learners are around 100 wpm, sometimes less, while the increment in rate of speech over time, or to intermediate or advanced learners, and often to NSs, tends to be 30–40 wpm faster. There is so much variability in these few studies that such absolute values cannot be considered fixed, although the trends toward separation between addressee levels are evident.

PAUSES

One feature observed in several studies which contributes to overall rate of speech, but which may independently aid learners' comprehension and processing of specific words, is amount and length of pauses. Pauses may be either intentionally made for comprehension, a result of the teachers' extra time spent planning how to phrase their speech to adapt to the listeners, or they may simply be a natural concomitant of slower, more articulated speech.

Downes (1981) found more of her native-speaking teachers than non-teachers (NSs recorded surreptitiously in service encounters with NNSs) using extended pauses (7 of 10, or 70%, of teachers vs. 2 of 6, or 33%, of nonteachers), and Henzl (1973, 1979) noted more and longer pauses in her subjects' speech to NNSs compared with NSs. They did not attempt to quantify the mean duration or number of pauses. Yet Håkansson (1986), wanting to explain the initially slower speech of her teachers, did examine one teacher's pauses using an oscillogram. She found that "the majority of pauses were approximately 95 centiseconds in length, and that the longest pauses were around 150 cs" (p. 87). She compared this finding with studies of standard Swedish, which show pauses typically around 60 cs, and rarely exceeding 100 cs.

Wesche and Ready (1985) also measured pauses in seven 2-minute segments and found the English professor pausing significantly longer when speaking to NNSs (six pauses of 5 + seconds or longer, 28 of 2 + seconds, compared to eight instances of either with NSs). The average pause length (for pauses 2 seconds or longer) was 3.25 (NNSs) versus 2.25 seconds (NSs). On the other hand, the French professor, who had fewer total pauses 2 seconds or longer and did not show differential lengths for listener groups, did have significantly more *filled* pauses (with "e," "hoo," "OK") when addressing NNSs than with NSs. Wesche and Ready argue, however, that this professor claimed to be consciously trying to avoid such pauses (she consequently had fewer total filled pauses than her English counterpart), so the significantly greater use of them was likely due to "distraction." This is again the plausible link between pauses and other planning phenomena, rather than the speaker's (un?)conscious attempt to segment her speech for improved comprehensibility.

Evidence for more conscious use of pauses to improve comprehensibility was noted in Chaudron's (1982) study of high school and university teachers' vocabulary explanations and elaborations in ESL classrooms. He observed a distinct tendency (although unquantified) for teachers to segment their speech with slightly longer pauses surrounding difficult words. This gave their utterances a sometimes choppy quality (e.g., "one of the . . . symbols . . . or emblems . . . of Canada").

PHONOLOGY, INTONATION, ARTICULATION, STRESS

Henzl (1973) observed that when the Czech NSs addressed NNSs, they spoke louder, using more standard literary Czech pronunciation than in the colloquial Czech spoken to NSs, which exhibited more consonant cluster reductions, vowel length reductions, and phonological variation.

These features served to make the full morphophonemic forms evident on the surface. The comparisons were not quantified, however. Her 1979 study reported very similar findings with teachers as subjects, again for Czech, and also for German and English subjects (e.g., "could you tell us" produced without reduced forms for NNSs). Mannon (1986) noted more careful enunciation and less reduction in the linguistics lecture to NNSs, and she observed significantly fewer contractions with auxiliary verbs (37%, versus 86% in speech to NSs).

Also reporting differences in articulation was Downes (1981), who stated that the NSs who were recorded in service encounters with NNSs ended to exaggerate their articulation (70% of them doing so), while 100% of the native-speaking teachers in L2 classrooms did so. She found it difficult to distinguish differences in loudness between subjects, however. Although Downes did not find the teachers exaggerating their intonation as much as the nonteachers, Chaudron (1982) observed a rising final intonation and marked stress in several teachers' speech to NNSs that had the effect of emphasizing and focusing on the teachers' speech in a way resembling a comprehension check (see Table 2.4).

The general lack of quantification of these features hinders definite conclusions regarding their distinctiveness as NS modifications for NNSs only, much less as specific characteristics of instructional modification. The failure to obtain appropriate comparison groups in these studies also precludes control over the independent variables of addressee and context simultaneously. On the other hand, the various findings for alterations in phonology and rate of speech strongly suggest that NSs will slow down their speech, exaggerate their pronunciation, and simplify regular forms when addressing NNSs. These appear to be quantitative modifications rather than unusual or distinctive features of speech to NNSs; that is, these features are clearly present in normal speech between NSs, and simply increase to various degrees in the presence of NNSs. Since there are few (Mannon 1986 and Wesche and Ready 1985 are the key exceptions) intra-individual comparisons across both contexts/tasks (conversations vs. instruction) and listeners (NS vs. NNS), it cannot be said to what extent these modifications fit systematically along a continuum. While the overall slower, accentuated speech likely enhances the learner's comprehension, other levels of linguistic adaptation (lexical and syntactic) are probably equally if not more important in their effects.

Modifications of vocabulary

Henzl (1973, 1979) claims that both nonteachers and teachers tend to use a more basic set of vocabulary items in their narratives told to L2 learners. She reports that the items selected were more stylistically neutral (e.g., less colloquial – "woman" instead of "young gal"), and they included fewer idioms, more concrete and proper nouns ("Mr. Brown" instead of "a gentleman"), and fewer indefinite pronouns. Mizon (1981) exhaustively lists the items produced by both a nonnative-speaking teacher of ESL in India and a British teacher in England each giving geography-orientation lessons. Her results are similar to those of Henzl concerning more proper nouns and less variety of content and function words.

Chaudron (1982) also observed one native-speaking teacher talking on the same subject on the same day, to both native-speaking and nonnative-speaking classes. This teacher had several comparable instances with more general high frequency vocabulary addressed to NNSs (e.g., "hold on very tightly" instead of "clinging"). Chaudron further illustrates a native-speaking teacher's evident awareness of the need to simplify speech to NNSs, citing the downshift to more basic vocabulary in one tenth grade teacher's utterance to a high beginner's class: "What do you think is happening in this picture, what's it supposed to depic- to show?"

The most common measure used in investigation of vocabulary simplicity is the ratio of number of different words to number of words produced ("type-token" – the smaller the ratio, the less diverse). Unfortunately, this measure has the deficiency of being laborious to calculate and not entirely indicative of the *complexity* of the vocabulary; rather it is only indicative of the *variety* of the vocabulary used. Analysis of the complexity of vocabulary would have to take into account the relative frequency and semantic complexity of all items. A few of the classroom studies have calculated this ratio. Mizon's (1981) finding reported previously was substantiated in a token-type ratio (the higher the value, the less variety, with 1 as the lowest possible value showing greatest variety). Her L2 teacher's ratios were 7 and 7.5 for content and function words, respectively, while for the L1 British teacher, the ratios were 2.3 and 4.3. Kliefgen's (1985) observation of a kindergarten ESL teacher's differential speech to three nonnative-speaking children and a native-speaking child also showed a higher token-type ratio for two of the NNSs (3.00 and 2.46) compared to the native-speaking child (2.07). One nonnative-speaking child was addressed with more varied vocabulary (although fewer total utterances), with a ratio of 1.69. Kliefgen suggests that this child was more skilled at initiating interaction, so the teacher was less compelled to direct additional utterances (or more simplified vocabulary) to her, under the instructional assumption that the less capable children required more assistance and activation. These interactional issues will be dealt with in greater detail in Chapters 4 and 5.

Henzl (1979) also compared verb token-type ratios across subjects, addressees, and stories. Since the range of values is somewhat broad (1.0–5.3), it is hard, without appropriate summary or inferential statistics, to judge the meaningfulness of her findings. There appears none-theless to be an increase in ratio for most subjects in their speech to beginner-level listeners (3 exceptions out of 11). The overall means are: native-speaking listeners, 1.5; advanced NNSs, 1.7; and beginner NNSs, 2.5.[3] The ratios for the first story tend, however, to be higher than for the second story.[4] In some cases, the ratios appear virtually equivalent across listener groups. Since Henzl appears not to have counterbalanced the order of presentation of the stories, it is not clear whether it was the second story, or the speakers' familiarity with the listeners by the second telling, that influenced the speakers' increased variety of verbs.

In contrast to these findings, which suggest that teachers use more basic, less varied vocabulary with nonnatives, Wesche and Ready's study (1985) revealed no significant differences between professors' speech to NSs and NNSs on any measure of type-token ratio or word-class distri-bution (content and function vocabulary). These comparisons were made on classes presenting identical content. Despite this finding, the authors report the transcript analyst's subjective impression that the French pro-fessor used more concrete (in contrast to more abstract) vocabulary with the NNSs, an impression that is difficult to quantify. It is very plausible that the more academically oriented nature of these classes, and the gen-erally advanced level of the learners, encouraged the professors to main-tain equivalent variety with both groups.[5] The evidence for vocabulary simplification for lower-level learners remains relatively uncontested.

Modifications of syntax

By far one of the most investigated and quantified characteristics of teacher talk has been teachers' syntactic modifications. These can be grouped into five types: measures of length of utterances, measures of subordination, measures of markedness, measures of grammaticality, and measures of distribution of sentence types.

MEASURES OF LENGTH OF UTTERANCE

There are conflicting findings on length of utterance. Some studies show that classroom speech to nonnatives is segmented into shorter utterances, and some studies find equal lengths of utterances addressed to native-

3 The mean ratio has been calculated across subjects, again based on Henzl's raw data, while disregarding probable differences in total tokens produced.
4 The first-story means are, respectively, 1.8, 2.2, 2.7, and the second-story means are 1.3, 1.3, 2.2.
5 Substantiation of this possibility is also seen in Mannon's (1986) report of (un-usually) high token-type ratios of 15.93 and 18.6 in teacher speech to NNS and NS addressees, respectively. With ratios this high, there is little difference between the two – type-token ratios would be the inverse, or 0.06 and 0.05, respectively.

TABLE 3.5. MODIFICATIONS IN LENGTH OF UTTERANCE

Study	Addressees			Significance of comparison between NS-NNS or other comp.
	NSs	NNSs		
Words per sense unit/utterance				
Mizon (1981)	7.2	6.3		Not tested
Kliefgen (1985) (MLU)	Subj. 4	Subj. 1	Subj. 5	
Time 1	5.27	3.18		Not tested
Time 2		3.81	3.59	
Time 3	5.52		3.75	
Words per sentence				
Henzl (1973)	10.96†@	6.8†@		Not tested
Henzl (1979)	19†@	5.8†@ (begin.) 10.1†@ (advanced)		Not tested
Håkansson (1986)	9.5			
Time 1		5.36†		
Time 2		6.28†		Not tested
Words per T-unit				
Gaies (1977b)	10.97	6.19 (mean) 4.3 (beginners) 5.75 (high begin.) 6.45 (intermed.) 8.26 (advanced)		Significant Differences across levels significant
Steyaert (1977)	12.87	11.01		Not significant
Dahl (1981) (ranges)	9.8–11.9	9.1–10.8		Not tested
Early (1985)	10.13–12.24	7.00		Significant
Wesche & Ready (1985)				
English	20.23	14.9		Significant
French	13.44	12.93		Not significant
Milk (1985)				
NNS		6.48 (low) 7.04 (mid) 7.97 (high)		Not significant
Ishiguro (1986)				
NS (in monologues)	15.26	10.24 (low) 10.19 (mid) 10.38 (high)		Significant

Study	Addressees		Significance of comparison between NS-NNS or other comp.
	NSs	NNSs	
NNS (in monologues)	12.67	9.64 (low) 9.63 (mid) 10.0 (high)	Significant
Mannon (1986)	15.98	13.59	Significant

†Means calculated from original raw figures.
@Means calculated for first story only.

speaking and nonnative-speaking listeners. The differences across studies may be attributable to analytical methods, which differ in the unit of analysis (e.g., utterance, sentence, or T-unit), in the segmentation of the speech itself, and in the definitions used for "word." Few researchers report their procedures for these analyses, making certainty about comparison difficult. Nonetheless, the absolute values found across studies, shown in Table 3.5, are of similar magnitudes, and the comparisons within each study suggest a trend toward shorter utterances directed to less proficient listeners.

Counting words per "sense unit," or utterance, which she segmented by intonation contour and pauses, Mizon (1981) found that teachers addressed the English native-speaking (L1) class with longer sense units (7.2 words) than the L2 class (6.3). Kliefgen (1985) used MLU (mean length of utterance, developed in L1 research), a measure involving a count of morphemes (bound and free) per utterance. Kliefgen does not specify more precisely how utterances were segmented, but since the addressees were kindergarten children, the low MLUs (relative to other length values in Table 3.5) of the teacher's address to two L2 children and one L1 child are plausible. Kliefgen found a slight increase in the teacher's length of utterance over three-month spans for all three children, and a larger MLU for speech to the L1 child.

Using words per sentence, where sentence was not defined, Henzl (1973, 1979) also found her subjects using shorter sentences in the narratives to L2 learners than in those for native speakers. Moreover, in Henzl (1979) the length of sentences addressed by NSs to nonnative-speaking beginners averaged 5.8, while those to advanced learners averaged 10.1, still far from the 19 words per sentence addressed to NSs. Håkansson (1986) evidently segmented Swedish sentences on a basis similar to that of a T-unit measure (as Henzl's measure may also be).[6] She compared teachers' classroom speech at five-week inter-

6 See Hyltenstam's (1983) discussion of this reanalysis, which, however, does not elaborate sufficiently on the specifics of the segmentation into units.

vals to data collected by others of informal speech among Swedish NSs. The mean words per sentence for each of the six teachers at Time 2 showed an increase over Time 1. (Only the overall means across teachers are shown in Table 3.5.) The mean for NS-NS informal conversation was 9.5.

The preceding studies suggest that teachers (as well as nonteachers, as in Henzl 1973) adjust their length of utterance downward for less proficient learners and gradually increase length as the learners improve in proficiency (a progress which is not entirely documented by Kliefgen or Håkansson) or as the teachers become more familiar with them. Yet these differences were not tested statistically, although the magnitudes and ranges appear to warrant a reasonably firm conclusion.

Gaies (1977b) was the first to perform a statistical test on length of T-units in L2 instructional settings.[7] He recorded and transcribed the classroom speech of teachers in training (who included some NNSs of English) at four levels of instruction (beginners, high beginners, intermediate, and advanced) and these same teachers' speech to one another in training discussions. On the basis of 500-word samples per subject at a given level (different subjects were recorded at each level), he found a significant overall trend toward longer teacher T-units (in words) for beginning- to advanced-level learners (means from 4.3 to 8.26). This effect was attributable specifically to the contrast between the beginner level and the pooled values for the remaining levels. The same teachers' speech among themselves in classroom discussions had a mean length of 10.97 (words per T-unit), compared to the overall mean of 6.19 for speech addressed to NNSs in classrooms, also a significant difference.

Early (1985) also compared length of T-unit in words of teacher talk in secondary-level social studies classes in Canada, where five teachers taught in each of two levels (junior and senior) to native-speaking students, and five taught social studies to ESL students. Following a significant analysis of variance result across conditions, Early tested the pooled means of speech to the two native-speaking classes against the ESL teacher talk. The difference was significant, with ESL students receiving much shorter utterances (7 words per T-unit vs. 10.13 and 12.24 for NSs).

Ishiguro (1986) compared length of both native- and nonnative-speaking teachers' one-way (monologue) speech to three levels of learners with speech among the teachers in evaluation discussions. Analysis of variance

7 Although Gaies (1977a) is the common citation for this research, there are a number of statistical and interpretive discrepancies between that report and 1977b, the dissertation on which it was based. Consequently, the discussion here assumes the dissertation report to be the more accurate.

was again significant for the addressee factor in both teacher groups. Post hoc comparisons for both groups of teachers showed significantly shorter utterances for L2 learners, with no difference in MLU between different levels of learners (see Table 3.5). Finally, Mannon's (1986) analysis of T-unit length also showed a significant difference on a *t*-test (two-tailed), with shorter utterances addressed to the NNS class.

Despite the apparently strong evidence that nonnative proficiency instills reduced length of teacher utterances, several studies have revealed little difference or no significant differences. All of these have used words per T-unit as the base measure. For example, Dahl (1981), discussed earlier in the section on rate of speech, reported values for mean words per T-unit (for six teachers) that are very close to one another for speech addressed to three supposed levels of L2 learner, and to NSs (recall, however, the weakness in her no-feedback design mentioned in the section on rate of speech). The only slight difference appears to be that the means for nonteachers compared to the teacher means are slightly higher, yet there were no significant differences revealed by analysis of variance.

Likewise, although Steyaert (1977) found a trend toward shorter T-units addressed to NNSs (for 8 out of 10 stories), the difference was not significant on a *t*-test. Wesche and Ready (1985) had mixed results, with the English professor showing a significant difference, but the French professor showing no significant difference. Still, the absolute values for the speech in the Dahl, Steyaert, and Wesche and Ready studies (range 9.1–14.9) are relatively higher than what was seen in other studies, thus raising some concern over the nature of the narrative task (in Steyaert and Dahl) or of the subject matter (in Wesche and Ready), which could be factors constraining the amount of simplification. Ishiguro's (1986) obtained values for differences in length of teacher utterance to levels of Japanese learners do not differ significantly from one another. Neither do Milk's (1985), in a test of the differences in his nonnative-speaking (Peruvian EFL) teachers' speech to three learner levels. The teachers' average length of utterance addressed to the researcher in interviews was, however, significantly higher than speech to the learners.

It should be evident that a variety of individual speaker and task variables will influence the overall magnitude of length of utterances, so that any positive or negative findings of differences in modifications should be viewed cautiously.[8] The interaction of length of utterance with

---

8 Note that several of Henzl's subjects produced extremely long sentences on their second story, a tendency which warranted their not being included in this calculation of means, for there may have been entirely unexpected factors influencing their changes.

other measures of complexity may also be a factor limiting direct conclusions. In fact, however, the results of other analyses of complexity are also conflicting.

MEASURES OF SUBORDINATION

For the comparison of subordination, shown in Table 3.6, the tabled values are mean number of clauses per T-unit, or equivalent base unit. Pica and Long (1986), who counted tensed and nontensed verb forms (a measure that approximates counting deep-structure sentoids), found that there were no differences in degree of subordination for teachers' speech to L2 learners (1.44) compared with NS-NNS conversations (clauses per T-unit = 1.30), or for experienced versus inexperienced teachers (1.48 vs. 1.52). In Dahl's one-way task, the teachers and nonteachers did not appear to differ from one another, or across levels of nonnative- and native-speaking listeners. Again, the evident lack of differences or trends could be influenced by the artificial nature of her task, but this is not a legitimate criticism of Pica and Long's results. The results of Steyaert (1977), Wesche and Ready (1985), and Mannon (1986) support these findings of no significant differences.

Yet the findings of other studies lend support to the hypothesis that teachers adjust the complexity of their speech downward when speaking to L2 or less proficient learners. Hyltenstam (1983) recalculated Håkansson's (1986) measures into T-units and found lower average degrees of subordination in teacher speech to nonnative-speaking learners than in the comparison NS-NS informal conversation data. (This difference was not tested statistically, yet the magnitudes are much farther apart than those in the previous studies.) Hyltenstam also found a tendency for the complexity to increase slightly from one time to the next (at five-week intervals). Milk (1985) supports this result. Milk's nonnative-speaking teachers used significantly more complex (one or more subordinate clauses) T-units relative to overall T-units in interviews with a NS than in classrooms (ratios of 0.29 and 0.15, respectively; these values are not entered in Table 3.6, as they are a different method of calculation). Since these separate findings compared two different speech contexts as well, one might question the results.

But Chaudron (1979) also reported trends toward greater complexity of speech (using the C-unit, the baseline unit described in Table 2.4 that is roughly equivalent to a T-unit; cf. Loban 1976) to more advanced-level learners in various subject matter classrooms, and in *intra*teacher comparisons for three teachers' speech to nonnative-and native-speaking students in similar classes. In his study, however, the fact that the teachers and subject matter changed at different learner levels is a confounding factor. Gaies's (1977b) results, from ESL lessons with teachers-in-training speaking to four NNS levels, show magnitudes similar to those in Chaudron's study, and he found the teacher speech to both low and high beginners each to be significantly less complex than the pooled values for higher levels. Also, Early (1985), who compared social studies teachers speaking to native- and nonnative-speaking students, found significantly less complex speech to L2 learners than the combined means of the two NS levels (NS levels = 1.63 and 1.46 S-nodes per T-unit, versus 1.19 for ESL students). Finally, Ishiguro (1986) found NS teachers' speech to peer teachers significantly more complex than to any level of learner.

Related to these findings is Henzl's (1973, 1979) comparison of frequency of subordinate clauses (no mention is made, however, of control over the baseline measure, namely, the length or segmentation of speakers' speech) in the native- vs. nonnative-speaking listener storytelling conditions. There was a tendency toward fewer subordinate clauses in the NNS condition. Similarly, Gaies (1977b) noted a trend for different types of subordinate clauses in teacher speech (adjective, adverb, and noun clauses per 100 T-units) to increase as the level of listener increased. Chaudron's (1979) data suggest such a trend only for adjective clauses, which Hunt (1966) had reported to be the most sensitive to advances in complexity in L1 students' writing. However, Wesche and Ready (1985) found no differences on any of these measures.

MEASURES OF MARKEDNESS

Regarding markedness (see for example, Rutherford 1982 for definition and discussion), other simplifications in speech to NNSs that have been reported include higher proportion of verbs in the simple present tense (Henzl 1973, 1979; Mizon 1981). Similarly, Long and Sato (1983) found a higher proportion of verbs marked for present than for nonpresent (future + past). This difference was statistically significant in Long and Sato's results, while for Wesche and Ready's (1985) English-speaking professor (actually a nativelike NNS), it was found significant only for the verb "to be." Wesche and Ready also report this professor using significantly more tensed verbs than nonfinite ones in speech to NNSs. Moreover, Henzl (1973, 1979) noted less inflectional complexity, less diversity in case roles, and lack of passive constructions, but she did not quantify these comparisons. She also reports (1979), as do Wesche and Ready for the English professor, a comparative avoidance of conditionals. The general lack of systematic comparability of measures of markedness across studies makes it more difficult to judge their value as modifications in teacher talk, yet it seems to be quite clear that teachers adapt their speech to less proficient learners to some extent by using less marked structures.

TABLE 3.6. MODIFICATIONS IN DEGREE OF SUBORDINATION[a]

Study	Condition and/or speaker	Addressee				Significance
		NSs	Advanced	Intermed.	Beginner	
Steyaert (1977)	Teachers	1.67	1.55			Not signif.
Gaies (1977b)	Practice teachers	1.60	1.38	1.21	1.14 (high) 1.02 (low)	#
Chaudron (1979) (ranges)	Teachers	1.61–1.77	1.36–1.67	1.24–1.46	1.10–1.15	Not tested
Dahl (1981) (ranges)	Teacher	1.1–1.2	1.2–1.3	1.1–1.2	1.2	Not tested
	Nonteacher	1.3–1.4	1.3	1.3–1.4	1.1–1.4	
Hyltenstam (1983) (reanalysis of Håkansson)	Teachers	1.55 (informal)				Not signif.
	Time 1				1.15	
	Time 2				1.22	
	Time 3				1.27	
Wesche & Ready (1985)	Teachers					
	English	2.2	2.02			Not signif.
	French	1.99	1.99			Not signif.
Early (1985)	NS teachers					Significant betw. pooled NS vs. ESL
	Senior	1.63				
	Junior	1.46				
	ESL			1.19		
Pica & Long (1986)	Teachers					
	Classroom			1.44		Not signif.
	Conversation			1.30		
	Experienced			1.48		Not signif.
	Inexperienced			1.52		

| Ishiguro (1986) | NS teachers | 1.79 | 1.38 | 1.35 | 1.29 | NS vs. each NNS signif. |
| Mannon (1986) | Teacher – content | 1.99 | | 1.72 | | Not signif. |

[a]Calculated on basis of clauses or sentoids per T-unit or equivalent.
#Beginner levels each significantly lower than pooled means of higher levels (see text).
Source: Adapted from Chaudron (1985b:223).

MEASURES OF GRAMMATICALITY

Although teachers and speakers to NNSs have generally been observed to use grammatical, well-formed sentences (Henzl 1973; Downes 1981; Håkansson 1986), frequent use of sentence fragments has been observed in some teachers' speech. Hyltenstam (1983) attributes this to the "didactic function of teacher talk"; fragments serve as elicitation devices, repetitions, and so on. Occasionally, ungrammatical speech has been reported (Downes 1981; Kliefgen 1985; Håkansson 1986; Ishiguro 1986). The ungrammatical utterances typically involve omissions of function words, of copula, of subject or object pronouns, articles, and so on. These instances appear to be rather rare in teachers' speech, although Kliefgen reports that about 24% of utterances in her teacher's speech contained some omission.

Pica and Long (1986) also examined dysfluencies in teachers' speech. These include false starts, hesitations, and interruptions. They found experienced teachers producing fewer dysfluencies than inexperienced ones, but teachers unfamiliar with the nonnative-speaking classes were not different from the regular classroom teachers. This variable appears to have more to do with the general competence of the teacher than with the learners' proficiency.

MEASURES OF SENTENCE TYPE DISTRIBUTION

This final type of syntactic analysis concerns the relative use of declarative/statement forms, interrogatives, and imperatives. While these forms have consequences for the pattern of classroom discourse, and thus for the sort of interaction that takes place, the basic comparison of their distribution is included here as a characteristic of teacher talk. We will have reason to reconsider these forms – especially questions – in later chapters, inasmuch as they affect the activation of learners in classroom tasks and possibly directly affect learning. Table 3.7 displays the percentages of the different types occurring in teachers' speech to L2 learners compared with L1 classrooms, NS-NNS conversations, and level of experience of the teacher.[9]

Long and Sato (1983) and Pica and Long (1986) found significant differences in the distribution of these types across comparison conditions. Early (1985) found each type to be significantly different between NS and NNS addressees. Mizon (1981) did not perform statistical tests, but a chi-square calculation on her reported frequencies reveals her data

---

9 For ease of comparison, the percentages in some cases are calculated based on the raw frequencies presented by the researchers. However, the statistical tests reported by the researchers are all calculated on the raw frequencies.

TABLE 3.7. MODIFICATIONS IN DISTRIBUTION OF SENTENCE TYPE

Study	Condition and/or addressee		Sentence type (%)			
			Declar. statement	Interrog.	Imper.	Significance[a]
Mizon (1981)	NNS		47	53	—	Signif.
	NS		78	22	—	
Long & Sato (1983)	Classroom		54	35	11	Signif.
	Conversations		33	65	1	
Pica & Long (1986)	(a) Classroom		65	24	13	Signif.
	Conversations		52	48	0	
	(b) Experienced teacher		66	20	13	Signif.
	Inexper. teacher		64	26	10	
	(c) Regular teacher		67	20	12	Signif.
	Visiting teacher		33	47	19	
Early (1985)	NS students (avg. jun. & sen. levels)		70	22	8	Signif. by type across conditions
	NNS students		52	30	18	(except interrog.)
Ishiguro (1986)	NS teacher	(low)[b]	53	43	4	Each was signif. for condition
		(mid)	54	41	5	
		(high)	54	40	6	
	NNS teacher					
		(low)	56	41	3	
		(mid)	60	38	3	
		(high)	56	42	3	

[a]Tests of significance are calculated on raw frequencies with the chi-square distribution when comparing among types; in the case of Ishiguro and Early, however, parametric tests were used.
[b]Low = beginner; mid = intermediate; high = advanced.

to be significant as well ($\chi^2 = 14.4$, df = 1, $p < .001$). The differences contributing to these significant findings appear to arise from a tendency for teachers to ask fewer questions of NS addressees than NNS addressees, and for more questions to be asked in conversations than in classrooms, presumably because of the pedagogical purposes of imperatives and declaratives. The greater the teacher's familiarity with the class and the more experienced the teacher is, the more this tendency is evident (Pica and Long 1986). Nevertheless, Mizon's and Early's findings reveal that this tendency toward a greater frequency of statements is not strictly a result of its being a second language class; rather, it may merely be a matter of general teacher talk. In other words, Mizon's and Early's higher proportion of questions addressed to L2 learners may be a result of the effort in those classes to check students' comprehension of the subject matter (geography and social studies, respectively). There is little doubt that the specific instructional goals and methodology adopted by the teacher will influence the extent of use of these forms.[10]

Modifications of discourse

FRAMING MOVES

Among more global aspects of teachers' discourse, conversational framing moves were examined by Early (1985) and by Pica and Long (1986). Early tested this difference in post hoc comparisons but found no significant differences, although there was a trend toward more frames for teachers addressing L2 learners compared with L1 instruction. Pica and Long (1986) believed that more experienced teachers would exhibit clearer and more frequent boundaries in their instruction through the use of framing moves (cf. Sinclair and Coulthard 1975, and Figure 2.3). This turned out to be false: the only significant difference in framing moves was that the visiting teachers used more, compared with the regular teachers. Pica and Long speculate that this was due more to the regular teachers' ability to structure the interaction through implicit signals.

SELF-REPETITIONS

Several researchers have analyzed teachers' self-repetitions quantitatively, on the assumption that repetitions may provide the learner with more opportunities to process the information or follow the teacher's model. Among a variety of teaching strategies which Hamayan and Tucker (1980) observed in grades 3 and 5 French immersion teachers' lessons, exact or paraphrase repetitions of the teachers' statements comprised 20% and 24%, respectively, of the strategies. (Commands and questioning were the other major strategies observed.) The frequency of repetitions was slightly lower, however, than for grades 3 and 5 teachers in comparison L1 French classes.

As a possible corrective on the previous finding, Wesche and Ready (1985) found *both* their French and English professors using significantly more words in exact and rephrased self-repetitions with their L2 classrooms than with their L1 classes. Early (1985) found ESL teachers using

10 The quite comparable distribution of types across learner levels in Ishiguro's study are possibly misleading, for they belie a high variability within the native- and nonnative-speaking teachers.

significantly more (about seven times as many) self-repetitions in their speech, compared with teachers speaking to NSs. Ellis (1985a) counted the same teacher's self-repetitions at two times in classroom interaction with two adolescent ESL students and found a significant decrease in frequency over the six-month period of observation. So self-repetitions are evidently used by teachers as modifications for improving comprehension.

Pica and Long (1986) did not find any differences in frequency of self-repetitions, either between the teacher levels of experience or of their familiarity with the L2 learners. This finding is not inconsistent with Early's, Wesche and Ready's, or Ellis's, for neither the factor of NS versus NNS addressee nor longitudinal changes were controlled variables in the Pica and Long study. It is possible, therefore, that Hamayan and Tucker's (1980) French L2 teachers made longer repetitions, albeit less often, than French L1 teachers. In a related result, Mannon (1986) counted repetitions (including paraphrases) to NSs and NNSs, while controlling for the separation between first utterance and repetition. Although an equal number of repetitions occurred within five T-units, the lecturer repeated substantially more often to the nonnative-speaking listeners (four times as much, compared to twice as much) after longer delays. This was evidently a strategy to ensure comprehension or retention of the material.

Summary of modifications

A wide range of phenomena in teacher speech have been reviewed which appear to some extent to adapt to the needs of L2 learners. The following are some examples of the findings concerning speech to lower-level NNSs:

1. Rate of speech appears to be slower.
2. Pauses, which may be evidence of the speaker planning more, are possibly more frequent and longer.
3. Pronunciation tends to be exaggerated and simplified.
4. Vocabulary use is more basic.
5. Degree of subordination is lower.
6. More declaratives and statements are used than questions.
7. Teachers may self-repeat more frequently.

Researchers have been concerned with the extent of teacher modifications for the primary reason that these are assumed to aid learners' comprehension. Although the current review is the first extensive comparison of results, it is perhaps not surprising that these same researchers have failed in most cases to investigate further the comprehensibility of teacher speech, given that the results are so mixed and difficult to document. (A few relevant studies on this topic will be considered in Chapter 6.) Since there has also been evidence of adjustments in teacher speech resulting from the teacher's general familiarity with the learners or the pedagogical purposes, the issue of whether the observed modifications truly result from teachers' sensitivity to learners' need for comprehension remains unsettled. (Cf. Chaudron 1986b for a study demonstrating teachers' possible sensitivity to simplification of discourse.)

Elaborated descriptions of teacher discourse

The final section of this chapter will consider one final feature of teacher talk which might be considered the epitome of the teacher's role, namely, vocabulary and grammar explanations.[11]

Explanations

One type of teacher behavior that has been surprisingly little investigated is the explanation, in the sense of providing information about grammatical rules, meanings of words, social uses of expressions, and so on. In Sinclair and Coulthard's (1975) system, explanations would typically be coded as "informative" acts, while in Fanselow's (1977a) system, "structuring" moves would be interpreted on the fourth dimension, "How are mediums used to communicate areas of content," in which most explanations would be types of "characterize" and "relate" (see Figure 2.1). It will be recalled from the section on functional allocation of teacher talk that J. D. Ramirez et al. (1986) found explanations to be the most dominant function of utterances in elementary bilingual education programs. Their category included both "procedural" explanations (i.e., many types of structuring of lesson activities) as well as explanations of concepts, names for things, and grammar rules (the latter two were rare occurrences). Regardless of the program type or level of class, procedural explanations consistently comprised almost two-thirds of the teachers' explanations, with concept explanations being used in about one-third of explaining utterances.

Faerch (1985, 1986) labels talk about the linguistic code "metatalk," stating that many lessons in traditional language teaching consist largely of such talk about the content of teaching. Faerch (1986) provides several examples of teachers providing pedagogical rules in class. These "rule-formulations" fit within a pedagogical sequence of acts which Faerch identifies as "problem-formulation," "induction," "rule-formulation," and "exemplification"; induction and exemplification are judged to be optional components of such a sequence. Faerch (1985) illustrates that teachers' "rules of thumb" and metatalk do not necessarily involve the

---

11 First language researchers have provided other useful descriptions of phenomena, such as teachers' directives (Holmes 1983).

use of grammatical terminology; he claims that, in fact, teachers' or students' metalinguistic attention to meaning, translation equivalents, and analogies between and within languages is an integral part of most early L2 learning experiences, at least in the foreign language context.

Chaudron (1982) illustrated a variety of ways in which teachers either explicitly or implicitly explain vocabulary by elaborating on the meaning of expressions – through paraphrase, definitions, exemplification, and naming. Yee and Wagner (1984) developed this approach with a more detailed description of the discursive segments of vocabulary and grammatical explanations. Their descriptive framework is illustrated in Figure 3.2, with several binary features listed as coincident with the different segments.

The optional *focus* segment may include + topic item, + metastatement, + teacher solicit; the obligatory explanation segment may include + explicit definition/rule and + direct usage; and the optional restatement segment can include + exact/partial repetition, + expansions, + examples. (See Faerch 1986 for more discussion on components of grammar explanations.) The following is an example of this sort of sequence in a vocabulary explanation:

Focus + metastatement	This expression "getting hitched" is kind of a popular...slang expression.
Explanation + explicit definition/rule	It means, "to get married"...ok? Hitched means "to put together"...ok?
Restatement + partial repetition	So getting hitched means to get married.

(Yee and Wagner 1984)

Yee and Wagner further distinguished between planned and unplanned explanations, and found the planned explanations tended especially to co-occur with certain other features: framing and focusing, examples, and restatements.

Conclusion

In this review, a variety of teacher behaviors have been described and compared across different contexts. Second language classroom speech involves a large number of modifications of normal conversational speech, although in no case do there appear to be entirely new qualities to the teacher speech, aside perhaps from ungrammaticality, and it appears to be limited. Only to the extent that quantitative differences are very extreme between L2 and L1 classroom discourse is it likely that there arise qualitative differences, in terms of the psycholinguistic or social effects on learners. The issue of what in fact learners might derive

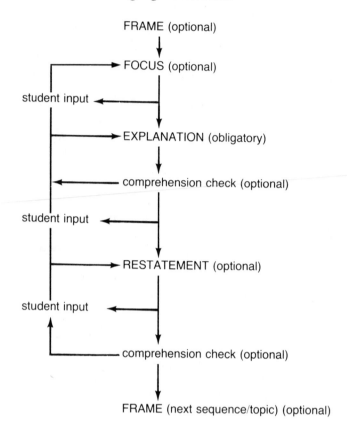

FRAME (optional)

FOCUS (optional)

student input

EXPLANATION (obligatory)

comprehension check (optional)

student input

RESTATEMENT (optional)

student input

comprehension check (optional)

FRAME (next sequence/topic) (optional)

Supercategory feature ($\pm$)	Subcategory feature ($\pm$)
Planned Teacher initiated Frame	
Focus	Topic item Metastatement Teacher solicit
Explanation	Explicit definition or rule Direct usage
Restatement	Exact/partial repetition Expansion Examples

Figure 3.2 Explanation sequence structure and binary system of analysis. (Adapted from Yee and Wagner 1984.)

from teachers' speech modifications, namely, their comprehension and acquisition of the L2, will be a topic of Chapter 6.[12]

Since a number of the features reviewed here had conflicting findings across studies, and factors such as the identity of the speakers and listeners were not consistently controlled, it is evident that greater rigor and a well-defined research agenda are needed for future studies of L2 teacher talk.

The next chapter balances this view of the teacher by looking at what classroom research has revealed about learners' classroom behaviors and language, and exploring the ways in which teachers and learners adjust to one another in classroom interaction. The evidence presented in this chapter has shown that teachers are aware of their learners' immediate but changing needs for comprehension and participation. But how they pursue communication and instruction in interaction with learners remains to be examined.

12 An important qualification is in order here. Throughout this chapter the concern has been whether observed differences were statistically significant, and when not, it had to be assumed that the differences might not in fact be real. The levels of significance employed have been the conventional ones of 0.05 or less. As was suggested in Chapter 2, however, researchers are entitled to alter their criterion levels of significance up (to smaller levels of probability) or down, thereby decreasing or increasing the power of the analysis to find significant differences, especially when it is believed that true differences are not being revealed or inferred at a given level. Since it is entirely possible that standard analyses and statistical distributions are not appropriate for use with linguistic analysis (i.e., we do not know the baseline distribution, or whether we are dealing with fixed or random effects – cf. Clark 1973), one must be cautious in assuming there are no differences between the complexity of speech in one situation versus another. Even if the statistics are correct, they do not necessarily reveal what the psychological effect of differences might be. A nonsignificant comparison might still be recognized by a learner as a difference, and one value in the comparison might have a true, psychologically significant effect on the learner's comprehension, learning, or attitude, resulting in differences with pedagogical and curricular value.

4 *Learner behavior in second language classrooms*

This chapter considers research on the contribution of the learner to acquisition of a second language. In L2 research since the early 1970s, an increasing emphasis has been placed on the role of the learner in L2 acquisition (Oller and Richards 1973; Richards 1986); classroom researchers have focused on learners' verbal and social interactions and have inferred learning strategies from learners' behavior in such interactions. In general in L2 research, learners as people have been considered more holistically than teachers have, with learners' personality and cognitive traits considered to be critical factors in the learning process.

The questions raised in this research have been of the following general types: What behaviors are characteristic of L2 learners in classrooms? What factors influence learners' classroom behaviors? What behaviors show the strongest relationship with positive learning outcomes? Although this last question will be addressed more fully in Chapter 6, research on learners' classroom behavior has developed several hypotheses concerning learners' contribution to L2 acquisition. The sources of these hypotheses in the data and tentative conclusions about relationships to learning are described in this chapter. The hypotheses are:

1. Learners develop in the L2 by producing the target language more frequently, more correctly, and in a wider variety of circumstances.
2. Learners develop in the L2 by generating input from others.
3. Learners develop in the L2 by engaging in communicative tasks that require negotiation of meaning.

These hypotheses will form the basis for organizing the results of studies on learner behavior.

In addition, a final section of this chapter examines studies of learners' learning strategies, a relatively recent area of investigation in second language classroom research.

The general findings of studies of learner behavior displayed in Table 4.1 are grouped under these categories: a) language performance (i.e., measures of linguistic output – quantity and quality), b) interaction-initiating behavior (e.g., hand-raising, asking questions, choice of interactant), and c) social-functional acts (i.e., speech acts and other pragmatic dimensions of linguistic interaction). Studies of learner-learner interaction are included here, especially several studies of learners interacting with NSs and other learners in experimentally constructed simulations of typical classroom language games or tasks (for example, problem solving, figure matching, and debates). Excluded from this table are aspects of these and other studies that analyzed learners' interactions with teachers. These findings will be reviewed in Chapter 5.

Language production

The first hypothesis, that learners will develop by producing the target language more frequently, and more correctly, follows the rather traditional notion that acquisition of a skill results from productive practice of the skill. Ellis (1980) argued in favor of this view, and the idea has received its most recent expression in the "comprehensible output hypothesis" discussed by Swain (1985:248):

One function of output is that it provides the opportunity for meaningful use of one's linguistic resources. [Frank] Smith ... has argued that one learns to read by reading, and to write by writing. Similarly, it can be argued that one learns to speak by speaking.

Swain goes on to suggest that the learner's output should be

pushed towards the delivery of a message that is not only conveyed, but that is conveyed precisely, coherently and appropriately. Being "pushed" in output ... is a concept that is parallel to that of the $i + 1$ of comprehensible input. (p. 249)

Swain offers evidence for this position from research comparing the proficiency of grade 6 French as a second language immersion students with 10 grade 6 native French speakers, in Ontario and Quebec, respectively. The L2 learners had had seven years of French immersion experience, that is, with most of their instruction in French from kindergarten through grade 6 (average about 80% each year). On most measures in a range of tests of oral and written proficiency, the learners proved to be significantly less proficient than natives, understandably enough, given the small number of contact hours with the target language compared to L1 peers.

The immersion students have developed, in the early grades, strategies for getting their meaning across which are adequate for the situation they find themselves in: they are understood by their teachers and peers. There appears to be little social or cognitive pressure to produce language that reflects more appropriately or precisely their intended meaning: there is no push for them to be more comprehensible than they already are. (p. 249)

The notable exception on the student test outcomes was on measures of written production evaluated on the basis of discourse performance,

TABLE 4.1. STUDIES OF LEARNER BEHAVIORS IN SECOND LANGUAGE
CLASSROOMS

Study	Class level(s)	Data collection	L1	L2	N of subjects
Naiman et al. (1978)	Grades 8, 10, 12	Classroom observation, interviews	English	French	12 classes, 72 students
Strong (1983, 1984)	Kindergarten (bilingual)	Classroom observation	Spanish	English	13 students
Peck (1985)	Kindergarten, 3 levels of proficiency	Peer tutoring NS-NNS (experiment)	Spanish	English	9 students
D. Johnson (1983)	Bilingual summer prog.; 5–9 yrs old	Peer tutoring NS-NNS over 5 weeks	Spanish	English	8 NS-NNS peer pairs; 8 teacher-NNS pairs
Pica & Doughty (1985)	University ESL, low intermed.	Classroom observation (experiment)	Mixed	English	3 classes
Cathcart (1986b)	Kindergarten bilingual ed.	Observation of activity situations	Spanish	English	8 pupils
Cathcart (1986a)	Kindergarten bilingual ed.	Observation of activity situations	Spanish	English	4 pupils

Language performance	Initiating behavior	Functional interaction
*S complete sentences + correlation w/imitation & comprehension	*S hand-raising + corr. w/ comprehension & imitation	*Student voluntary clarification, correction, elaboration, all + corr. w/comprehension
*S continuing responses − corr. w/comp. & imitat.		
*S correct responses + corr. w/comp. & imitat.		
*S partially correct & incorrect responses − corr. w/ comp. & imitat.		
*S responding above 10 times + corr. w/comp. & imitat.		
*S no response − corr. w/ comp.		
*Responsiveness + corr. w/ structure, vocab., pronunciation	*Gregariousness + corr. w/ vocabulary	
*Talkativeness + corr. w/ structure, vocab.		
*Across high/med./low Ss: descending type/token vocab. ratio, slower rate of speech, fewer words relative to peer tutor		Lower students show more lack of understanding
*Children w/NS tutors spoke more to NS children in other contexts than controls	*Children w/NS tutors initiated more interactions than controls	
*S production grammar = between peer group & teacher group		
*More production in peer group vs. teacher-fronted group		
Trend for more student turns in peer vs. teacher group		
Complexity of requests for action increases when *joint* goal involved w/ peers	NNSs use more control acts than NS peers	
	To adults: info. requests most frequent, successful in getting response	

TABLE 4.1 (*continued*)

Study	Class level(s)	Data collection	L1	L2	N of subjects
Cathcart (1986a) cont.					
Porter (1986)	University ESL intermediate, advanced	Experiment pairs/triads	Spanish	English	12 students
Duff (1986)	University ESL	Experiment pairs in tasks	Chinese/ Japanese	English	8 students
Seliger (1977)	University ESL	Classroom observation	Mixed	English	6 students
Day (1984, 1985)	Pre-university ESL	Classroom observation	Mixed	English	5 classes, 58 students
Scarcella & Higa (1981)	Elementary and secondary	Experiment pairs in task	Spanish	English	14 students
Sato (1982)	University ESL	Classroom observation	Mixed	English	2 classes, 31 students
Saville-Troike (1984)	Elementary 2nd–6th grade	Classroom observation	Mixed	English	19 pupils
Long et al. (1976)	University ESL intermediate	Classroom observation & experiment	Spanish	English	—
Gaies (1983b)	University ESL	Experiment triads & pairs in tasks	Mixed	English	12 subjects

Language performance	Initiating behavior	Functional interaction
	To children: info. requests & labeling objects most successful, state intent most frequent, calls for attention *not* successful for verbal response	
Advanced learners produced = quantity of words as NS (but lower quality & ratings) All learners produced more words in interaction w/ NNS than w/NS		More prompts in NNS-NNS than in NNS-NS NNS-NS = NNS-NNS in repairs (confirmation check, comprehension check; clarification requests)
*Quantity of words = betw. tasks (Problem solving & Debate) *C-units, turns more in Prob. solv. vs. Debate *Words/turn, words/C-unit, S-nodes/C-unit more in debate vs. Prob. solv.	*Chinese Ss dominate in turn-taking	Prob. solv. superior to Debate: *Total questions *Questions per subject *Total confirmation checks *Total referential questions
	Students' frequency of interaction & initiated interaction + corr. w/final grammar & aural comp. No corr. between initiated interaction and proficiency	
	*Adolescents initiate new topics > than children or NS adults	*Adolescents use clarification requests & signals of noncomprehension > than children *Adolescents use initiates in cooperative dialogues more
	*Asians self-select < others *Asians bid more frequently before turns	
Verbal interaction small corr. w/reading achievement *Verbal interaction + corr. w/syntax proficiency		
		Pedagogical moves, social skills, rhetorical acts greater for groups than teacher-fronted Variety of pedagogical & social skills greater for groups Reacting moves the dominant feedback type

TABLE 4.1 (*continued*)

Study	Class level(s)	Data collection	L1	L2	N of subjects
Doughty & Pica (1986)	University ESL intermediate	Classroom observation & experiment	Mixed	English	—
Rulon & McCreary (1986)	University ESL	Classroom observation peer- and teacher-led groups	Mixed	English	2 classes
Gass & Varonis (1985)	University ESL	Experiment triads and dyads in tasks	Mixed	English	9 subjects

*Denotes a significant result, with the relationship or direction indicated.

where the L2 learners' mean scores tended in fact to surpass the native learners on all discrete measures. On the basis of factor analysis, Swain argues that the learners' performance in written French was distinct from their oral performance, and the relative superiority of the former is attributable to the greater amount of demanding practice the learners had had with writing tasks.

The research that has examined learners' production in classrooms is remarkably sparse in terms of associations of these measures with learning outcomes or with independent factors, such as type of classroom activity. Nevertheless, several of the studies shown in Table 4.1 reveal some degree of differentiation among overall proficiency of learners and among activities, in measures of quantity, accuracy, and complexity of learner speech.

One large-scale study of grades 8, 10, and 12 French as a second language (FSL) classes (Naiman et al. 1978) found significant correlations between learners' classroom production measures, and their performance on standardized listening comprehension tests (IEA test of French achievement) and elicited imitation tests (see the first entry in the "language performance" column in Table 4.1). The more proficient the FSL learners were, the more likely they were to produce correct and complete responses, and to be among the most frequent responders. On the other hand, there was a significant negative correlation between the

Language performance	Initiating behavior	Functional interaction
		*Comprehension check, confirmation check, clarification requests, repairs, preventive moves, reacting, and self/other repetition a) = betw. tasks in teacher groups b) *greater* for groups w/required info. exchange c) *more* in groups than teacher-fronted class
*Productivity & complexity = betw. peer groups & teacher-fronted discussion		*Confirmation checks, clarification checks on lesson content greater in group vs. teacher-fronted
		*Indicators of noncomprehension = between one- and two-way information exchange tasks

proficiency measures and learners' amount of continuing responses, and partially correct or incorrect responses. Learners' failure to respond was also negatively correlated with the comprehension measure. These findings are not too surprising, in that they support the virtually self-evident notion that successful learners will perform more, and more correctly, in language classrooms. Since the classroom performance may be a *consequence* of the learners' proficiency, and prior proficiency was not controlled by Naiman et al., no causal conclusion can be drawn from these correlational relationships about the effectiveness of correct or more frequent responses in promoting greater TL competence.

Strong (1983) supports the notion that greater proficiency is related to responding in a longitudinal observation of 13 kindergarten children in bilingual education. He reported that the children's responsiveness as measured by responses to utterances of others showed significant correlations with proficiency measures. Talkativeness and gregariousness also correlated with at least one of the proficiency measures.

Peck (1985) also found a positive relationship between proficiency in kindergarten ESL learners (high, medium, or low, as measured by teachers' ratings) and the learners' production in amount (number of words) and rate (words per minute). These children were observed in a dyadic game-playing, tutoring encounter with a slightly older native-speaking child. An inverse relationship held for vocabulary variety, however. Although they used fewer words, the lowest proficiency group had a significantly higher type-token ratio (0.46) than the other two groups (0.28 and 0.27).

Learner production and situational factors

Learners' production measures have also been investigated with regard to the situational factors that influence quantitatively more, and more proficient, production. Several studies of this sort have necessarily been, like Peck's, quasi-experimental in design, but since the learners' tasks have been typical of the sort used in second language classrooms (and not, for example, like testing situations, interviews, or conversations), the results are included in the present review.

Peer interlocutors may be beneficial to learner production. D. Johnson (1983) conducted an experiment with 16 ESL children (L1 Spanish; 5–9 years old) in a summer bilingual program. She paired eight of these children with English native-speaking peers for a tutoring session every day for five weeks. Each pair alternated in the tutor and tutee roles, while the eight control children did the activities in a teacher-directed group. The treatment group and a matched control group were observed for parts of the rest of each day in regular play and class activities. From a regression analysis on measures of interaction over time, Johnson found a trend over time for the treatment group to increase in amount of speech with fluent English-speaking interactants. The only indication of the treatment group's development in proficiency was that their comprehension of vocabulary (Peabody Picture Vocabulary Test) showed a significant positive increase over time, compared with the control children. A supporting finding is that of Pica and Doughty (1985). They compared adult ESL students' production in peer groups with that in teacher-fronted class discussion. The learners produced significantly more T-units and fragments, and no less grammatical language, in the group work.

Cathcart's (1986b) finding helps to interpret the effect of an interlocutor. She observed eight Spanish L1 kindergarten children in a variety of activities over the course of one year and analyzed the children's production principally in functional terms. She reports differences in numbers and surface forms of several communicative acts across the observed situations. For example, Cathcart found that the children used longer and more complex requests for action in addressing an adult, compared with those addressed to peer interlocutors. An increase in utterance length or complexity was found, however, in those peer-peer interactions involving tasks with a joint goal (as in a joint block-building activity). The difference in effect of an adult interlocutor may be a result of the more personal interactions that Cathcart observed, compared with the instructional contexts in Johnson's (1983) and Pica and Doughty's (1985) studies. Cathcart points out, moreover (personal communication), that the more complex child utterances in speech to adults were those which the children initiated.

Porter (1986) also studied the effect of an interlocutor on learner production, by experimenting with dyads and triads of adult intermediate and advanced NNSs and NSs. Porter's L1 Spanish learners produced more words in interaction with nonnative-speaking peers than with NSs, on three problem-solving tasks (values clarification games). Furthermore, the advanced learners produced an *equal amount* of words to NSs' production on the tasks, although the overall *quality* (measured by objective means and by holistic ratings) of the NNS speech was lower.

In an attempt to determine the effect on production of particular task types, Duff (1986) distinguished between convergent and divergent tasks on the basis of the goals set for participants in two problem-solving and two debate tasks. She matched four dyads of university ESL learners for proficiency and found no significant differences in the quantity of total words or communication units (C-units; see Table 2.4 and Loban 1976) produced by learners in the two task types. But she did find the learners taking significantly more turns each in the problem-solving tasks than in the debates. Consequently, the learners produced more words per turn and per C-unit in the debates than in the problem-solving discussions. Moreover, the debate C-units were more complex (in S-nodes) than those in problem solving. Other differential effects for different types of information exchange tasks will be noted in a later section on interaction.

Summary

In support of Swain's (1985) argument, there is some evidence that more production and more correct production is associated with TL proficiency (Naiman et al. 1978; Strong 1983; Peck 1985). However, these studies demonstrate a correlation rather than causation. A more direct causal relationship is investigated in studies to be discussed in Chapter 6.

Furthermore, several of these studies suggest that more language, possibly more complex language, and no less grammatically correct target language, can be encouraged if learners interact with their peers, in small groups, or on convergent tasks (D. Johnson 1983; Pica and Doughty 1985; Duff 1986; Porter 1986); yet it appears from other studies that production alone may not be sufficient to ensure progress. The following sections will consider the roles of input generation and of interaction in promoting target language development.

Input generation

In Chapter 3 the notion was considered that the teacher's input to learners could influence L2 acquisition by being modified in various ways. The counterpart notion concerning the learner is that those learners who initiate interactions that result in speech directed to them will derive more benefit from the input than if they are exposed to the input in a more vicarious manner. Seliger (1977:266–7) expressed this notion in relating it to the general principle that such learners would thereby engage in more practice with the language:

Some students, the high input generators, are actively involved and, like the child, cause input to be directed at them by calling out, answering out of turn, and working out answers to questions or drill cues directed to others. Such students can often be observed talking to themselves during language drills. Still other students, the low input generators, sit quietly but rarely and in some extreme cases never participate unless specifically asked to do so.

Seliger operationalizes the notion of input generation by measuring behaviors that reflect the learners' initiative to produce language. This may seem to be a spurious approach. One might prefer to observe behaviors like requests for information or assistance, or initiations of new topics. Yet the argument could be made that precisely those learners who are most eager to provide responses are those who would also initiate interactions. Such a relationship would of course require independent corroboration, but it has not been studied directly. Nevertheless, several studies provide analyses pertinent to this issue.

In the Good Language Learner Project, discussed previously (Naiman et al. 1978), a variety of learner behaviors had been observed, but only the measures of "hand-raising" and "student-teacher questioning" (number of times a student asked a question) were explicit input-generating actions. The measure for hand-raising in fact correlated the highest of all the observed behaviors with the dependent measures of imitation and comprehension proficiency. For all grade levels together, the best predictor of these dependent measures, in stepwise regression analysis, was hand-raising. Yet when the individual grade levels were analyzed, this relationship held true only for the lowest grade 8, and the hand-raising variable was deleted from the regression model in later steps as other observed behavioral measures (especially "complete responses") combined to explain more of the variance in proficiency. A possible explanation for this outcome may be that student initiative in the beginning classes is more important than other factors; alternatively, the variability in such L2 productive measures as "complete responses" may not have been as great for the early stages of learning, thus not as highly correlated with achievement measures.

Nevertheless, hand-raising did show a significant positive correlation with measures taken of the learners' motivation, and integrative and instrumental orientation. These results suggest that attitudinal variables and students' proficiency may underlie the overt initiating behaviors, instead of a relationship in the other direction. As further confirmation of this suspicion, the student-teacher questioning measure showed no significant relationship to any proficiency measures, rather only to cognitive measures of field independence, and to behavioral measures of self-initiated repetition and callouts.

It will be recognized, however, that these last two positive correlations precisely support Seliger's proposed association among initiating behaviors, although the Good Language Learner Project results did not test the *causal* relationship between them and acquisition. Seliger (1977) chose to test the effects of input generating behavior on the *change* (improvement difference) in learner proficiency over a 15-week semester. One upper-intermediate level intensive university ESL class was observed for four hours, and students' total number of "speech acts" were tallied as a measure of interaction. Of these, the number of interactions that were "initiated" was coded, and six learners were selected whose total interactions and percentage of initiated interactions would rank them as either high- ($N = 3$) or low- ($N = 3$) input generators. Significant positive correlations were reported between these learners' percentage of initiated interaction and both a) course-final aural comprehension scores and b) change (percentage of improvement) in grammar scores from placement test to final score (identical pre- and posttest). In addition, *total* number of interactions correlated with these, and also with final grammar scores. Seliger also found significant positive correlations between the two classroom behavior measures and a quantification of the learners' self-reports of amount of contact and interaction with the L2 in extracurricular activities. He claims that these results support the notion that learners who engage more in interaction with others (inside and outside the classroom) will get more focused input and thereby develop faster. There are methodological problems with Seliger's analysis, however, which render his conclusions questionable.[1]

---

1 Seliger does not report that his coefficients of correlation were Spearman rho rank-order correlations, which are more liberal than Kendall's tau when ties are found. Since several of the coefficients appeared unusually high, these were recalculated from the data reported in Table 1 (1977:269), using the SPSSX NONPAR CORR procedure. This recalculation did not replicate all the coefficients reported in Table 2 (1977:272); four of the significant tabled values are too high, and two of these are no longer significant — those of final aural comprehension with total interac-

Day (1984, 1985) attempted a replication of Seliger's study on a larger population, since findings on a sample of six subjects can hardly be considered generalizable. Day also refined Seliger's coding of input generation and limited the measure of interactions to those initiated spontaneously by the learner. Day thus coded only learners' responses to (teacher) general solicits (and not to teacher-initiated solicits directed to specific learners) and learners' self-initiated turns. Day also believed that Seliger's inclusion of the learners' L1 interactions was an inappropriate indicator of L2 input generation. Four-hour observations of learners were made twice over a span of eight weeks, and special proficiency tests were administered. Out of 58 observed learners, 14 high-input generators and 12 low-input generators were selected for comparison on the proficiency measures. Day reports, however, that no significant correlations between the classroom measures and proficiency were obtained, thus providing no support for the hypothesis that high-input generators would have greater proficiency.

Day's inability to replicate Seliger's findings led him to question several aspects of the earlier study. He points out a) the refinement in the behavioral measures of input generation may be one source of failure to replicate, but also b) the use of an integrative proficiency measure (the Bachman-Palmer oral interview), as compared with Seliger's discrete point test of grammar, was another possible source. It should also be noted that Day tested subjects' change in proficiency over the observation period using a regression analysis in which class level was controlled for (the observations in the study had been made on five separate class groups originally placed on the basis of proficiency, and there was a significant correlation between class level and results on the end-of-observation period oral interview $- r = 0.47$). So the removal of variance attributable to the learners' degree of fluency at the start of observation should better reveal the relationship between subsequent behavior and proficiency at the end.[2]

tions ($\rho = 0.725$), and percentage change in structure score with total interactions ($\rho = 0.657$). Given the large number of correlations tested, the low sample size, and Seliger's use of a one-tailed test, it is difficult to have confidence in the findings of significance in this study.

2 Seliger's use of percentage improvement was not the best form of adjustment for development over the period in question. Such "change score" measures automatically bias against a more proficient learner and in favor of the lowest proficiency learners at starting time. Seliger should at least have established equivalence of the two groups on the pretests. Analysis of covariance or the regression procedure used by Day would have been more appropriate.

On the other hand, Day's study would also have benefited from a pretest of the sort used as posttest, instead of relying on the classroom placement to differentiate beginning proficiency. Furthermore, there are several weaknesses in Day's study. One was pointed out by Seliger in an exchange at the Seventeenth Annual TESOL Convention in Toronto, 1983, namely, that Day's subjects were predominantly

Although these studies differ in their operationalization of learners' initiating behavior, and the relationship of such behavior to target language development is not established, several other studies have revealed interesting relationships between degree of learners' initiation of interaction and other situational factors or learner characteristics.

Age and initiating

Scarcella and Higa (1981) compared the amount of initiation of new topics by nonnative (L1 Spanish) children and adolescents in experimental block-building interactions with native-speaking adults. The authors found that the adolescents initiated new topics at a significantly greater rate than did either the L2 children or native-speaking adults in interaction with other native-speaking adults. They conclude that older learners may be better at sustaining the conversation in ways to obtain the most comprehensible input. As a qualification on Scarcella and Higa's finding, there is evidence in data from a longitudinal study of L1 Spanish ESL kindergarten children (Cathcart et al. 1979; Cathcart 1983, 1986a; Strong 1983, 1984) that young L2 learners can nonetheless be effective in initiating and controlling conversations.

Social contexts and functions of initiation

Among a variety of functions of children's speech, Cathcart (1983, 1986b) distinguishes "control acts" from "information acts," "social routine," and "play with language." She noted unequal distributions of these types of acts across situations, where some situations (recess, a playhouse activity, individual seat activity, free play) involved larger percentages of controlling acts that could be interpreted as initiating ("call for attention," "request object," and "request action"). The information-sharing act "request for information" was also relatively frequent in seat work. Cathcart also found that L2 learners used more control acts than their TL-fluent peers (some of whom were also pro-

Asian, thus limiting generalizability of the findings (although there was considerable variability in the frequency of input-generating measures). A second problem is that Day's classification of learners, like Seliger's, was based on observations at one time. However, Day is unclear about the exact criteria used for selecting the high- and low-input generators included for proficiency testing. On the basis of the data reported for the two classroom observations, the subjects selected do not appear to fall consistently into well-defined groups. The classification should not matter greatly in this case, since Day's analysis involved parametric correlations between test scores and frequencies of classroom behaviors, and the selection of the predominantly more extreme high- and low-input generators should in fact tend to *bias in favor of* a significant correlation, because of the somewhat artificial spread in variance resulting from this sample.

ficient in the L1), presumably because these allowed them to participate in play with a minimum of linguistic production.

In a narrower study of these children Cathcart (1986a) analyzed the responsiveness of native-speaking children and the adult observer to four of these L2 children's functional acts. She calculated the rate of response and the number of responses that expanded the child's utterances. While the adult responded to 100% of the children's requests for information (the most frequent act), requests for action, calls for attention, labeling of objects and actions, and statements of intent, the native-speaking peer interactant responded to about 50% of the acts, with requests for information and labeling objects the most elicitative of responses. However, expanded responses occurred most for requests for information. Expanded responses also occurred frequently for statements of intent, an interesting result, for it raises a new consideration, that cooperative interaction involves a responsiveness to the speaker's announcement of intentions. Cathcart's observations suggest an important corrective to the previous research on initiating behaviors: that learners' initiating behaviors may be differentially effective depending on the social circumstances and the nature of the initiations.

Strong's (1983, 1984) study of the same group of learners related measures of the learners' proficiency and social-psychological characteristics to their social interaction. He found (1983) that the children's talkativeness (i.e., initiations of conversation) and gregariousness (i.e., number of different interlocutors) had a significant positive correlation with their L2 vocabulary skills, as well as (for talkativeness) with L2 structural skills. Yet, as a corrective on the notion that talkativeness, gregariousness, and so on imply the generation of target language input, Strong (1984) claims that the more proficient children did not tend to associate more with native-speaking children during the early stages of learning than did slower learners. Thus, the faster learners do not necessarily get more target language input (their gregariousness may just be general social behavior); rather, they make more effective use of the input they receive. This result concurs with the finding reported by Saville-Troike (1984), who observed 19 ESL elementary learners in both playground and classroom interaction.

Strong's finding is consistent with D. Johnson's (1983) experiment in the summer bilingual program with young children (see the section on learner production and situational factors). She had found that the experimental children who had engaged in tutoring with native-speaking peers initiated more interactions with nonnative-speaking playmates, but that there was no relationship between the amount of interaction with NSs and growth in L2 proficiency (measured by correlations on posttest measures with pretest scores partialed out).

Cultural factors and initiation

A final issue in learner initiation of language concerns cultural differences in learners' classroom production. Sato (1982) investigated this question in a study of two university ESL classes. She was especially concerned with the different turn-taking styles of Asian and non-Asian students. One variable studied was the number of self-selected turns taken by the groups, that is, student-initiated turns that were not dependent on prior solicits. Research on classes with ethnic minorities illustrates differential cultural expectations for the manner of participation in school class-rooms (e.g., Cazden et al. 1972; Philips 1972; Brophy and Good 1974; Laosa 1979; Malcolm 1986b; cf. also Trueba et al. 1981). Some students (e.g. blacks, some Hispanics, native Americans) tend to be less direct or aggressive in initiating interaction with the higher-status teacher. Sato suspected that Asian students might differ, although no directional or qualitative hypotheses were made. She found that the Asians as a group (Chinese, Japanese, and Korean), although greater in numbers than non-Asians (Latin Americans, Europeans, and Middle Easterners), took significantly fewer self-selected turns than non-Asians (34% vs. 66%, respectively, of the total turns) with the Asians adhering more strictly to a pattern of bidding for turns in class (38% of turns were bid for by Asians, vs. 18% by non-Asians), instead of just speaking out. Thus, in these classes, Asians' expectations for appropriate turn-taking proce-dures may be denying them their possibilities for manipulating input. The teachers' reactions to this behavior, to be discussed in the next chapter, clearly distinguished between the groups.

Nevertheless, ethnic or cultural effects on participation need to be ex-plored more fully. Duff's study (1986) of Japanese and Chinese dyads re-vealed a significant tendency for the Chinese subjects to dominate the interaction in every measure of linguistic productivity (turns, length of ut-terance, etc.). There are surely a number of factors involved, including the specific ethnic group concerned and, possibly, age and personality vari-ables (although in Naiman et al. 1978, no personality variables – specifi-fjcally extroversion, sensitivity to rejection, and empathy – were correlated with participation behaviors). Also, some data collected in a pilot anal-ysis of different ethnic group response rates in secondary ESL classrooms (Kocher and Potter 1985) supports the speculation that the proportion of an ethnic group in the class could influence their degree of participation.

Summary

A direct relationship between learners' initiating behaviors and development in proficiency is not supported by the preceding studies. Yet it does appear that more subtle distinctions in the factors involved, for example, functional types of initiations, and social or age relationships, may influence the amount of initiation and interlocutors' response to initiating behaviors. Cultural differences may furthermore influence the extent to which particular learners engage in classroom interaction at all.

With such limitations, it seems inappropriate to regard initiating behaviors and the presumed input generated from them as the ultimate factors responsible for language acquisition in classrooms. As will be seen in the following section, features of learners' interactions with one another are equally plausible factors that can influence the way in which learners acquire the target language.

Interaction between learners

Several features of learner behavior examined thus far ultimately involve interaction in the classroom (e.g., responsiveness and initiations), yet there are theoretical grounds for distinguishing between these forms of participation and what are sometimes referred to as "negotiating" behaviors in interaction. Following the arguments that Long (1983b) has made for the importance of NSs' negotiation for meaning as a contribution to learners' development, and that Ellis (1984b:ch. 5) has proposed concerning the mutual construction of meaning in language classrooms, a number of recent studies have focused on the interactive discourse between learners who are engaged in L2 learning tasks.

The behaviors considered in this section include speech acts that are contingent on previous utterances and that in some way negotiate meaning or maintain conversation by reacting to the preceding discourse: clarifying, modifying, repeating, asking for clarification, and so on. Here learners are not merely interacting; they are interacting to clarify meanings. The effects are presumed to differ from the previous behaviors we have reviewed, in that the linguistic, semantic, and pragmatic rules of the learners' interlanguage are presumably put to the test, in terms of their communicative results, when learners are negotiating for meaning as opposed to when they are simply responding or initiating.

Such a distinction may seem arbitrary, but it is probably warranted, considering the failure of "interaction" to correlate with school achievement in Saville-Troike's (1984) year-long study of 19 ESL children. This study will be examined in more detail in Chapter 6, but it is sufficient to note here that Saville-Troike's operationalization of "interaction" (in which the interlocutor – child or adult – was distinguished) amounted simply to a tally every 30 seconds as to whether the learner was engaged in some verbal exchange with an interlocutor. Although functions were evidently noted, they were not fully reported, and there is no way of knowing to what extent the learners were negotiating meanings in Long's or Ellis's sense, or merely "verbalizing." A finer distinction of this sort could differentiate more from less effective "interactions" in Saville-Troike's study. Whenever it makes a difference, the term "interaction" used alone will refer henceforth to the narrower sense of negotiation of meaning in learner-learner or teacher-learner communicative exchanges, and the more general sense of interaction will be appropriately qualified.

While a number of issues concerning interaction from the teacher's point of view will be treated in Chapter 5, this section will compare the results of several classroom studies of learner-learner interaction, and of several quasi-experimental studies involving learners in communicative tasks resembling classroom activities. Both the influence of classroom organization (e.g., group vs. teacher-fronted) and of task types will be considered.

Classroom organization

L1 research has shown the viability of peer group organization for classroom instruction (see Peterson, Wilkinson, and Hallinan 1983). In L2 contexts as well, learner-learner interaction may be more valuable than NS-NNS, for as Varonis and Gass (1985) showed, NNS-NNS dyadic interactions involved more meaning-negotiating exchanges than NS-NNS interactions. They argued that NNSs feel more free with one another to indicate noncomprehension and negotiate for meaning. Five studies of adult ESL learners have investigated the effects of group organization on interactive behaviors, usually by comparing teacher-fronted classes and peer-group dyadic discussions.

Long et al. (1976) reported that there was a significantly greater *number* of students' pedagogical moves, social skills behaviors, and rhetorical acts (the first two of which include interactional acts) in group work than in a teacher-fronted ("lockstep") classroom. Dyads also exhibited a significantly greater *variety* of pedagogical moves and social skills. The researchers point out that the greater quantity in peer group discussion is less surprising and perhaps less important than the finding for greater variety.

Doughty and Pica (1986) performed a similar quasi-experimental comparison between teacher-fronted and group work on a problem-solving task. They also made a comparison with Pica and Doughty (1985) between *types* of task, which is relevant to the topic of the following subsection. Whereas Pica and Doughty (1985) used an "optional" information exchange task, Doughty and Pica (1986) used a "required" information exchange. The interactive behaviors (termed "conversational adjustments") that were the dependent variables were comprehension checks, confirmation requests, clarification requests, self- and other-repetitions, and repairing, preventive, or reacting acts. Doughty and Pica found these behaviors significantly more frequent in the group activities with required information exchange than in the teacher-fronted classroom. This was unlike the finding of Pica and Doughty (1985), where teacher-fronted work had slightly more conversational adjustments than the optional information exchange task in groups. Even in the comparison for task effects in the group condition, the required information exchange had more conversational adjustments.

Rulon and McCreary (1986) also conducted a comparison between teacher-fronted and group work negotiation for meaning. Student triads were separated from the remaining class groups and their instructors, in order to discuss a videotaped lecture that all had heard in the regular class. Both the small groups and the remaining classes followed the same outline of questions for discussion. The peer groups produced target language speech which was equal in quantity and complexity to that in the teacher-led classes, and which had equal frequencies of confirmation and clarification checks. Rulon and McCreary argue that the nature of class and group discussion requires a distinction between negotiation of *linguistic* meaning, owing to lack of understanding of the target language or of the formal aspects of the current discourse, and negotiation of *content* meaning, which may arise due to a lack of clarity about the lesson material. The measures just noted referred to linguistic/formal points of negotiation; Rulon and McCreary found the peer groups producing significantly *more* confirmation and clarification checks in regard to the lesson content. Thus, although they acknowledge that in one case a peer group failed to correct a point being discussed (that the American Revolution took place in England), and risked being uninformed about the matter, they suggest that enhancing the negotiation of content by using peer group discussion may be the best way to promote interaction and, subsequently, target language acquisition.

Finally, Gaies's (1983b) study illustrated the variety of interactive phenomena possible in small group tasks, by analyzing interactions among learners and native speakers in dyads and triads engaged in a one-way picture description and identification exercise. He was exploring the ways in which learners would provide feedback to their interlocutors about their success or lack of comprehension, or other negotiation of communication. The most dominant type of feedback by far (about 60%) was "reacting" moves (as in Fanselow's 1977a analysis), such as confirmation by repetition, utterance completion, confirmation by paraphrase, request for definition, and halt signal. Gaies does not provide a breakdown of the frequency of these subtypes, however. He noted that there was a greater tendency for one learner to dominate the interaction in triads than in dyads.

Task type

Two experimental studies also involved learners' interactional behaviors as dependent variables and task type as an independent variable (see Crookes 1986 for an extended discussion of tasks and L2 research). Duff's study (1986), discussed previously in the section on production, compared a variety of interaction variables within learner dyads on two problem-solving and two debate tasks. Calculating ratios of behaviors to total turns, she found the problem-solving task significantly superior to debates only on 1) the rate of questions posed by the subjects, 2) the rate of "referential" questions (see Chapter 5), and 3) the rate of confirmation checks. The problem-solving tasks involved participant-shared goals of deciding on what items to take for a boat rescue operation, and of determining who was to blame for a medical accident. Evidently, these demanded a greater amount of checking of the partner's point of view.

Gass and Varonis (1985) were concerned with the effect on learners' indications of "non-understanding" of "one-way" and "two-way" tasks. The dependent variable appears to be the same as clarification requests, but the task types involve a differentiation of the number of participants who have information necessary to accomplish the task (i.e., one or two in most cases). There were no differences in mean number of indicators on the two types of tasks, although on the one-way task, the partner who lacked the primary information produced significantly more.

Summary

The results of these studies of interaction between learners reveal no clear trends in differences between different classroom organizational structures. Some studies favor one organization over the other, and some find organizations and tasks equal. The important qualification appears to be that the language task is the critical factor, as Pica and Doughty (1985) and Duff (1986) have found. Further evidence in Chapters 5 and 6 will support this point. The effect that negotiation arising from interaction has on eventual L2 acquisition is, however, unknown at this time.

Learner strategies

The foregoing discussion has considered a rather small variety of behaviors that may contribute to successful L2 acquisition; these have principally been behaviors classified under classroom processes. Yet an important area of research on language learning has been concerned with the cognitive operations that learners apply while in classrooms or

TABLE 4.2. STUDIES OF LEARNER STRATEGIES

Study	Class level(s)	Data collection	L1
Naiman et al. (1978)	Grades 8, 10, 12	Classroom observation, interviews	English
Bialystok & Fröhlich (1978)	High school	Questionnaire	English
Politzer (1983)	University	Questionnaire	English
Politzer & McGroarty (1985)	University graduate preparation	Questionnaire	Mixed
Chesterfield & Chesterfield (1985)	Preschool & grade 1	Classroom observation	Spanish
Willing (1985)	Adult immigrants	Questionnaire	Mixed
O'Malley et al. (1985a)	High school	Interviews, classroom observation	Mixed

*Denotes a significant result, with the relationship or direction indicated.

other learning situations. These behaviors, termed "learning strategies" (see discussion of the notion of strategy in Faerch and Kasper 1980, 1983; and O'Malley et al. 1985a), amount to the operations performed on the TL input as it is being comprehended and after negotiation of meaning. The methodology and descriptive framework for observing or eliciting such behaviors is not well developed, so there have been a variety of categorizations and constructs proposed for differentiating learning strategies. Moreover, recent studies have revealed (Rubin 1981; O'Malley et al. 1985a) that many behaviors included on lengthy lists of hypothetical strategic behaviors may not be observed with great frequency in actual classrooms, even if one could make reliable judgments as to the units and categories of analysis. As a result, it is difficult for classroom research to produce solid evidence of which specific learning strategies are the most fruitful ones to investigate.

Table 4.2 lists several of the studies concerned with learner strategies. Three of these are classroom based, and although others used learner

L2	N of subjects	Learner strategies in relation to other proficiency measures
French	12 classes, 72 students	*Attitudes toward correcting others + correlated with comprehension and imitation
French	Not provided	*Overall use of strategies (practicing, inferencing, monitoring) second best predictor of listening, speaking, reading skills
French, German, Spanish	90 students	*Student paying attention, Student asks for teacher explanation, Student asks for explanation of vocabulary, Student corrects other Ss mistakes to him/herself + correlated with grades and Teacher evaluation
English	37 students	No correlation of learner strategies with proficiency
English	14 students	Scale of use of various strategies over time (see text)
English	517 students	Consistent strategy performance across social ethnic groups
English	22 classes, 70 students	Frequencies of use of strategies observed, some uncommon

interviews or questionnaires, they have been included because of the additional perspective they provide on the issue.

Naiman et al. (1978) observed students' self-initiated repetitions, self-corrections, and attitudes toward correcting others. Only the last of these, a measure derived from interviews with the students rather than from the classroom observations, showed a significant correlation with the proficiency measures. This finding was apparently attributable to the correlation for the eighth grade learners.

In an attempt to investigate a more theoretically motivated set of learning strategies, Bialystok and Fröhlich (1978) administered a questionnaire to high school FSL learners, asking for their perceived use of specific learning strategies – practicing, inferencing, and monitoring. They correlated these student self-reports with independent measures of the learners' attitudes, motivation, language aptitude, and French achievement. In three out of four stepwise regression analyses – on reading, listening, and grammar achievement scores, but not on writing

– the overall use of these strategies was the second best (significant) predictor, after aptitude. Yet the change in explained variance (R-squared) attributable to the strategies was not great. Moreover, these measures did not constitute observations of classroom behavior, nor even necessarily classroom learning strategies. Bialystok and Fröhlich did not report what specific strategies had the strongest relationship to achievement, but they point out that the strategies investigated are the most likely candidates for instructional manipulation from among the predictor variables.

Politzer (1983) followed a similar, though less rigorous, procedure. He had 90 university-level learners of L2 French, Spanish, and German rate a variety of descriptions of learning behaviors on a 5-point scale by their perceptions of degree of use. Politzer correlated these ratings with the learners' grades and teacher evaluations of their progress, effort, and participation. Three general complexes of items were used: "general behaviors," "classroom behaviors," and "interactions with others outside of class." The classroom behavior scale items had the strongest correlation with the evaluation ratings (possibly because these learners have less chance outside the class to engage in TL use or learning processes, so the variability in outside interactions was lower relative to the scale means). The highest correlations from among the classroom behaviors were for "when I do not understand an FL expression or construction, I ask the teacher to explain it immediately," and "I ask the teacher to explain subtle differences in the meanings of FL words." In contrast to this finding, however, Politzer and McGroarty (1985), using a similar self-report measure with ESL learners, found no significant correlation between the classroom behavior scale and students' gains on several proficiency tests. This nonreplication may be attributable to the use of only a binary response format, the correlation with proficiency measures instead of grades, or to confounding with other within-subject factors (e.g., ethnic group differences were significant on some items and scales).

Willing (1985) and his colleagues administered questionnaires to 517 adult immigrant ESL learners in Australia. These consisted of 30 questions asking about preferences for general strategies of learning grammar and vocabulary, preferences for modality (listening, speaking, etc.), in- and out-of-class activities, and so on. The large number of subjects allowed Willing to compare these strategies and preferences on levels of various demographic factors, such as ethnic group, age, sex, and length of residence. The complex results allow few generalizations; perhaps the most important one was that "for any given learning issue [i.e., strategy], the typical spectrum of opinions on that issue will be represented, in virtually the same ratios, within any ethnic group, any age group, either sex, etc." (p. 100). Differences between demographic subgroups on any particular issue were marginal, rarely more than 15% differences from an overall mean.

Two papers by O'Malley and his colleagues report a study of similar learners' strategies. O'Malley et al. (1985a, b) interviewed teachers and learners, and observed classrooms in order to develop a classification of learner strategies. They group strategies into three types: 1) metacognitive, which involve knowledge about or regulation of cognition (planning, monitoring, and evaluating), 2) cognitive, which are "operations of analysis, transformation, or synthesis," and 3) socioaffective, that is, operations of social interaction with others (cooperation, questioning). The complete list is presented in Table 4.3, which includes all strategies defined by them, whether or not they occurred in the interview or observations.

As O'Malley et al. (1985a) point out about their own and previous studies, the reliable identification of strategies is quite difficult, a fact indicated as well by the continuous modification of strategies on every such study (note also a different collection in Willing 1985). Evidently, the different analytical techniques – interview and observation procedures, inferencing of internalized strategies from observations, and units of analysis of learner discourse – can lead to conflicting and variable constructs. This is an area in which further careful research with learner diaries may help explore the critical psychological constructs of learner strategies (for example, Schmidt and Frota 1986). O'Malley et al. (1985b) applied their three categories of strategies in a teaching study, the results of which have some bearing on learning outcomes; this study will be discussed in Chapter 6.

A final study (Chesterfield and Chesterfield 1985) dealt with young L2 learners. In this study eight L1 Spanish children were observed twice during an experimental preschool bilingual program, with concomitant proficiency measures being obtained. Six more children were added to this sample when all 14 were in regular bilingual first grade classrooms, and two more observations of their classroom behaviors were made. Chesterfield and Chesterfield coded 12 learning strategies for their frequency of occurrence:[3]

repetition
memorization
formulaic expression
verbal attention getter

---

3 While Chesterfield and Chesterfield acknowledge that their analytical categories for learning strategies "are a mixture of different units of speech performance" (p. 48), *intra*coder reliability checks on the data at later times resulted in high coefficients of agreement. Nonetheless, *inter*coder reliability should also have been checked, given the range in behaviors to be coded as exclusive categories.

TABLE 4.3. LEARNING STRATEGY DEFINITIONS

Learning strategy	Description
Metacognitive strategies	
Advance organizers	Making a general but comprehensive preview of the organizing concept or principle in an anticipated learning activity.
Directed attention	Deciding in advance to attend in general to a learning task and to ignore irrelevant distractors.
Selective attention	Deciding in advance to attend to specific aspects of language input or situational details that will cue the retention of language input.
Self-management	Understanding the conditions that help one learn and arranging for the presence of these conditions.
Functional planning (advance preparation)[a]	Planning for and rehearsing linguistic components necessary to carry out an upcoming language task.
Self-monitoring	Correcting one's speech for accuracy in pronunciation, grammar, vocabulary, or for appropriateness related to the setting or to the people who are present.
Delayed production	Consciously deciding to postpone speaking in order to learn initially through listening comprehension.
Self-evaluation	Checking the outcomes of one's own language learning against an internal measure of completeness and accuracy.
Self-reinforcement[a]	Arranging rewards for oneself when a language learning activity has been accomplished successfully.
Cognitive strategies	
Repetition	Imitating a language model, including overt practice and silent rehearsal.
Resourcing	Using target language reference materials.
Directed physical response	Relating new information to physical actions, as with directives.
Translation	Using the first language as a base for understanding and/or producing the second language.
Grouping	Reordering or reclassifying, and perhaps labeling, the material to be learned, based on common attributes.
Note-taking	Writing down the main idea, important points, outline, or summary of information presented orally or in writing.
Deduction	Consciously applying rules to produce or understand the second language.
Recombination	Constructing a meaningful sentence or larger language sequence by combining known elements in a new way.
Imagery	Relating new information to visual concepts in memory via familiar, easily retrievable visualizations, phrases, or locations.

Learning strategy	Description
Auditory	Retention of the sound or a similar sound for a word, phrase, or longer language sequence.
Keyword	Remembering a new word in the second language by 1) identifying a familiar word in the first language that sounds like or otherwise resembles the new word and 2) generating easily recalled images of some relationship between the new word and the familiar word.
Contextualization	Placing a word or phrase in a meaningful language sequence.
Elaboration	Relating new information to other concepts in memory.
Transfer	Using previously acquired linguistic and/or conceptual knowledge to facilitate a new language learning task.
Inferencing	Using available information to guess meanings of new items, predict outcomes, or fill in missing information.
Socioaffective strategies	
Cooperation	Working with one or more peers to obtain feedback, pool information, or model a language activity.
Question for clarification	Asking a teacher or other native speaker for repetition, paraphrasing, explanation, and/or examples.

[a]Items appearing only in O'Malley et al. (1985a).
Source: O'Malley et al. (1985a:33–4; 1985b:582–4).

answer in unison
talk to self
elaboration
anticipating answer
monitoring
appeal for assistance
request for clarification
role play

The students were classified by language dominance. The order of frequency of use (calculated binarily, for two or more occurrences vs. fewer than two occurrences) of the learning strategies over the four observations in two years was compared with proficiency, in order to determine a dominant sequence in use of these strategies. The investigators found high coefficients of reproducibility and scalability for the ordered sequence listed above, with repetition the earliest used strategy, memorization next, and so on. There were some inversions in the data, however, and role play appeared to be out of order (i.e., used more) for the more English-proficient children.

Chesterfield and Chesterfield acknowledge the variability in the data:

There were individual differences in the rates of development and in the time periods in which certain strategies were employed. Whereas individual children were found to expand their use of language learning strategies greatly at a particular point in time, others of the same language proficiency relied on a few initial strategies and a number of non-verbal ones throughout the study. (1985:57)

Yet they characterize the general progression in use of strategies as being one of increasing interactive use of the target language:

Strategies that were largely receptive, in that they did not elicit further interaction, such as repetition and memorization, were used first. These were followed by strategies which permitted children to initiate and maintain interactions. Strategies demonstrating awareness and monitoring of grammatical errors were the last to be developed, and were exhibited by only a few children at the end of the first grade. (p. 56)

Just as Bialystok and Fröhlich (1978) had suggested, Chesterfield and Chesterfield also emphasize the possibility of structuring classroom activities to match the developmental tendencies of the children.

Summary

The study of classroom learning strategies is still in early stages of development. As Chesterfield and Chesterfield admit, and as is evident in Rubin's and O'Malley et al.'s work, the units of analysis for what might constitute a "strategy" are inconsistent both within and across studies. Furthermore, the definitional constraints on specific labels such as "memorization" and "monitoring" can vary considerably from one study to another, leading easily to noncomparable results. The degree of conscious and unconscious employment of particular strategies by the learner is also a probable factor that has eluded focused study in classrooms.

There is a need for more controlled research on classroom learning strategies, especially in the form of experimental training of learners to employ selected strategies, in order to determine learning effects. Yet exploratory research on learners' strategy use needs to apply more carefully defined, reliable categories before it can point to targets for more controlled classroom-based research.

Conclusion

Research on learners' classroom behaviors addressed several major hypotheses (see beginning of this chapter). The first, pertaining to the influence of learner production, was supported by several studies which found a relationship between learners' productivity in classrooms and their target language proficiency. Yet the evidence does not support a causal relationship between the mere production of correct target language utterances and learning. Learners' production appears contingent on various situational factors, such as group structure and task. Arguments have been proposed that the critical factor relating learner production to learning is possibly 1) learners' initiations and input generation (the second hypothesis) and 2) learners' involvement in interactive negotiation of meaning (the third hypothesis). The former argument does not appear to be well supported, whereas interaction and negotiation of meaning among learners has the potential of being more directly related to their target language acquisition. The research reviewed here has demonstrated the sensitivity of interactive behaviors to specific group structures and communicative tasks, although a precise categorization of structures or tasks that most affect interaction remains to be determined. Furthermore, a demonstration of the effect of these on learners' acquisition remains to be considered. The next chapter will take a much closer look at the richness of the classroom interaction (in the broader sense). It will review the complexity of teacher-student interaction and its likely influence on language learning outcomes.

As for learner strategies, there are clearly fruitful topics for further research. It is evident that the strategies identified to date constitute a very mixed set of phenomena, not all of which can be investigated under classroom conditions. The anecdotal evidence of use of such learning operations and processes is vast (as in the diary study literature, which has, however, given greater attention to affective factors and their effects on learning). Also, a large body of psycholinguistic research on the learning of artificial languages has explored certain of these processes (e.g., Reber 1976). A thorough review of this literature is, unfortunately, beyond the scope of this book, not only because of the multitude of potential cognitive processes involved, but primarily because most such studies involve experimental learning tasks and tests that are too unlike those seen in classrooms.

5 Teacher and student interaction in second language classrooms

In the previous two chapters ways in which teachers' and students' language use in classrooms might contribute to learning a second language have been described. In several places, especially in the sections on learners' interactive behaviors in Chapter 4, the importance of teacher-student interaction was proposed. In the view of many researchers and practitioners, conversation and instructional exchanges between teachers and students provide the best opportunities for the learners to exercise target language skills, to test out their hypotheses about the target language, and to get useful feedback. In this chapter, therefore, several of the factors that have been considered to influence the quality and quantity of teacher-student interaction are examined. The interaction which occurs as a result of these factors is described, and some of the likely consequences of the interaction for learners are suggested.

Four major areas are reviewed which exemplify the nature of interaction and its possible effects on TL learning: 1) selectivity of teachers' speech to L2 learners in mixed NS and NNS classes, 2) the variability in teachers' choice of language in addressing learners, 3) the pattern of questioning behavior, and 4) characteristics of feedback to learners following errors of L2 production or subject matter content. As was pointed out in Chapter 2, the particular perspective adopted by each researcher, whether from an ethnographic, discourse analytical, or interaction analytical position, results in different categories and units of analysis, making comparisons across studies difficult.

For instance, Enright (1984) takes an ethnographic perspective, in which the types of interactions between participants are seen to take place within different "event" types that are generally defined by the teacher's perception of purpose. These interaction activities are guided by usually implicit rules or norms of behavior ("constitution"). What constitutes an interaction of a particular size or purpose, and the degree to which the nature of the interaction is negotiable, depends on the rules of speaking established by the teacher. Enright found the two classroom teachers he studied differing in the degree to which student contributions and negotiation were possible. One teacher's constitution was the traditional teacher-centered one of "do not speak unless you are spoken to," while the other's "open or child-centered" constitution was characterized by "if you have something to say, say it," among other rules. In order to quantify these differences, Enright compares the classroom interaction of these two teachers in terms of time spent on events and proportion of adult-to-student speech acts within events.

Ellis (1984b), on the other hand, adopts an essentially discourse-analytical approach to the specific interpretation of two adolescent students' acquisition of linguistic structures through classroom interaction. In order to discover how the discourse structure results in the children's either reproducing modeled TL forms, generating new TL utterances, or otherwise reconstructing the TL grammar, Ellis characterizes interaction in terms of the goals and participants of interaction ("address types"). Various interactions illustrate how changes in goals (e.g., from the lesson content to the language as medium) or in address types (pupil-to-pupil versus teacher-to-pupil) might lead to quite different TL production and comprehension by the learners. The detail of a discourse-analytical approach can lead to very interesting insights into the implicit rules of interaction that must be acquired by learners, as in van Lier's (1982, in press) study of turn-taking and of repair in classrooms, which merges certain ethnographic interpretations with a discourse-analytical approach.

Whatever the particular orientation to interaction in the classroom, most of the research reviewed here is concerned with the extent of TL learning resulting from interaction, although the association of precise measures of learning to any types or quantity of interaction are rarely tested. In the following, the nature of major interactive phenomena will be described; the few explicit associations of interaction with learning outcomes will be summarized in Chapter 6.

Differential allocation of teacher speech to learners

A fundamental concern of some language researchers and educators is the apparent disparity in treatment of limited-proficiency students compared with NSs in mixed classrooms. Much evidence suggests that a mismatch between teachers' and students' cultural norms results in a differential in teacher interactions with students in classrooms (see research cited in Chapter 4 on cultural factors and student initiations). In a review of this research, Laosa (1979) argues that teachers in academically, socially, or ethnically heterogeneous classrooms behave differently toward students who are perceived either as low-achieving, of low socioeconomic status, or belonging to a minority ethnic group. The different behavior is often more negative, in that teachers address these students less, react less positively to their contributions, criticize them more, and so on. Laosa further argues that this tendency toward differential treatment would result in fewer educational advantages for minority-language children who are mainstreamed in regular majority-language classrooms.

To investigate this problem, Laosa (1979) studied 14 kindergarten and second grade classrooms in five schools in a predominantly Mexican-American school district where a Spanish-English bilingual curriculum was instituted. He observed 51 sets of three students matched on social and academic measures, but different in ethnicity and language dominance (that is, English-dominant Anglo-Americans vs. English-dominant Mexican-Americans, vs. Spanish-dominant Mexican-Americans). Comparing grade levels, he found that language dominance, rather than ethnicity, was the major variable which contributed to negative teacher behavior. Thus, only for the Spanish-dominant Mexican-American group was there an increase in amount of disapproving teacher behavior from the kindergarten sample to the second grade sample. There was a parallel decrease in disapprovals for English-dominant children, regardless of ethnicity.

Schinke-Llano's (1983) data corroborate this finding in fifth and sixth grade English-medium classrooms with monolingual English students, and NNSs either fluent in English or of limited English proficiency (LEP). Twelve teachers were recorded for approximately one hour each, and the type of interaction and choice of student interlocutor was tallied. There was considerable variability among teachers, but the LEP students were spoken to half as frequently on average as the non-LEP students, with almost half (45%) not spoken to at all (compared with only 14% of non-LEP students being ignored). Although such a finding might be explained by reasoning that the LEP children's low proficiency inhibited interaction (the study was nevertheless conducted at the *end* of the school year), Schinke-Llano demonstrates that interactions with LEP students also tended to be managerial in function (60.9%), as opposed to instructional (39%), in contrast to the reverse proportion for non-LEP students (27.7% vs. 64.9%).

These results do not, however, establish that language proficiency is the only factor in differential occurrence of teacher-student interaction. Sato (1982, discussed in Chapter 4 with respect to learners' initiations) studied this issue of teacher selection of students by ethnicity in two university-level ESL classes. The two teachers tended to select the non-Asian more than the Asian students. Significant differences in the teachers' allocation of turns to specific individuals in the groups (48% to Asians, 60% to non-Asians) could in part be explained by the teachers' perception that non-Asians were more ready to participate, and by the similarity between the teachers' expectations and the non-Asians' norms of interaction.

Although conclusions as to eventual learning of subject matter or L2 acquisition cannot be drawn from these studies, the implication is that lack of attention or negative functional treatment will at least not promote, and may inhibit, students' progress. There is clear evidence that in mixed classrooms, second language learners risk being less involved in exchanges with the teacher, and possibly less involved in instructionally relevant interactions. If different interactional goals affect language learning in different ways, as Ellis (1984b) proposed, differentials in teacher-student exchanges that neglect L2 learners need rectification.

Choice of language

A second issue, choice of language addressed to L2 learners, also has bearing on the general quality of the language environment that L2 learners experience in the classroom. Depending on the type of language program and the theoretical analysis of learning processes that influence acquisition, quite different expectations exist for the effects of use of the target language by the teacher in interaction with L2 learners. Thus, in the maintenance bilingual education program model strongly advocated by some in the United States (see Trueba 1979; Cummins 1981), the teacher is encouraged not to submerge the learner in the target language; development of native language skills is believed to be important for adequate cognitive, social, and educational growth for the minority child. On the other hand, for the majority language child in an L2 "immersion" class (see Swain and Lapkin 1982; California State Department of Education 1984), where there is no conflict between the social prestige of the native and target languages, greater use of the TL is encouraged. Similarly, in the typical foreign language classroom, the common belief is that the fullest competence in the TL is achieved by means of the teacher providing a rich TL environment, in which not only instruction and drill are executed in the TL, but also disciplinary and management operations.

As a consequence of these quite different viewpoints, investigations of teachers' language choice in L2 classrooms have taken distinct positions upon discovering the extent of L1 or L2 use. In bilingual education with minority-language children acquiring a socially dominant L2 (as in the United States), surprisingly low rates of L1 use have been observed, even when bilingual teachers and aides have been employed for L1 maintenance. Several studies document this, showing that only certain influences, such as student preferences, subject matter, or strong program influences, can lead to greater L1 use. Legarreta (1977), for instance, found the total teacher or aide talk in L1 Spanish in five bilingual kindergarten classes ranged from 16% to 47%, with only a special "Alternate Days" program (switching language by days) achieving the nearly 50%–50% split that is the goal of these programs.

Bruck and Schultz (1977) found that either a non-L1 subject content (math, English), the teacher's language dominance, or a "transitional" philosophy toward L2 development during the school year can influence increased use of the socially dominant L2. They studied two teachers' interactions with two bilingual Spanish-English (Spanish dominant) children in a grade 1 half-day transitional bilingual program. Two teachers (one English- and the other Spanish-dominant) were recorded teaching different subjects at three sample times throughout the year. Bruck and Schultz show that despite the teacher's attempt to use the L1, the two children observed would often initiate and respond in L2 English, thereby revealing their perception of the social norms. This is shown in the following example:

Teacher: Dónde está número dos?
Rosa: This is one, I did number five already.
Teacher: Este, ésa es mala, mira cambia ésta y ésta.
Rosa: Which one is wrong?
Teacher: Las dos están malos.
Rosa: Which one?
Teacher: Las dos. Allí están.

(pp. 76, 78)

Nonetheless, both the teachers and the children (in peer-peer interactions) demonstrated sensitivity to the language dominance of the child being addressed, so that frequent L1 Spanish use was observed throughout the year in many interactions.

Wong-Fillmore (1980) also found a range in L1 use depending on the classroom activity and the degree of individualization in teacher-student interaction. In an exploratory study of kindergarten classes, she observed one child in a bilingual Chinese-English class and compared it to a Chinese child in an ESL kindergarten class. The teacher in the bilingual class spoke between 0% and 92% in English: Chinese writing involved the most teacher talk in Chinese (100%), interaction with individuals in seat work was next with 28% Chinese, and whole-class instruction involved the most English (92%).

In preschool classes, the language preference of the children may be a more important factor. Chesterfield et al. (1983) did a longitudinal ethnographic study of five bilingual (L1 Spanish, L2 English) preschool classes in two distinct locations. The teaching staff (teachers and aides) maintained fairly high L1 use throughout one school year, with one location tending to be more dominant in English (range of 53% to 78% across classes and observation times), compared to the other (range of 33% to 52% English). Chesterfield et al. suggest that the greater use of

L1 Spanish in the latter location may have resulted from the greater preference for Spanish use by the children.

Chesterfield et al. also intimated, when referring to higher use of Spanish as a result of the program's encouraging translation in various instructional activities, that program emphases can make a difference. Findings in accord with this were also obtained in a study by J. D. Ramirez et al. (1986; see section on amount and types of teacher talk in Chapter 3). While the 74 kindergarten and first grade immersion classes observed used between 93% and 100% L2 English, the 7 kindergarten late-exit transition classes averaged 66% L1 Spanish, and 11 grade 3 late-exit classes averaged 51% Spanish.

On the other hand, two studies demonstrate that very little L1 may be used, in spite of program specifications requring L1. Strong (1986) investigated 10 third and fifth grade bilingual classrooms (either Spanish or Cantonese L1) throughout one year, comparing them to grade 3 and 5 "submersion" classrooms with mixed minority LEP children and monolingual English children. Instead of segmenting instances of each language used, as Legarreta had done in timed intervals, Strong timed the total duration of L1 and L2 speech, as well as silence, for an average of almost six hours per teacher. This measure, he argues, is the most appropriate assessment of amount of language input. Although slightly less time was spent speaking English in the bilingual classrooms compared to the submersion ones (47% and 53%, respectively), there was no significant difference in the amount of English spoken. The remainder of the time in *both* groups was occupied by silence, with the bilingual teachers using the L1 an average of only 6% of the time (range 0% to 23%). A second study, by Nystrom, Stringfield, and Miron (1984) of three "bilingual" and five ESL junior and senior high school classes, found similarly low or no levels of L1 use in the bilingual classes, with the principal users of L1 being teachers' aides. In fact, the ESL classes revealed L1 use equivalent to that in the bilingual classes.

The emerging picture here is thus one of a limited use of the native language in favor of the socially dominant L2, depending on the program emphases. Only very conscious administrative and pedagogical concern can increase use of the L1. As will be seen later, moreover, the dominance of the L2 in these situations is also revealed in the distribution of the L1 and L2 for particular classroom functions.

The use of the L2 target is encouraged in foreign language and immersion classrooms, and it is virtually unavoidable in second language classrooms with mixed L1 students and no L1-speaking teacher aides. Thus, it is not surprising that Fröhlich et al. (1985) found very high uses of French or English L2 (about 90% or more) in the four program types they observed in Canada (13 grade 7 classrooms in core French, extended

French with subject matter courses, French immersion, and ESL). However, Mitchell et al.'s (1981) study of 17 Scottish secondary school FFL classes found a minimum average of only 21% use of English L1.[1] Mitchell and Johnstone (1984) also observed one teacher throughout a 30-week term and found about 70% (range 52% to 87% in seven selected lessons) French use. These are respectably high levels of TL use for a foreign language educational environment.

These researchers of language use in L2 classrooms are aware, however, that the total proportion of L1 or L2 use alone is probably not the critical variable in determining the degree of L1 maintenance or L2 acquisition. As several have argued and attempted to demonstrate in their data, it is the *functional allocation* of the TL relative to the L1 (or the balance between the two in a bilingual context) which would indicate to the learner the priorities of the extended social environment that schools and teachers represent.

Functional allocation of language choice

Just as functionally negative teacher treatment may inhibit learning (see the argument by Laosa 1979 above), an unbalanced differentiation of L1 or L2 use may signal to the child that one or the other is undesired. This can at the least generate negative attitudes toward an L1 or L2, but it can also simply limit the learner's exposure to the full range of L1 or L2 use. This is, of course, the argument made by a communicative methodology that advocates use of the target medium (whether L1 or L2) in as complete a repertoire of functions as possible. The findings of several studies of bilingual education are, on the whole, discouraging in this regard.

Townsend and Zamora (1975) was an early study distinguishing teacher functions by language. Using a modification of a Flanders-type interaction observation scheme, they observed 56 teachers in a bilingual preschool (three- to four-year-olds) over a two-year period. While they do not report the relative amounts of L1 Spanish and L2 English use, they note the following results for functional distribution:

During lessons taught in Spanish, there was a greater percentage of questions asked..., a greater percentage of student responses..., a greater percentage of rejecting of a student's answer..., and a greater percentage of incidences in which a student response was followed by teacher acceptance.... [I]n English, subjects had a greater percentage of direction-giving behavior..., a greater percentage of incidences in which a student response was followed by

---

1 "Minimum" because the authors coded by activity segment rather than an actual timing of language use; as Strong (1986) has pointed out, the method of timing and segmentation used can substantially over- or underestimate the total time of teacher talk as well as the breakdown into language.

a teacher praise..., and a greater percentage of the use of two or more consecutive reinforcing behaviors...(p. 199)

These results concur to some extent with those of Legarreta (1977), who studied L1 Spanish/L2 English bilingual classes. Legarreta found that in general, English was dominant, used more often to direct pupils, to correct and discipline them, and to provide positive feedback ("warming, accepting, amplifying"), and Spanish was used to a relatively greater extent to direct the children (almost 30% of the time) than it was used for other functions. Yet the teacher with the most balanced amount of the two languages, from the alternative days program, used much more Spanish for positive functions and directing (72% and 62%), but much more English (61%) for correcting and disciplining the children.

Guthrie (1984) studied two teachers in a grade 1 Cantonese-English bilingual program where the one reading teacher was a fluent bilingual. Evidently because of a perceived need to introduce the L2 in the English reading class, this teacher used the L1 in only 7% of the coded speech acts (in contrast to a more balanced use in other subject classes). Guthrie notes that the uses of L1 in this class were for various purposes, namely for translation, classification, checking understanding, procedures and directions, and as a "we-code," or solidarity marker. Similarly, Wong-Fillmore (1980; see previous section) noted that the small amount of Chinese used in whole-class instruction was primarily for explanation and clarification. Thus, not only instructional and managerial but social functions can inspire use of the L1, albeit a small amount, even when the L2 is assumed to be preferred.

Milk (1982) found a similar uneven distribution of English L2 versus Spanish L1 for different functions in a grade 12 bilingual civics class. English dominated in the teacher's directives (92%) and metastatements (63%). In other functions (elicitation, expressives, replies, informatives), there was greater balance between the two languages.

Finally, J. D. Ramirez et al. (1986) noted a variety of differences in emphases among the three programs investigated in the functional distribution within L1 or L2 use. Most of these they believed to be consistent with program goals. What they found to be unusual, however, was the disproportionate L1 Spanish use of "modeling" in the highly L2-dominant immersion programs (about 28% of L1 use versus 12% or less in the more L1-dominant early- and late-exit programs). The investigators state that "this is not consistent with immersion strategy program goals" (pp. 64, 66), yet they caution that the absolute frequency of the acts was rather low.

Summary

Although the preceding studies indicate that many bilingual programs may be failing to provide balanced amounts and functions of the L1 and the TL, it is probably premature to condemn them in general, for the influence of program type and pedagogical emphasis has not been fully explored. More investigation is needed of the causes of TL or L1 use and functional distribution. (For example, the effects of teacher attitudes and training, subject content, and learner age on language choice need further investigation.) Perhaps more important, however, is the need to study the effects of TL and L1 use and functional distribution on development of L2 proficiency.

Questioning behavior

Teachers' questioning behavior has been examined in a few L2 studies concerned with the extent to which teachers' questions might facilitate either TL production or correct and meaningful content-related responses by students. Teachers' questions constitute a primary means of engaging learners' attention, promoting verbal responses, and evaluating learners' progress, although there is considerable debate as to whether language teaching methodology requires this sort of interaction. Typically, a question is the initiation of the three-part solicit-response-evaluate sequence of moves typical of classrooms:

Teacher: What is your name?
Student: Rosalie.
Teacher: Good.

Recall from Chapter 3 that, although questions constituted only about 20% to 40% of major syntactic types in classrooms (see Table 3.7), Mizon (1981) and Early (1985) found teachers using questions more with nonnative-speaking students than with NSs. The reason for this is perhaps, as Long (1981b) argued, that questions probably facilitate interaction by clearly establishing both the topic and who is expected to speak next. Yet, on the other hand, the nature of the question may severely limit the possibilities for the student to respond at any length, if at all. Although students' failure to respond to teachers' questions may result from their lack of knowledge or insufficient L2 proficiency (factors to which teachers become more sensitive over time), researchers have been concerned with influencing teaching practices, studying how teachers can construct questions in less vague and less restrictive forms. Several factors have been considered important in either limiting or enhancing the productivity of students' responses to questions.

Type of question

An early study of L1 classrooms distinguished between "closed" and "open-ended" questions (Barnes 1969); L2 researchers discriminated "specific" and "general information" questions (cf. Naiman et al. 1978;

Bialystok et al. 1978). Both of these distinctions separate those questions which expect a particular (usually brief), closed set of responses (e.g., "Where were you born?" "Did you sell your house yet?") from those which leave open the nature (and length) of the expected response ("What did you do on your trip?"). With the growth in concern for communication in language classrooms, a further distinction has been made between "display" and "referential" questions (see Long and Sato 1983 for discussion), which involves determining whether the teacher is asking for information which he or she already knows (display) or does not know (referential). While referential questions may be either open or closed (display questions would tend to be closed), the supposition is that open/general questions, or referential questions, would promote greater learner productivity, and the latter would likely promote more meaningful communication between teacher and learner.

Long and Sato (1983) found that ESL teachers used significantly fewer referential questions than display questions in classrooms, compared to NSs in conversations with NNSs. Pica and Long (1986) also found that L2 teachers asked proportionately more display than referential questions. This significant finding was corroborated by further within-teacher comparisons in other groups of experienced and inexperienced teachers. The trends in Dinsmore (1985) and Early (1985) also support this finding. In Early's study the ratio of display to referential questions with ESL social studies students was almost 6 to 1 (but only 1.5 to 1 for teacher speech to L1 grade 11 and 12 social studies students). In primary level bilingual classrooms, J. D. Ramirez et al. (1986) also found consistent trends across program types and grade levels for twice as many display questions as referential ones.

The only finding possibly discrepant with these trends was that of Bialystok et al.'s (1978) comparison between core and immersion French. There, the immersion teachers were found to use more general information (potentially referential) questions. The implication is that the more language-oriented the classroom, the more the teacher finds it appropriate to elicit linguistically constrained student contributions in order to promote practice in the language. Some direct effects of display and referential questions on student responses will be discussed in Chapter 6.

Modification of questions

In addition to the fact that display questions are so readily used in classroom situations because the teacher is supposed to be evaluating the learners, White and Lightbown (1984) point out that teachers will persist in asking questions by repeating or rephrasing them. They found three secondary ESL teachers asking up to four questions per minute, with overall about 40% of the questions receiving no response and up to 64% being repetitions of previous questions, with as many as nine repetitions of the same question. They claim that the success rate of students responding to subsequent repetitions of questions was quite low, lower often than rate of response to questions asked only once. This, of course, may be an artifact of the difficulty of the question and the consequent need to repeat or rephrase more difficult questions several times. A second factor in improving questions is, therefore, to provide the right sort of modification of a question initially or in subsequent rephrasings so as to make it appropriately comprehensible and answerable within the learners' subject matter and L2 competence.

It is natural enough to modify a question which has not been understood, by aiding the respondent with perhaps a clue to the expected answer, with some limiting of the possible range of responses. Buckheister and Fanselow (1984) show that only about 15% of ESL or L1 secondary teachers' classroom questions contain such "narrowing" by means of clues, including in their count the initial questions asked. They list a number of different types of clues that might be used to help the respondent focus on the domain of appropriate answers; for example, clues that would describe the attributes of an expected response, compare or contrast the expected response to something, or assign a label to the expected response.

Another modification of questions is by rephrasing with alternative, or "or-choice" questions: "What would you like to drink? [pause] Would you like coffee, tea, beer?" Long (1981b) found or-choice questions to occur proportionately twice as much in NS-NNS interactions than in NS-NS ones. Yet Long provides some support for White and Lightbown's skepticism about rephrasing of questions, with an example of an overly modified NS question from an NS-NNS conversation:

Are the islands the same – do they look the same? . . . as Japan as . . . the country in Japan? Are the houses, for example, are the houses the same on Osima . . . as say in the country . . . Sapporo or (Akairo)? Do the people talk the same or do the houses look the same? . . . Or are the trees the same? (p. 152)

A final factor that has been considered is "wait-time," or the amount of time the teacher pauses after a question and before pursuing the answer with further questions or nomination of another student. Although this factor has been shown to be important in L1 classrooms as well (Rowe 1974), additional wait-time should especially allow L2 students a better opportunity to construct their response, and it may fit better with their cultural norms of interaction. Holley and King (1971) proposed at least a 5-second wait and claimed that teachers who waited that long in college German classes obtained an increase in student responses following initial hesitations. White and Lightbown (1984) and

Long et al. (1984) also argue for greater wait-time. Long et al. conducted an experiment to determine the possible influence of training on teachers' wait-time and the effects of increased wait-time on learners' responses. These empirical results will be discussed in Chapter 6.

Shrum and Tech (1985) provide some data on wait-time in five first-year high school foreign language classes (Spanish and French) in the United States. They measured the teachers' wait-time both following teacher solicitations and following the subsequent student responses. The means were 1.91 and 0.73 seconds, respectively. The relatively short postsolicitation wait-times indicate that the students were responding quite rapidly to teacher solicits, which the authors suggest may be due to the relatively drill-like nature of second language classes (they do not verify whether this was the case in the classes under study). The most interesting finding was that when the language of the solicitation was coded (L1 English or TL), L1 solicits resulted in significantly longer wait-time than TL solicits (2.33 vs. 1.70 seconds). The authors consider that this may also be a result of the low difficulty level (drill-like behavior) of the TL questions, thus allowing rapid student responses. The post-response wait-time relates to teacher feedback, and will be considered in the section on feedback.

Questioning patterns

In addition to these rather concrete means of improving on the content and form of questions in order to promote greater student responsiveness, it should be recognized that teachers use questions in more complex ways. The practice of teaching is considered at times to involve a structuring of information for the learner, either as a direct presentation of information or as the facilitation or generation of a dialogue between a source of knowledge (teacher, book, material) and the learner (cf. Hyman 1974:439–526). Some constrained version of the "Socratic" method is, therefore, often adopted by teachers, where questions are used to guide the learner toward particular bits of knowledge. Thus, a sequence of questions might help specify the topic of interaction by focusing on a subordinate category or an exemplification of that dealt with in a more general question. The following examples from Chaudron's (1983a) study of ESL classes (secondary and university) illustrate such use of questions:

1) Teacher: If, a state, if a state only has, under 20 inches of rain in a year, [Student's name] what kind of climate does it have? Is it like Canada, or is it like Lebanon?
2) Teacher: What is a capital city?...[no appropriate response] OK. Ottawa is the capital city of Canada. Ottawa is the capital city of Canada. Just like what is the capital city of Italy? (p. 133)

On the other hand, Chaudron also illustrates ways in which teachers' attempts to simplify the question in order to obtain a response risk obscuring the point of the instruction, as in the continuation of the first example above, where the characterization of the climate in geographical terms gets lost:

S: Like Lebanon...
S: There is hot, you know...
T: ...OK. It's a hot state [Reference to Nevada] Because Lebanon is very hot also, and there's very little rain. Uhm, [Student's name] you said there's desert there, that's true,
S: It will be the same as the capital.
T: It will be the same as,
S: The capital of Lebanon.
T: The capital of Nevada?... [Ss attempt several inexact responses] OK. If you looked at something in the East Coast, uhm what would that climate be like, what would it look like there?...There's a lot of rain, but when you have a lot of rain, what do you have, then?
S: Thunderstorm?
T: No, what *grows* when you have a lot of rain?
Ss: [speaking together; some unintelligible] Forest.
T: Yeah, forests.

(pp. 133–4)

Note the vagueness, the nonspecificity of the question, "When you have a lot of rain, what do you have then?" compared with "What *grows*...." But this sequence also ended here, before geographical terms for climate were elicited.

Questions in interaction

In the last examples, it is evident that teachers modify the form and content of their questions in adapting to apparent difficulty or noncomprehension by L2 learners. Three subtypes of question have the specific function of maintaining interaction by ensuring that the interlocutors share the same assumptions and identification of referents. These are *comprehension checks, confirmation checks,* and *clarification requests.* These types of questioning acts were discussed in regard to the interaction resulting from different classroom tasks and group organizations in the section on learner interaction in Chapter 4. However, several researchers have investigated these primarily in teachers' speech, in order to determine the extent to which they improve the interaction by promoting more student negotiation, again in accord with the theory that more negotiated interaction would enhance L2 acquisition.

As discussed in Long and Sato (1983), these three types of question indicate "the direction of information-flow in preceding utterances." A comprehension check elicits assurance from the listener that a message has been received correctly, whereas confirmation checks and clarification requests allow the speaker to correctly interpret reactions by the listener, the former presupposing a positive answer and the latter being much more open-ended. If measured for both teacher and students, these types should contribute to an index of interaction or negotiation in the classroom.

Ellis (1985a) observed these features in teachers' interactions with two adolescent ESL students. He found relatively few of them, with little change in use over two observation times, four to five months apart. In Early's study (1985), involving more teachers and classes over more time, only comprehension checks occurred with any substantial frequency. Early compared secondary-level social studies lessons with ESL students and with L1 students, twelve lessons each, with four teachers in each group. There appeared to be virtually no use in either group of confirmation checks or clarification requests, but the ESL teachers used significantly more comprehension checks. Both Long and Sato (1983) and Pica and Long (1986) compared classroom teachers' use of these three question types in beginning-level classes with frequency of question types in a set of data obtained from native speakers in dyadic information gap tasks with L2 learners. In both Long/Sato's, and Pica/Long's comparisons, while comprehension checks were the least frequent (10%) in the dyadic NS-NNS tasks, they were the most frequent in the classroom interactions (between 52% and 67% of the three types). Confirmation checks, which were the most frequent in the dyads (72%), were 35% and 14%, respectively, in the two classroom data sets. Clarification requests were low in frequency in all conditions (between 12% and 19%).

Under the assumption that more interaction is an aid to acquisition, Pica and Doughty (1985), whose study was also discussed in Chapter 3, investigated the extent to which these indicators of interaction were greater in teacher-fronted activity compared with group activity in classrooms. They found, contrary to their hypothesis, more of these question types in the teacher-fronted activity than in the group activity, although students in the groups took more turns, produced more language, had more input directed toward them, and had more utterances completed or corrected by interlocutors.

Summary

The general picture of classroom interaction that results from teachers' questions is that the questions alone may not promote a great amount of learner TL production or other interaction, unless the teacher is aware of the pitfalls of too closed, too fast, or too vague questions, or worse, too many repetitions of the same non-understood question. Although modifications of questions to improve comprehensibility may be an eventual aid to the learner, the teacher probably cannot rely on multiple questions to solve a problem of noncomprehension. Nonetheless, as seen in the previous section and in the section on interaction in Chapter 4, in tasks requiring exchange of information, it is likely that the special kinds of questions that negotiate comprehension and sharing of information will be needed and potentially useful to the learner.

Feedback

The aspect of interaction in classrooms with the widest scope is probably that generally referred to as feedback, which includes the notion of error correction. Feedback has been widely investigated in information theory and general communication research outside classroom or language learning contexts (Annett 1969). In any communicative exchange, speakers derive from their listeners information on the reception and comprehension of their message. This information may be actively solicited (by means of comprehension checks, as seen in the previous section), implicit in the listeners' lack of any signals of noncomprehension, or explicit in other sorts of behavior of the listeners, such as questioning looks or prompts, interjections or rejecting comments, and "backchannel" cues (such as "Oh, I see, uhm hm"). Participants in natural communication actively exchange and negotiate this sort of information in ways suggested in the previous discussion on questioning. In the classroom, on the other hand, the special circumstances of the teacher having superior knowledge and status results in an imbalance in expectations as to who provides feedback and when it is provided.

Aside from general instruction, the primary role of language teachers is often considered to be the provision of both error correction, a form of negative feedback, and positive sanctions or approval of learners' production. In most other social interactions, no one participant is specified as having the automatic right to impose judgment on the other's behavior, especially linguistic behavior. If correction of another is to be done, it is done discreetly, with deference, since there is a strong preference to allow speakers to correct themselves (see Schegloff, Jefferson, and Sacks 1977). Repair of the communication by another is usually only allowed in the form of noncomprehension signals such as those discussed in the previous section – clarification requests and confirmation checks.

The differential right to the floor in classrooms results in the final step of the classic exchange cycle of teacher initiation/solicitation–student response–teacher feedback/evaluation, where the evaluation step is the most unusual in comparison with natural conversations. Teachers are expected to execute their vested instructional authority to evaluate any and all student behavior, nonverbal or verbal. Yet the impossibility of consistently applying standards of appropriateness or correctness leads to the possibly unwanted result that learner behavior not receiving admonishment or correction is by default taken to be appropriate or correct. Feedback, as contrasted with the narrower notion of "correction," is therefore an inevitable constituent of classroom interaction, for no matter what the teacher does, learners derive information about their behavior from the teacher's reaction, or lack of one, to their behavior.

From the language teacher's point of view, the provision of feedback, or "knowledge of results" (Annett 1969), is a major means by which to inform learners of the accuracy of both their formal target language production and their other classroom behavior and knowledge. From the learners' point of view, the use of feedback in repairing their utterances, and involvement in repairing their interlocutors' utterances, may constitute the most potent source of improvement in both target language development and other subject matter knowledge. Yet the degree to which this information in fact aids learners' progress in target language development (or in subject matter content) is still unknown. In this section, the nature of feedback in classroom interaction and its possible effects will be addressed; several studies point to characteristics of feedback that are potentially successful promoters of target language improvement.

Feedback as a factor in learning theory

The study of feedback in learning situations has a long history, closely tied to behaviorist learning theory, programmed learning, and instructional technology (see Kulhavy 1977 for a critical review of this research in L1 content teaching). Adopting the notion of reinforcement of behavior as a fundamental factor in learning, learning theory tended to equate feedback with positive or negative reinforcement. These two aspects of feedback, as consequences of a student behavior (response), bring about a strengthening or weakening of the response, respectively. The audiolingual approach to language teaching took this view (Lado 1957; Brooks 1964), with positive feedback usually being considered either positive praise – "Very good" – or repetition of the student's correct response. For negative feedback, however, the traditional approach relied on grammar explanations and modeling of the correct response, usually assuming the ability of learners to recognize the difference between the model and their errors, which, as will shortly become clear, is a problematic assumption.

Without detailing the historical developments in language teaching theory (see critical discussion in Lucas 1975; Chaudron 1977b; Long 1977; Hendrickson 1978; and Courchêne 1980), we must now recognize that the adequacy of this view of feedback in language learning has been discounted. In a cognitive view of learning (one general alternative to behaviorist theories), the function of feedback is not only to provide reinforcement, but to provide information which learners can use actively in modifying their behaviors (see Zamel 1981; and Annett's 1969 tripartite function of feedback —"reinforcement," "information," "motivation"). Several models of L2 acquisition now include the process of hypothesis testing as an integral part of learners' interlanguage development (see Faerch and Kasper 1980; Krashen 1983; Schachter 1983a, b, 1984; and a comparison of these views in Chaudron 1985a). The information available in feedback allows learners to confirm, disconfirm, and possibly modify the hypothetical, "transitional" rules of their developing grammars, but these effects depend on the learner's readiness for and attention to the information available in feedback. That is, learners must still make a comparison between their internal representation of a rule and the information about the rule in the input they encounter. The nature of this comparison remains to be elaborated on by L2 learning theorists.

As to readiness and attention, Vigil and Oller (1976) pointed out that the effect of feedback consists not only of the positive or negative information about target language forms but of the further continuum of positive, neutral, or negative affective support present in conversation (Annett's motivational function), which can interact with cognitive information factors and influence learners' efforts to attempt revision of their production. MacFarlane (1975) emphasized the importance of this motivational aspect of feedback in the classroom, the need to release students from the anxiety of representing corrections as "failures." Krashen (1982, 1983) has argued repeatedly that learners must be affectively positive and receptive in order for "natural" acquisitional processes to function. For these reasons, articles on feedback and error correction have frequently noted the importance of whether or not a positive affective tone or climate is present in teachers' or other NS conversants' interactions, as difficult as it may be to measure this.

Feedback as error correction

The multiple functions of feedback and the pressure to be accepting of learners' errors lead, however, to the paradoxical circumstance that teachers must either interrupt communication for the sake of formal TL correction or let errors pass "untreated" in order to further the communicative goals of classroom interaction. Moreover, a number of L2 researchers have pointed out that many teachers' attempts to "correct" learners' errors are in fact ambiguous, misleading, and potentially inconsistent (e.g., Allwright 1975a; McTear 1975; Stokes 1975; Chaudron 1977a; Long 1977; Walmsley 1978; Stratton 1986; Bradshaw 1986; see also Mehan's L1 study, 1974). The following example from Stokes (1975:7) illustrates the inconsistency of an error correction attempt which is dropped, apparently for the sake of moving on with the lesson:

S3:   When did you leave Venezuela?
Eulyces: I left Venezuela the eleventh of January.
Teacher: Good.
          ... [later in lesson]
Teacher: When was he born?
Eulyces   Twenty ... twenty-first of January nineteen sixty-three.
Teacher: Come on, Eulyces, you missed something here. Just say it over again.
Eulyces: Twenty ...
Teacher: the twenty-first.
Eulyces: twenty-first of February nineteen sixty-three.
Teacher: Good.

To reveal the causes and possible solutions to this problem, as well as other issues in feedback, the same questions dealt with by Hendrickson (1978) in his review of research on L2 feedback will be examined here. Hendrickson's answers to these questions were tentative and based largely on nonempirical work. Yet the empirical work which is summarized here largely supports his conclusions. Although his review also dealt with written error correction, this update will be restricted to research on classroom oral error correction.

1. Should learner errors be corrected?
2. If so, when should learner errors be corrected?
3. Which learner errors should be corrected?
4. How should learner errors be corrected?
5. Who should correct learner errors?

SHOULD LEARNER ERRORS BE CORRECTED?

Hendrickson (1978) arrived at an affirmative answer to this question, with the argument following the hypothesis-testing rationale noted in the previous section. His justification was primarily theoretical, with one empirical study of learners' preferences cited. Cathcart and Olsen (1976) compiled 149 adult ESL learners' responses to a questionnaire. They showed a strong preference for correction of all errors. However, when one teacher involved in the study attempted to provide such treatment, her class agreed it was undesirable, since it rendered communication impossible. A more recent survey by Chenoweth et al. (1983), of over 400 adult ESL learners' attitudes to interactions with native-speaking friends, also found a strong preference for more error correction, in this case in the context of social encounters. These subjects' desire for more correction, which was rated on a relative scale, may arise from the very low rate of correction (about 9% of errors) that this population encountered in NS-NNS social conversations, which the same researchers found in another study of the same population (Chun et al. 1982). Whether learners' errors *should* be corrected may not, however, depend entirely on their preferences, although satisfaction of their perceived need may be important for a positive attitude. The answer should follow primarily from evidence of the effectiveness of error correction, a distinctly difficult phenomenon to demonstrate.

WHEN SHOULD LEARNER ERRORS BE CORRECTED?

Hendrickson concluded that error correction should be confined more to "manipulative grammar practice," leaving communicative activities free from a focus on error correction. He again considered theoretical views and one empirical survey. As with the first question, research would have to demonstrate differential effectiveness for correction at different times. Several studies of error correction in L2 classrooms have since demonstrated the degree to which teachers correct errors, and these patterns appear to reflect the priorities Hendrickson suggests. Table 5.1 displays several design features of studies in L2 classrooms, the results of which will be compared in this and the following sections.

Several of the studies in Table 5.1 reveal that classroom teachers will likely correct learners' errors either when they pertain to the pedagogical focus of the lesson or when they significantly inhibit communication (the latter are sometimes referred to as "global" errors, as opposed to "local" errors; see Burt and Kiparsky 1974). For instance, Courchêne (1980), Nystrom (1983), and Chaudron (1986a) elicited teachers' rationales for correcting errors.

Chaudron's (1986a) three subjects were grade 8 and 9 French immersion teachers, two of whom expressed a preference for correcting formal French errors only during French language classes, and not during other subject classes (math, science, geography). The third teacher did not believe students had problems with the content of his history class, so he emphasized target language corrections even there. Yet, in a count of classroom error corrections based on transcripts of 12 lessons, the three teachers demonstrated a priority for correcting errors of subject matter content in all classes (from 75% to 100% of such errors were corrected), while grammatical errors (morphological and syntactic) were corrected most in French classes (77% on average), but not in other subjects (37% on average). Moreover, late in the school year (April), the rate of correction of grammatical errors in French class was lower (66%) compared to early in the year (October – 95%), indicating a gradual acceptance of deviant forms in the learners' production (morphological errors especially contributed to this decrease).

Courchêne (1980) observed a similar strong preference among 10 teachers in pre-university and university level adult ESL courses. These teachers corrected 100% and 97% of subject content and lexical errors, respectively, compared with 46% and 41% of grammatical and phonological errors. From interviews and observation, Courchêne also determined that the principal criteria teachers used for correction were pedagogical focus and both global and local errors.

Nystrom (1983) found an extreme case of a teacher intentionally omitting correction of formal errors in learners' production. She compared four teachers in bilingual Spanish-English elementary classes with respect to their selection of error sequences viewed in videotapes of their lessons. She found one teacher consciously not treating learners' deviant forms, because "she did not regard her role as one of a correcting machine," but also because the errors the students made were predominantly ones in a nonstandard dialect, during noninstructional activities at transition times between lesson activities (namely, times at which the children were most likely to be communicating their real needs).

A further justification for the claim that pedagogical focus is a major determinant of when errors get treated is the extent to which errors were ignored. Slightly different criteria are adopted for identifying errors and "corrections," yet a comparison of the studies in Table 5.1 is quite revealing. In the two studies of English as a foreign language classrooms with nonnative-speaking teachers – Lucas's German study (1975) and Yoneyama in Japan (1982) – the percentage ignored was only between 10% and 15%, reflecting presumably a high priority for error correction in such grammar-based instruction.

In adult ESL classes, on the other hand, Salica in the United States (1981), Courchêne in Canada (1980), and Lucas in Israel (1975) found that the percentage of errors ignored was between 42% and 49%. Furthermore, Lucas contrasted native and nonnative teachers in Israel (five teachers each). She found that natives were more tolerant of errors, ignoring 53% of all errors in contrast to 31% for nonnatives. It should be noted that this contrast held especially for phonological errors, somewhat for syntactic errors, and not for lexical ones. Second language contexts presumably permit a freer communicative use of the target language with less emphasis on formal correctness.

In a different sort of program, elementary bilingual education or immersion, teachers appear to be more attentive to errors. With the exception of the one teacher who corrected nothing, Nystrom's (1983) teachers ignored between 13% and 24% of errors, similar to EFL teachers. Likewise, Hamayan and Tucker's (1980) grades 3 and 5 immersion

TABLE 5.1. QUANTITATIVE STUDIES OF FEEDBACK IN SECOND LANGUAGE
CLASSROOMS

Study	Level	Teacher N	Classroom N	L1	L2
Lucas (1975) I	Grades 6–12 EFL	21	26	German	English
II	Grades 9–10 EFL/ESL	10	20	Hebrew	English
Fanselow (1977b)	Adult ESL	11	11	Mixed	English
Chaudron (1986a)	Grades 8–9 French immersion	3	3	English	French
Hamayan & Tucker (1980)	Grades 3, 5 French immersion	6	6	English	French
Courchêne (1980)	Adult pre-university & university ESL	9	10	Mixed	English
Salica (1981)	Adult ESL	5	6	Mixed	English
Yoneyama (1981)	High school EFL	10	10	Japanese	English
Nystrom (1983)	Grade 1 Bilingual education	4	4	Spanish	English

and regular French class teachers rarely ignored errors (between 4% and 36%, average 19% – the one native-speaking teacher ignoring 36% of errors contributed greatly to the average). Presumably, these teachers still consider language form to be important, regardless of the particular content being taught (which varied considerably in these elementary classes). This tendency contrasts with the overall average frequency of ignoring errors (of all types, including content) in Chaudron's (1986a) secondary immersion classes, which was more similar to the ESL classes at 40%.

The one apparent exception to these tendencies is Fanselow's (1977b) average of only 18% errors ignored in 11 adult ESL classes. However, this result might be explained by the fact that, for reasons of equivalence

Duration of observation	Coding analysis	Reliability of analysis
1–2 hours each class	Direct observation, with adaptation of L1 coding system (Zahorik 1968)	Spearman rank order on subsample of lesson
1–2 hours each class	4 categories (from audiotape?)	Spearman rank order on subsample of lesson
One lesson each	Discourse analysis (from audiotape?) 16 categories	Not provided
1–3 hours per teacher (total 12) early & late in year	Discourse analysis from audiotape	None estimated
4–8 hours per teacher	3 categories of teacher response (from audiotape?)	Correlation on sample
10–20 minutes per teacher	Adaptation of Fanselow's (1977b) categories from videotape	Not provided
1 hour per class	Chaudron's (1977a) model from audiotape	Consensus on sample with 2 raters
1 hour per class	Adaptation of Fanselow's (1977b) categories from audiotape	Not provided
5 hours per teacher average	Adaptation of Chaudron's (1977a) model from audiotape (only error sequences selected by teachers)	Not provided

across classrooms, Fanselow had all of his subject teachers perform the same grammar-based lesson, where the focus (for the sake of the lesson, as well as perhaps due to the presence of the observer) would likely be more on formal target language production.

In general, these tendencies across different L2 contexts demonstrate the prevalance of the principles that Hendrickson suggested: when instructional focus is on form, corrections occur more frequently. There is, however, another possible meaning of the question, "When should learners' errors be corrected?" – namely, at what time following commission of the error? The answer to this question is addressed in later sections discussing *how* and *who*.

WHICH LEARNER ERRORS SHOULD BE CORRECTED?

Hendrickson (1978:392) again summarizes theoretical views and several empirical studies of NS reactions to learners' errors:

> Correcting three types of errors can be quite useful to second language learners: errors that impair communication significantly; errors that have highly stigmatizing effects on the listener or reader; and errors that occur frequently in students' speech and writing.

Although these criteria are appealing, they of course need to be studied empirically to see whether in fact correcting such errors is effective. The notions that L2 learners' interlanguages progress at a rate determined by other factors (universal sequences, communicative necessity) would mitigate direct application of Hendrickson's principles. Nevertheless, if communicative interaction and feedback have a role to play in aiding learners' progress, these three criteria probably have some validity, for such errors would be the most noticeable in communicative interaction.

In Table 5.2, data from all studies which reported relative proportion of types of error and amount of teacher correction of those types is presented. For the most part, comparable categories of error were used, but when not, the types have been situated in the most commonly accepted category. There are also differences in criteria for determining "correction." As a result, comparisons across studies should be interpreted cautiously. Taking into account some studies' lack of error counts in some categories, there is remarkable similarity in general proportion of error types. Of total errors, the median percentages of errors produced among the studies are: phonological, 29%; grammatical, 56%; lexical, 11%; content, 6%; and discourse, 8%. The trends for proportion of errors corrected (see medians) appear to reflect the general rate at which errors are made in classrooms, in an inverse relationship, where the more a type of error is made, the less likely the teacher appears to be inclined to correct it. Whereas Hendrickson's third principle suggests correcting the most frequent errors, this may in fact be the *opposite* of teachers' tendencies, although Hendrickson may have been referring to the most frequent type of errors within a given category.

In addition to the disclaimer that these patterns do not *justify* particular priorities in error correction, these data on treatment of errors in classrooms do not reflect the extent to which the teachers involved made substantial efforts to correct the errors. The proportions refer to any "treatment," and it now deserves qualification that error treatment comprises a wide range of behaviors. This brings us to the crux of the problem of error correction.

TABLE 5.2. RATE OF ERROR PRODUCTION AND TEACHER TREATMENT (IN %)

Type of error	Salica (1981)[a]	Courchêne (1980)	Chaudron (1986a)[b]	Fanselow (1977b)	Lucas[c] (1975) NS	NNS	Median
Phonological							
% of total errors	—[d]	32	29	28	28	32	29
% treated	—	41	54	17	67	61	54
Grammatical							
% of total errors	75	56	42	53	63	55	56
% treated	51	46	50	76	36	47	49
Lexical							
% of total errors	11	11	3	12	9	13	11
% treated	67	97	75	94	97	92	93
Content							
% of total errors	6	3	19	—	—	—	6
% treated	85	100	90	—	—	—	90
Discourse							
% of total errors	9	—	8	7	—	—	8
% treated	94	—	61	95	—	—	94

[a]Does not include phonological errors.
[b]Collapsed across both observation times.
[c]Separated by teacher type because significant difference found.
[d]Dashes indicate that the category was not evaluated; percentages (% of total errors) thus total 100 for each column.

HOW SHOULD LEARNER ERRORS BE CORRECTED?

A large number of empirical studies of error correction in classrooms and of repair of communication breakdown in natural conversation have been primarily concerned with the forms and functions of the teacher or listener's feedback. (For studies in natural L1 conversational repair see Schegloff et al. 1977. For studies of L1 teachers' reacting moves see Bellack et al. 1966; Zahorik 1968; Hughes 1973; Sinclair and Coulthard 1975. For studies of NS-NNS or NNS-NNS conversations see Gaskill 1980; Schwartz 1980; Chun et al. 1982; Day et al. 1984; Varonis and Gass 1985; Faerch and Kasper 1985b. For L2 classrooms or tutoring see Allwright 1975a; Stokes 1975; Chaudron 1977a, b; Fanselow 1977b; Long 1977; Bruton and Samuda 1980; Wren 1982; Rehbein

1984; Kasper 1985; Pica and Doughty 1985; Stratton 1986; Bradshaw 1987; van Lier in press.) To varying degrees these studies identify the choices available to participants in reacting to a perceived error or miscommunication.

Feedback turns.   Figure 5.1 is a slight adaptation of Day et al.'s (1984) flow of feedback in NS-NNS exchanges, which is representative of several such diagrams (cf. other studies of turn-taking in NS-NNS conversations and in L2 classroom interaction: Allwright 1980; Glahn and Holmen 1985; Kramsch 1985; Lörscher 1986; Kumaravadivelu n.d.; van Lier in press). The left column for NS turn refers to the listener's (teacher's) utterances, and the right column to the NNS's (the speaker's) utterances. The diagram is simplified, omitting the fact that the listener who initiates and provides the feedback/repair sequence (box 2) may eventually include more than one individual; teachers may in fact prompt other listeners to provide some feedback. The error occurring in the speaker's utterance (box 1) is perceived by the listener, who initiates the repair sequence. There are several points to note about the subsequent interaction.

First, the pattern of interaction depends initially on the listener waiting for the appropriate moment when a turn can be made (a "possible transition point," discussed in Schegloff et al. 1977), which is usually after the speaker pauses sufficiently (following the rules of speaking of the particular culture) or ends a syntactic unit with final intonation. Any other turn taken by the speaker will be judged as an interruption. Second, the abbreviated sequence of turns that constitutes the repair indicated in the diagram (from listener back to the speaker's acknowledgement – box 3 – and back to the listener's possible confirmation – box 4) may be prolonged to the extent that the repair requires a segmenting into portions (box 6, etc.), or the speaker fails to perceive the point of the listener's reaction. Such recursive cycling through the first sort of listener and speaker turns, before acknowledgement and confirmation, has been noted by many researchers and was suggested in other models of feedback (e.g., Chaudron 1977a; Varonis and Gass 1985). Finally, exit from the repair exchange (box 5) will result in a return to the main topic or line of conversation, the "main sequence," usually when the interlocutors have reached mutual satisfaction on recognition of the repair.

The L2 classroom is a special case of this general model for several reasons (see also discussion on these points in Kasper 1985 and van Lier in press):

a) The teacher has a preferred option on a turn at any transition point in reaction to a student response, unlike in natural conversation where the speaker has the first option for self-repair. The teacher even has the option of interruption,

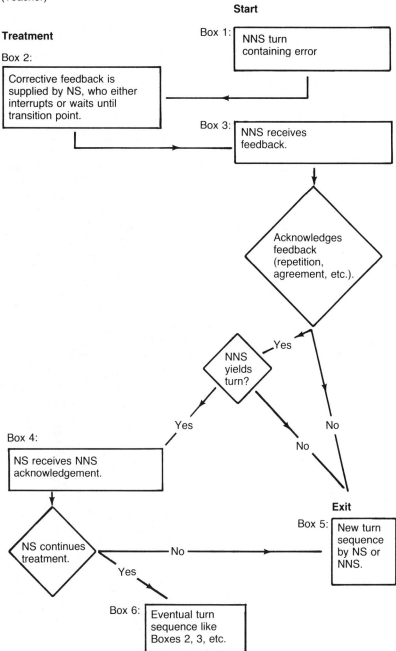

NATIVE SPEAKER TURNS
(Teacher)

NONNATIVE SPEAKER TURNS

Start

Treatment

Box 1: NNS turn containing error

Box 2:

Corrective feedback is supplied by NS, who either interrupts or waits until transition point.

Box 3: NNS receives feedback.

Acknowledges feedback (repetition, agreement, etc.).

NNS yields turn?

Yes

No

Yes

No

Box 4:

NS receives NNS acknowledgement.

NS continues treatment.

No

Yes

Exit

Box 5: New turn sequence by NS or NNS.

Box 6: Eventual turn sequence like Boxes 2, 3, etc.

Figure 5.1 Flow of corrective feedback in native–nonnative discourse. (Adapted from Day et al. 1984:38.)

which is not evidenced in natural conversation except in cases of serious misunderstanding, erroneous content or facts, or assistance when the speaker is searching for words. Schegloff et al. (1977) suggested that a differential in competence (adult-child) could result in a change in the priority of the speaker for self-correction. The differential competence between NS and NNS should lead, therefore, to a more probable breaching of this priority, even more so in the case of the institutionally assumed greater competence of the language teacher.

b) There is much greater likelihood that the source of the teacher's correcting turn is a formal error that does not substantially impede communication.

c) The rules of classroom interaction and assumptions about proper learning style may require the speaker being corrected to acknowledge the correction in a more explicit, complete manner than in natural conversation; the teacher may in fact elaborate on the correction with explanations about the psychological or physiological source of the error, linguistic descriptions of its rectification, demands on the speaker to repeat the correction, and so on – all of which would be highly unusual in natural communication.

d) The teacher has the option of nominating other participants to provide either the correcting feedback or evidence of comprehension of the correction (the latter was termed "verification" in Chaudron's 1977a model – see Table 5.3). The speaker and other participants are often held accountable for the correction long after it has occurred.

Types of feedback.   Within this basic model of turns that can be taken, the essential options available to the teacher for providing feedback, whether negative or positive, comprise virtually every sort of discourse act mentioned in this and the previous chapters: confirmation checks, clarification requests, repetition, models, explanations, and so on. These acts can be constructed in perhaps an infinite variety of ways to indicate several basic feedback functions or purposes, of which Allwright (1975a:104) lists the following:

Fact of error indicated
Blame indicated
Location indicated
Model provided
Error type indicated
Remedy indicated
Improvement indicated
Praise indicated
Opportunity for new attempt given

Thus, not only cognitive information regarding the fact, location, and nature of the error is possible, but motivational and reinforcement functions are possible. Numerous other researchers have proposed various sets of categories of feedback types, but as Chaudron (1977a) noted, these usually do not consist of elemental discourse units. General descriptors, such as "explicit" and "implicit," "correcting" and "helping," like Allwright's functions (which he called "features"), require high-level inferences about the interactants' intentions, and knowledge to be derived from the discourse structures and the context, or from independent inquiries. While such inquiries may be a legitimate undertaking of the discourse analyst, Chaudron proposed a more elementary, low-inference set of structural types and features of corrective discourse which involve fewer assumptions about intentions, effects, or context. These types and features are listed in Table 5.3.

"Types" were deemed to be capable of standing independently, like free morphemes, whereas "features" were bound, dependent on the context. For example, an "interruption" is a feature, because it depends on the context, whereas there are identifiable exponents of "acceptance" and "negation." Some structures can be either types or features, however.

Problems with feedback. The usefulness of such a set of feedback acts is most evident when one considers the problems that researchers have noted regarding inconsistency, ambiguity, and ineffectiveness of teachers' corrections. Many of these problems stem from the multiple functions that very similar discourse structures can perform.

First, one of the most noted problems with corrective feedback is that "repetition" of a speaker's utterance can serve several functions, of either a negative (correcting) or a positive nature (agreeing, appreciating, understanding – these terms are from Gaskill 1980). Repetitions are among the most common types of corrective feedback. In two studies adopting Chaudron's (1977a) model, Salica (1981) found three types of repetition (including approving repetition) among the four most common corrective treatment acts (a total of 32% of acts), and Nystrom (1983) found three teachers using repetition 15%–20% or more of the time. Also, Speidel (1984) found 47% of a teacher's responses to be exact or modified imitations of nonstandard dialect learners' utterances.[2]

As Chaudron (1977a) pointed out, correcting repetitions usually contain some additional information or a discourse feature that signals them to be corrections instead of confirmations, such as a slight modification of the original utterance (reduction or addition or substitution), an emphasis in stress or lengthening of a segment, a questioning intonation, or other correcting acts. Thus, a second problem is that, for L2 learners, whose grammar may not encompass the target rule, the modification or emphasis may be imperceptible, or perceived as merely an alternative to

---

2 Several other studies do not provide enough information about the error treatments to determine whether "model," "gives correct response orally," "expansion," or "gives part of correct response" (very frequent treatments in these studies) are in fact repetitions of the learner's utterance.

TABLE 5.3. FEATURES AND TYPES OF CORRECTIVE REACTIONS IN THE MODEL
OF DISCOURSE

Feature or type of "act" (F and/or T)	*Description*	*Example of exponent of expression*
IGNORE (F)	Teacher (T) ignores Student's (S) ERROR, goes on to other topic, or shows ACCEPTANCE* of content.	
INTERRUPT (F)	T interrupts S utterance (ut) following ERROR, or before S has completed.	
DELAY (F)	T waits for S to complete ut. before correcting. (Usually not coded, for INTERRUPT is "marked")	
ACCEPTANCE (T)	Simple approving or accepting word (usually as sign of reception of ut.) but T may immediately correct a linguistic ERROR.	Bon, oui, bien, d'accord
ATTENTION (T-F)	Attention-getter; probably quickly learned by Ss.	Euhh, regarde, attention, allez, mais.
NEGATION (T-F)	T shows rejection of part or all of S ut.	Non, ne...pas.
PROVIDE (T)	T provides the correct answer when S has been unable or when no response is offered.	S: Cinquante, uh... T: Pour cent.
REDUCTION (F) (RED.)	T ut. employs only a segment of S ut.	S: Vee, eee...(spelling) T: Vé...
EXPANSION (F) (EXP.)	T adds more linguistic material to S ut., possibly making more complete.	S: Et c'est bien. T: Ils ont pensé que c'était bien?
EMPHASIS (F) (EMPH.)	T uses stress, iterative repetition, or question intonation, to mark area or fact of incorrectness.	S: Mille. T: Mille?
REPETITION with NO CHANGE (T) (optional EXP. & RED.)	T repeats S ut. with no change of ERROR, or omission of ERROR.	T: (les auto-routes) n'a pas de feux de circulation.
REPETITION with NO CHANGE and EMPH. (T) (F) (optional EXP. & RED.)	T repeats S ut. with no change of ERROR, but EMPH. locates or indicates fact of ERROR.	S: Mille. T: Mille?

Feature or type of "act" (F and/or T)	Description	Example of exponent of expression
REPETITION with CHANGE (T) (optional EXP. & RED.)	Usually T simply adds correction and continues to other topics. Normally only when EMPH. is added will correcting CHANGE become clear, or will T attempt to make it clear.	S: Le maison est jaune. T: La maison est jaune.
REPETITION with CHANGE and EMPHASIS (T) (F) (optional EXP. & RED.)	T adds EMPH. to stress location of ERROR and its correct formulation.	S: Doo tout… T: D*u* tout. (stress)
EXPLANATION (T) (optional EXP. & RED.)	T provides information as to cause or type of ERROR.	
COMPLEX EXPLANATION (T)	Combination of NEGATION, REPETITIONS, and/or EXPLANATION.	S: Uh, E. (spelling 'grand') T: D. Non, il n'y a pas de E.
REPEAT (T)	T requests S to repeat ut., with intent to have S self-correct.	
REPEAT (implicit)	Procedures are understood that by pointing or otherwise signaling, T can have S repeat.	
LOOP (T)	T honestly needs a replay of S ut., due to lack of clarity or certainty of its form.	
PROMPT (T)	T uses a lead-in cue to get S to repeat ut., possibly at point of ERROR; possible slight rising intonation.	S: Petit. Grande. T: Petit…
CLUE (T)	T reaction provides S with isolation of type of ERROR or of the nature of its immediate correction, without providing correction.	S: Les stations-services sont rares. T: *Sont* rares? Au présent?
ORIGINAL QUESTION (T)	T repeats the original question that led to response.	

TABLE 5.3. *(Continued)*

Feature or type of "act" (F and/or T)	Description	Example of exponent of expression
ALTERED QUESTION (T)	T alters original question syntactically, but not semantically.	
QUESTIONS (T) (optional RED., EXP., EMPH.)	Numerous ways of asking for new response, often with CLUES, etc.	
TRANSFER (T)	T asks another S or several, or class to provide correction.	
ACCEPTANCE* (T)	T shows approval of S ut.	
REPETITIONS* (T)	Where T attempts reinforcement of correct response.	
EXPLANATION* (T)	T explains why response is correct.	
RETURN (T)	T returns to original error-maker for another attempt, after TRANSFER. A type of VERIFICATION.	
VERIFICATION (T-F)	T attempts to ensure understanding of correction; a new elicitation is implicit or made more explicit.	
EXIT (F)	At any stage in the exchange T may drop correction of the ERROR, though usually not after explicit NEGATION, EMPH., etc.	

*Asterisk indicates acts that occur as approving feedback, although they resemble the analogous correcting feedback acts.
Source: Reprinted by permission from Craig Chaudron, "A descriptive model of discourse in the corrective treatment of learners' errors," *Language Learning* 27/1 (1977), pp. 38–39.

their own utterance, because accepting, approving, confirming repetitions occur frequently in the same contexts. The classic case of this sort of confusion is an example from Fanselow (1977b:588):

Teacher: It's blue.
Student 1: It blue.
Teacher: It's blue.
Student 2: It's blue.
Teacher: It's blue.
Student 1: It blue.
Teacher: It's blue.
Student 1: It blue.

As illustrated in Chaudron's (1977a) comparison among types of repetitions, one way to be more successful in such a situation, if success is in fact desirable, is probably for the teacher to provide more explicit emphasis on the modification, by reducing the repetition ("It's") and/or by stressing the /s/.

A third problem, noted by many (see especially McTear 1975; Stokes 1975; and Fanselow 1977b; or Mehan 1974 in L1 research), is the inconsistency with which teachers correct learners' utterances, at times accepting a faulty TL form for the sake of the communicative purpose, at times correcting the same or a similar error, at times correcting minor errors or altering learners' meaningful communications for the sake of the example. Research is not clear as to the solution to this problem, although the consensus among various studies (including those mentioned earlier with NS-NNS or NNS-NNS conversational interactions) is that correction should be kept consistent within a focused domain of types of errors. Teachers should not expect learners to perceive and retain "corrections" that are provided in their "modeled" utterances or modified repetitions of learners' statements, if these corrections are not followed upon by verification of the learners' perception.

A final problem is perhaps the most general one. Even a cursory reading of the literature on feedback will reveal that the term "correction" is used in a variety of meanings. Chaudron (1977a) pointed out that there are several increasingly narrow denotations of this term. The most general is equivalent to "treatment of error," which appears to be the most widely employed meaning, used to refer to any teacher behavior following an error that minimally attempts to inform the learner of the fact of error – the treatment may not pursue correction further. Note that such treatment may be evident only to the outside observer or only to the teacher providing it. The next most general meaning refers to some treatment which is explicit enough to elicit (or which makes great efforts to elicit) a revised student response. And finally, there is the "true" correction which succeeds in modifying the learner's interlanguage rule so that the error is eliminated from further production.³

These three meanings are not clearly or consistently distinguished at times, leading to assumptions about the "explicitness" or "implicitness" of treatments and their subsequent effects. There is no study of classroom error correction which investigates the third, most narrow meaning. There are, however, several studies (including studies of tutoring and NS-NNS interaction) which investigated the second meaning of correction and noted the extent of learners' incorporation of corrections and models in their interlocutors' speech. These will be discussed in Chapter 6, as the best suggestion of learning outcomes that might be derived from feedback.

WHO SHOULD CORRECT LEARNER ERRORS?

The apparent possible answers to this question are: the teacher, the learner making the error, or other learners. We have already seen what the teacher might do or fail to do in correcting errors. Depending on the importance or likely success of the error correction, it is incumbent on the teacher to be as consistent and thorough as possible, to follow through with a correction until the learner evidences understanding of the error problem.

Otherwise, it may be more appropriate to allow the learner to self-correct. Certainly it should be the goal of instruction to improve learners' ability to monitor their own target language speech. In tutoring interaction, Wren's (1982) advanced student managed self-correction for 14% of her errors, and for another 29% of her errors she initiated Wren's assistance for either confirmation or help in correcting. So besides explicit grammar instruction to improve monitoring, it may be appropriate to train learners in the particular communication strategies that are useful for appeals for assistance. Recall also the observations made by Holley and King (1971) about the advantage of increasing wait-time following teacher questions. Fanselow (1977b) found teachers' treatments of error involving only the indication of error to occur for about 1% of the errors, but students' self-correction occurred for almost 4%. Courchêne (1980) found similar frequencies. More extensive research has yet to be conducted to determine the extent of learner self-correction possible if teachers wait before providing treatment, or merely indicate the fact of error.

Hendrickson's (1978) conclusion to this question cites several studies of composition correction to suggest that NNS peers may be very ef-

---

3 The now archaic sense of correction, meaning only positive or negative evaluation – praise or reproof – is omitted from this list.

fective correctors of one another's writing.[4] Although there are no studies comparing success of oral NNS peer correction and teacher correction in classrooms, several studies of classrooms and experimental conversations have demonstrated that NNS peers will provide substantial amounts of feedback and other negotiation of meaning in interaction with one another. This research is reviewed by Long and Porter (1985), from which the following summary deserves quotation:

> Correction. The frequency of other-correction and completions by students is higher in group work than in lockstep teaching (Pica and Doughty 1985) and is not significantly different with NS and NNS interlocutors in small-group work, being very low in both contexts (Porter 1986). There seems to be considerable individual variability in the amount of attention students pay to their own and others' speech (Gaies 1983b; Morrison and Low 1983), however, and some indication that training students to correct each other can help remedy this (Bruton and Samuda 1980). During group work, learners seem more apt to repair lexical errors, whereas teachers pay an equal amount of attention to errors of syntax and pronunciation (Bruton and Samuda 1980). Learners almost never *mis*correct during unsupervised group work (Bruton and Samuda 1980, Porter 1986). (p. 222)

Several of these points are rather important, for the intuitive judgment would be that NNSs would not provide enough correction or would provide incorrect feedback. This belief is not supported by the studies just cited, for although Porter (1986) found NSs correcting grammatical and lexical errors more frequently than NNSs, the overall frequency was low in both cases (8% and 1.5%, respectively), and only one-fifth of the low number of NNSs' corrections were erroneous. Porter also found that other negotiation of meaning (termed "repair," and including clarification requests, confirmation checks, and similar negotiating acts, but not corrections) was practiced equally frequently by the NNSs and the NSs in the study. In their classroom study, Pica and Doughty (1985) also found that learners produced no more correct target language utterances in the teacher-fronted (lockstep) activities than in the peer group activity.

These studies support the practice of enlisting learner involvement in correction of peers, although it is clear that the particular group task employed will influence the amount of negotiation: tasks involving exchange of information from both learners necessitate more negotiation. Yet it is evident that NSs, and presumably trained teachers, will be more alert to particular target language problems besides lexical ones or gen-

---

4 Although more recent studies and reviews by Chaudron (1984, 1987) and Zhang (1985) tend to support this view, Zhang found that teachers' corrections of grammatical and mechanical errors on compositions resulted in superior revisions, when compared with groups receiving peer correction or only self-generated revisions. However, a review of writing experimentation is beyond the scope of this book.

eral miscommunication, and their provision of feedback could appreciably aid learners' attention to the problems. Unfortunately, the evidence for such additional success of teacher correction is not available.

Summary

Feedback in L2 classrooms lies at the core of research on teacher-student and student-student interaction in L2 classrooms. The research demonstrates both the inherent danger in assuming that learning is occurring because the teacher is performing an instructional act ("correcting") and the potential benefit that learners may derive from 1) the appropriate sort of information about their target language speech, 2) the incentive to monitor their speech, and 3) the opportunity to interact with one another to improve their competence.

The research reviewed here has suggested that error correction does not constitute a major proportion of the activity in L2 classrooms which focus on communicative activities, such as subject matter instruction. Also, communicative interaction in group work may provide as much, and possibly more, appropriate corrective feedback to learners as teacher-fronted classroom tasks. While some studies to be reviewed in the next chapter provide suggestions on what constitutes effective feedback, longitudinal research is greatly needed to determine the extent of learning possible from feedback, or the types of feedback that would best succeed in promoting progress in the target language.

Conclusion

The nature of interaction in L2 classrooms is perhaps the most critical issue concerning formal second language learning, and although the research cited in this chapter suggests important ways in which current instructional practice may be both effective for and detrimental to promotion of TL skills, the complete picture remains to be developed. The classroom research has shown that teachers may be less likely to address L2 learners when they are mixed with native speakers. Even in uniquely L2 classes, teachers may have inappropriate priorities for how and when to elicit learners' contributions, and they may employ less of the target language than intended, or use it for less authentic purposes. It has also been revealed that teachers' different questioning strategies may be either helpful for or inhibiting of communication in classrooms. Teachers need to pay greater attention to the content and timing, as well as the clarity, of questions. Finally, teachers' feedback was seen to be a complex phenomenon with several functions. The greatest error teachers make may be the assumption that what occurs as "correction" in classroom interaction automatically leads to learning on the part of the student.

The study of L2 classrooms has reached an important stage where the potentially significant phenomena have been identified, described to some degree, and even quantified. The next step in research must then be to establish clear relationships between the occurrence of these phenomena – types of questions or feedback, the amount of target language use, functions of teacher talk, or the other teacher and learner variables studied in Chapters 3 and 4 – and student learning outcomes. These relationships are the topic of the next chapter.

6 *Learning outcomes*

The previous chapters have discussed research on teacher speech – its functions and qualitative or quantitative modifications, learner behaviors in response to instructional activities or interaction with other learners, and classroom interaction phenomena such as questioning and corrective feedback. In several cases, the behaviors described have been linked to L2 learning, so the present chapter will review research on L2 classroom processes that have a potentially positive effect on learners' perception and incorporation of the forms and functions of the target language.

Teacher input and learner comprehension/production

An initial consideration in Chapter 3 was the quantity of teacher talk. Although the typical dominance of teacher speech in classrooms was considered to be undesirable, several classroom studies suggest a relationship between the frequency of certain structures in teacher input and learners' target language development. These will be discussed in a section on frequency of input. A second issue, the principal focus of Chapter 3, dealt with modifications of teacher classroom speech. To what extent might teachers' modifications influence learners' comprehension, and consequently learning? Among the modifications of classroom target language input that were described, two have been investigated with regard to comprehensibility: rate of speech and syntactic complexity. These studies will be considered first.

Rate of speech

Hatch (1983:183) has suggested several benefits of slower speech to L2 learners, among which are especially that it should allow more processing time and clearer segmentation of the structures in the input. Although several of the studies reviewed in Chapter 3 revealed that teachers' speech to less proficient learners tended to be slower, Dahl (1981) was the only one of these researchers who directly investigated the relationship between rate of speech and the comprehensibility of the message. She found

that although a group of 16 L2 college students judged the more un-
derstandable messages to be spoken more slowly, the judgments did not
in fact correlate with the measured speech rate. Dahl considers that
perhaps some unmeasured characteristics regarding clarity of articulation or conciseness of information are related to perceived rate of speech,
since these positive qualities were also attributed by the subjects to the
less comprehensible messages.

A related support for slow rate of speech as a positive influence on
comprehensibility was an experiment by Kelch (1985). He found that
university L2 students had significantly greater success in dictation when
the rate of speech of lecture listening passages was slowed down from
about 200 wpm to 130 wpm. Note that this slower rate of speech also
approaches the lower rates noted for teacher speech to beginner-level
learners (see Table 3.4). Consequently, there is some support for the
intuitive notion that slower speech to learners improves comprehension.
Further research is needed to determine whether this effect is attributable
to the slower speech or to other prosodic features in teacher talk (see
discussion in Chapter 3), and whether it has any specific effects on target
language development.

Syntactic complexity and repetition

Although the studies of degree of subordination summarized in Chapter
3 suggest that speech to lower-proficiency learners tends to be simplified,
research on the comprehensiblity of such syntactically reduced speech
is surprisingly quite limited. The supposition is again that less complex
speech could contribute to comprehensibility by aiding the perception
of segmentation and the clarity of form/meaning relationships, yet there
are no studies investigating this effect.

The general approach of classroom-oriented research on this issue is
to present experimentally manipulated material to L2 learners and measure their overall comprehension of the content. For example, Long
(1985a) constructed two versions of an academic-style lecture, one of
which was an NS version and one of which was a "foreigner-talk"
version. The latter version was modified from the former by reducing
both the syntactic complexity (average words and S-nodes per T-unit)
and the rate of speech, and by the addition of rephrasings and restatements. In two different studies with these lectures, Long found that L2
college students who heard the foreigner-talk version were significantly
better at answering comprehension questions about the lecture, and rated
their perceived comprehension significantly higher, than similar students
who heard the NS version. Since several factors were modified simultaneously in the foreigner-talk lecture, it is difficult to ascertain the source
of this advantage. For example, the repetition of information had been

shown to aid its immediate recall in an L2 listening comprehension experiment with simulated lectures (Chaudron 1983b), and similarly in a dictation experiment by Cervantes (1983). So, since Long's subjects were allowed to answer their comprehension questions *during* the lectures, one might suppose that the repetition modification alone could have led to the improved comprehension for the foreigner-talk version.

A similar study by Speidel, Tharp, and Kobayashi (1985) involved 120 second grade pupils in Hawaii, who all heard the same three stories, but in one of six conditions. The stories were recorded in six versions, combinations of simple or complex syntax, and spoken in either standard English, Hawaiian English, or standard English with local Hawaiian pronunciation. Half the children spoke standard English and half Hawaiian English. While the preferred, familiar dialect was superior for both groups in measures of the children's comprehension, the unexpected result was that the simple syntax versions (simpler by a factor of one-half on a morphosyntactic complexity measure) did not lead to superior comprehension. Similar results have been obtained, in addition, by several experimental studies of the greater comprehensibility for L2 learners of syntactically simplified written passages (P. Johnson 1981; Blau 1982; R. Brown 1985). These studies suggest that lesser complexity alone does not result in significant improvement in reading comprehension; in most cases, it was less effective than other passage versions.

Recent studies dealing with syntactic simplification do not fully resolve this issue. Long's (1985a) study was modified in a second experiment. Fujimoto et al. (1986) developed three versions of an academic-style lecture: 1) a "native speaker" version with no modifications (2.11 S-nodes per T-unit, and judged to be at a ninth to tenth grade level of readability), 2) a "modified input" version in which difficult lexical items were replaced with simpler ones and complex sentences were simplified (1.15 S-nodes per T-unit, and a fifth to sixth grade readability level), and 3) a "modified interaction" version in which greater redundancy of information was provided by inserting, for example, definitions, synonyms, paraphrases, and missing elements of ellipsis (2.15 S-nodes per T-unit and ninth to tenth grade readability – i.e., approximately the same level of linguistic complexity as the native-speaker version). L2 college students performed significantly better on a postlecture multiple choice test after hearing the modified input version than after the native-speaker version. The modified interaction version just missed the post hoc comparisons criterion (Tukey's Honestly Significant Difference) for being significantly different from the native-speaker version (the means were 9.8, 12.9, and 12.1, for the three versions, respectively, out of 20 possible points). It is worth noting, however, that despite quite different levels of syntactic complexity, the two modified versions were not significantly different from one another. Thus, the modifications, whether lexical and syntactic simplification, or the addition of redundancy, appear to enhance comprehensibility. In this study, however, the rate of speech in the passages was confounded with modifications, for both the modified versions were spoken more slowly than the NS version (117 and 124 words per minute, vs. 140).

In the most realistic study of this sort, Mannon (1986; see discussion in Chapter 3) showed videotapes of two lecture versions (NS and NNS) to two other classes of L2 students from the same NNS population. She noted several trends favoring comprehension for the students hearing the simpler NNS lecture version. Lack of significance in this study may have been a result of the sometimes subtle and uncontrolled differences in complexity between the lecture versions.

Although more research is clearly called for, with more explicit tests of syntactic complexity in L2 listening comprehension, the current results do not look promising. The other factors involved in simplification of input, namely, elaborations by way of redundancy − restatements, repetition, synonyms, and so on − need to be more extensively examined, as in Fujimoto et al. (1986). Furthermore, longitudinal studies need to be conducted on the question of whether or not learners' interlanguage development, not simply comprehension, can be improved through exposure to comprehensible TL input. At present, the line of reasoning that would establish a causal link between simplification modifications and learning outcomes (discussed in Long 1983b, 1985a) has received some supporting evidence for the first step in the argument, namely, that speech simplification (of a certain sort) enhances comprehensibility. The second step, the influence of comprehensibility on learners' grammar, is untested.

Frequency of input

MORPHEME FREQUENCY RANK ORDERS IN INPUT

The hypothesis that L2 learners acquire what they hear the most may seem tautologous. Nonetheless, extensive research on the acquisition of L2 grammar does not tend to support the notion, although its potential in the case of vocabulary acquisition, or other higher-level linguistic structures in discourse, such as conversational patterns, is still perhaps viable, albeit untested. The initial proposal of this hypothesis generally considered in SLA research was that concerning the frequency of input of a collection of English morphemes, although Hatch (1974) proposed this for the case of input frequency and question development. (The literature on this topic is extensive; see Pica 1983, or any of the earlier cited SLA texts, especially Ellis 1985b:218−20, where the evidence points against classroom instruction resulting in any changes in the natural order of morpheme acquisition.)

A simple relationship may nonetheless hold between input and acquisition. Several correlational studies comparing frequency of input of various morphemes in teachers' speech, and their accurate production in learners' interlanguage, have revealed positive associations. An early study of this relationship was that of Larsen-Freeman (1976, a follow-up of Larsen-Freeman 1975), who examined the correlation between the frequency rank order of nine English morphemes in the speech of two ESL teachers, and the accuracy order of those morphemes in other studies of adult and child ESL learners' oral productions. The correlation was significant ($p < .05$, one-tailed) in four of six comparisons with the adults and in all six comparisons with the children. The teachers' frequency of production also correlated significantly (one-tailed) in four instances with that of native-speaking adults in R. Brown's (1973) study of first language acquisition.

Long and Sato (1983) also investigated the correlation between rank order of morpheme frequency in six ESL teachers' speech and Krashen's (1977) "average order" of morpheme accuracy, which was based on a synthesis of numerous second language acquisition studies. They did not find a significant correlation, however. In contrast, their ESL teacher rank order did correlate with the rank order of the morphemes in NS input to NNSs during conversations (taken from Long 1980b), and this latter rank order also correlated with Krashen's average order.

In order to achieve some perspective on these relationships, these rank orders and selected correlations are displayed in Table 6.1. Aside from the correlations already mentioned, the additional rank order correlations displayed in Table 6.1 show that Larsen-Freeman's learner accuracy order correlates significantly ($\rho = 0.83$, $p < .01$, [critical value = .783, one-tailed]) with Krashen's average order, and with Long and Sato's teacher frequency order ($\rho = 0.65$, $\rho < .05$ [critical value = .60, one-tailed]).[1] Three of six of Larsen-Freeman's teacher orders correlate significantly with Krashen's average order (range of $\rho = 0.63$–0.68, $\rho < .05$, one-tailed), and all six of them correlate significantly with Long and Sato's average teacher order (range of $\rho = 0.78$–0.98). Larsen-Freeman and Long and Sato's teacher input orders appear most in agreement with one another. They diverge from Krashen's average learner order in their high relative rank for article frequency and third-person singular, and low relative rank for the progressive-*ing* form and the progressive auxiliary (the latter two being closely related to one another in input). Long and Sato argue that the discrepancy in matching

---

1 Note here that Long and Sato used two-tailed tests, while Larsen-Freeman and the present study used a less stringent one-tailed test.

TABLE 6.1. NINE GRAMMATICAL MORPHEMES IN ESL TEACHER SPEECH AND LEARNERS' PRODUCTION

Morpheme	A. Krashen's (1977) "average (NNS) order" rank	B. Larsen-Freeman's (1975) NNS rank order of accuracy	C. Larsen-Freeman's (1976) ESL Teacher rank order in input						D. Long and Sato's (1983) ESL Teacher rank (N = 6)	E. Long's (1980b) NS to NNS input in conversation
			Teacher 1			Teacher 2				
			t1	t2	t3	t1	t2	t3	t3	
Progressive -ing	1	1	4	4	4	4	5.5	6	5	4.5
Plural	2	5	3	3	3	2	3	2	3	3
Copula	3	2	2	2	2	3	2	3	2	2
Auxiliary (progressive)	4	4	7	8	8	8	8	8	7	4.5
Article	5	3	1	1	1	1	1	1	1	1
Irregular past	6	8	9	6	7	7	4	5	8	6
Regular past	7	6	7	7	6	5	5.5	4	6	7
Third-person singular -s	8	7	5	5	5	6	7	7	4	8
Possessive	9	9	8	9	9	9	9	9	9	9

Rank order correlations:
(ρ, N = 9)

	B	C1 (t1	t2	t3)	C2 (t1	t2	t3)	D	E
A	.83**	.43	.67*	.63*	.68*	.47	.43	.46	.75*
B	—	.78*	.65*	.68*	.65*	.49	.43	.65*	.61*
D	—	.98***	.92***	.97***	.91***	.79**	.78*	—	.77*

* $p < .05$ (one-tailed)
** $p < .01$ (one-tailed)
*** $p < .001$ (one-tailed)

their teacher input with an average learner order of acquisition may be explained by the different levels of learners involved in the classes studied (primarily intermediate and advanced learners in Krashen's synthesis, intermediate learners in Larsen-Freeman's studies, but beginners in Long and Sato's study). Yet this neglects the very high correlations between their teacher input frequency and those of Larsen-Freeman. An alternative possibility is, as they imply, and as J. D. Brown (1983) has clearly illustrated, that slight changes in frequency of one item can quickly alter the rank placement of the item, resulting in borderline or extreme (non)significant correlations.

This point raises, in fact, two important caveats on frequency of input studies. First, in that they regularize the distance between items, rank order associations will thus obliterate potentially meaningful differences in *raw frequency*, which from the theoretical view should be the critical factor. Product-moment correlations between frequencies and percentage accuracy could be more appropriate in some cases. Second, average input frequencies of phenomena that are displaced in space and time from the learners studied are much less likely to be interpretable, even if significant correlations are obtained. There was no real connection between the teachers and the learners observed in Larsen-Freeman's and Long and Sato's studies. Thus, instead of suggesting a direct effect of input in instruction per se, these correlations may be related to a more general effect of the natural frequency of occurrence and obligation to produce the morphemes in English.

Nevertheless, a point in the study by Hamayan and Tucker (1980) suggests a direct input effect: they also found significant rank order correlations between teachers' frequency of production of nine French syntactic structures in classroom speech, and the accurate oral production of the structures in the elicited speech of students from the same classes. This was found for both FSL children in immersion classrooms and native French-speaking children in L1 classrooms. This is interesting, for the rank orders for the different teachers were different from one another, yet the correlations held true for each class. In all likelihood, therefore, whether merely through frequency or focus on specific forms, instruction can make some difference in the acquisition of target language structures. Pica (1983) demonstrates, for instance, that six instructed learners, who were matched with six naturalistic learners (as well as a "mixed" group) on language background (Spanish L1) and length of experience with the TL English, attained better TL accuracy overall on the nine morphemes seen in Table 6.1. They were especially superior to the other groups on their accuracy with plural -*s* and third-person singular. Pica points out that, among other possible explanations for success, these morphemes have been considered easy to learn. Ellis (1985b) argues, however, that these differences are slight, since they involve perhaps only one or two "overlearned" features of the morphemes involved. The stronger implication is that a natural order of acquisition is followed regardless of instructional input, for uninstructed learners' order tends to match that of instructed learners. The next section provides more detail on this issue.

INSTRUCTIONAL FOCUS AND FREQUENCY OF INPUT

Although there have apparently been no classroom studies investigating frequency in input and incorporation in production during interactive turns (beyond an occasional suggestive example, as in the cases cited in Ellis 1985a:79–80), two longitudinal studies (Felix 1981; Lightbown 1983) suggest the extent to which instructional focus can influence learners' incorporation of target language forms.[2]

Over a period of eight months, Felix (1981) observed a fifth or sixth grade (not "high school," as Felix refers to them – the students were 10 to 11 years of age) EFL class in northern West Germany. Based on analysis of transcripts of the first three months, Felix illustrates two target language forms (negation and interrogation) which the students appeared to be acquiring following the orders recognized from naturalistic L2 studies. Despite frequent practice with the target structures in the class, the students' acquisition was notably nontargetlike. For example, even with continuous drilling with elliptical responses ("No, it isn't"), the students persisted until the third month in producing mismatches ("No, I can"), and produced utterances with negatives placed externally to the verb phrase ("Britta no this...no have...this," "Doesn't I drink a cup of tea" – the latter was not a question). For two other TL forms, pronouns and "There is a N in NP / It's a N," the students also showed rates of error (63% and 24%, respectively) and failures to absorb the explicit instruction in these forms, which indicates their adoption of either random responses or natural developmental processes. Felix prefers the latter explanation. In defense of instruction, it might be remarked that except in the case of pronouns, the rate of accurate production of all these forms was over 50%. Yet Felix derived

2 On the other hand, for many years anecdotal reports have maintained that formal instruction could *hinder* L2 acquisition by overemphasizing certain structures, by teaching structures out of context, or by incorrect models in text materials or in teachers' input (cf. Selinker's 1972 "transfer of training" strategy in interlanguage). Kasper (1982) illustrates pragmatically inappropriate L2 English in German learners' speech that was likely derived from too formal a register in EFL text materials and from the artificiality of L2 classroom discussion. While such examples are probably numerous (a case of overemphasis will be noted in this section), the fact that instruction can have such an effect, whether appropriate or not, is not, of course, an argument against the effectiveness of instruction (on the contrary!), but against *bad* instruction and materials.

his interpretation from the students' classroom L2 productions, which were highly constrained by the teacher's drill-like exercises, so it is likely that the error rate would have increased in the learners' spontaneous speech.[3]

Whereas Felix did not quantify the target language input frequencies, Lightbown (1983) provides several quantified comparisons of teachers' classroom production with learners' classroom and elicited production. For two years, Lightbown and her colleagues followed several sixth, eighth, and tenth grade students who were studying English in French-speaking communities in Quebec, where English virtually has the status of a foreign language. Thus, especially for the sixth (and later seventh) grade learners discussed in the article, she considers that the classroom language and textbook constitute the principal source of input for the learners. Several of the verb and noun phrase morphemes analyzed by other researchers (as in Table 6.1) were studied in detail.

Comparing cross-sectionally over grade levels, Lightbown observed that the learners' accuracy in elicited production of progressive -*ing* was low relative to the other morphemes. This finding clashes with the high ranking of the progressive in Krashen's average order, but coincides with Larsen-Freeman's (1976) and Long and Sato's (1983) observations of lower frequency for -*ing* in teacher input. Lightbown found, indeed, that despite a rather high frequency of -*ing* in early lessons from the grade 6 textbook, and a corresponding high frequency and accuracy for the grade 6 students, the teacher generally did not produce many verbs inflected with -*ing* during that year (the frequency rank order being virtually identical to that of Larsen-Freeman's ESL teachers, seen in Table 6.1). In the following year (grade 7), these students' accuracy of -*ing* in elicited production dropped substantially (from 55% to 25%), unlike other verb inflections. This corresponded to a total absence of the form in the textbook series for that year. Thus, Lightbown concludes that the students had initially practiced -*ing* forms from the textbook to the point of overlearning, but owing to the later absence from instruction, the students' appropriate use of the form declined.

There is a recent important line of experimental instruction research which has taken seriously the issues of natural-universal sequences of acquisition. As discussed in Chapter 1, Pienemann (1985) argued that underlying psycholinguistic principles constrain learners' movement through developmental sequences, and therefore, learners who are exposed to the right sort of input relative to their state of readiness will

---

3 Felix and Hahn (1985) describe an extension of this study in support of the argument that the learners were acquiring pronouns following a sequence of universal features (e.g., personal vs. possessive first, followed by case, number, person, and gender). Felix and Hahn do not describe the extent or nature of the formal instruction on these forms in the class studied, however.

acquire target language forms at the next stage of development. This proposal for more explanatory principles that apply to a variety of language structures is not intended to apply to all language forms; only those target language structures that are constrained by language universals are deemed by Pienemann to be developmental, while others are considered variable and are acquired according to learners' affective states, amount of exposure, or other factors (see Meisel et al. 1981 for an exposition of these arguments). Pienemann (1984) tested this notion in a simple experiment with 10 Italian children learning L2 German (GSL). Two groups identified as being at successive stages (2 and 3) in GSL word-order development were provided two weeks of instruction in the fourth stage. Only the stage 3 learners appeared to progress.

In an analogous manner, Zobl (1984, 1985) investigated 76 L1 French learners' developmental acquisition of L2 English possessive pronouns ("his" and "her"), according to a markedness analysis of the primary feature (+HUMAN) of the object of the pronoun. His detailed findings (1985) suggest that even limited instructional input on the marked +HUMAN domain ("her arm" versus "her book") led to improved production of both +HUMAN and −HUMAN possessive NPs, while the −HUMAN group did not progress.

Ellis (1984a) attempted an instructional experiment with Wh-question pronouns and subject-verb inversion with 13 adolescent ESL learners, but he failed to find improvement. As Long (in press) points out, Ellis's selection of target language structures may have been too advanced for his learners' stage of development, even though they were attested to be using Wh-pronouns to some extent. The time allotted may have been too little as well (three hours), although Zobl's results were obtained after only 15 minutes of exposure to the TL structures. Much may depend, therefore, on the precise state of readiness to progress in a natural sequence.

There is thus some indication in these studies of a fruitful area of investigation, namely, stage-appropriate instruction, or instruction in marked features of TL structures (see further discussion in Hyltenstam and Pienemann 1985). However, even if the principle of stage-appropriate target language instruction is valid, it is regrettably not possible to determine from these studies whether frequency in the input, a formal focus, or the communicative practice (and thus "natural" intake) is responsible for the learners' improvement.

Summary

From these studies of the form and quantity of the target language input, there is only an inkling of a relationship between comprehensibility or frequency and learners' progress. Lightbown's results suggest, however, that while frequency may influence learners' production temporarily, their interlanguage will follow other developmental paths once the variability in exposure changes. There is little doubt that most language syllabi and instructional practices present structures that are inappropriate for learners' stage of acquisition or natural-universal sequences in development of specific TL forms. Nonetheless, it should be recognized that the measures employed in the previous studies are usually gross, average summaries, and therefore many specific effects of instructional input have inevitably been overlooked. For the learner to recognize some morphological segment, syntactic rule, or a specific vocabulary item, surely more complex linguistic events and communicative interaction will contribute as much as the simple frequency of occurrence of the item. Lightbown (1983:240) states the problem this way:

> The fact that our learners' accuracy orders differ from those observed in previous studies may be due to the exposure they had to a distorted version of the English language and to the fact that they were required to repeat and practice sentences whose grammatical complexities were far beyond what they would have included in their speech if they had been acquiring English through communicative interaction involving more varied natural language.

Formal language instruction

If, as suggested in the previous sections, natural teacher input and the wide range of materials and methods in L2 instruction may not be providing the right sort of instructional input or focus, one might wonder in what ways teachers, as instructors rather than simply as conversants, can influence learners' progress. Recall from Chapter 1 Long's (1983a) argument that the advantage of instruction over natural exposure might lie in part in the formal focus on language that occurs in the classroom. In Chapter 3, teachers' explanations were briefly considered, and both Yee and Wagner (1984) and Faerch (1985) believed that such metatalk might contribute to L2 learning. Classroom research has addressed this question, either in observational/correlational studies or in experimental and quasi-experimental comparisons between methods and programs. Regrettably, however, most research conducted on specific methods or materials has not been conducted in classroom contexts. A complete survey of experimental work on grammar learning is beyond the scope of this book.

Focus on form

Spada (1987; see also 1986) observed three adult ESL classes in Toronto, Canada, over a six-week period, using the COLT system for a process analysis (Allen et al. 1984; see discussion in Chapter 2, this volume) and several proficiency measures as pre- and posttests. On the basis of the weight of several COLT categories, Spada found the classes to be different with respect to their focus on syntactic forms; one class spent one and a half to three times as much time as the other two on a focus on code-related features. Yet the classes did not differ in relative grammatical improvement estimated by analysis of covariance on posttest scores.

On the other hand, Mitchell et al. (1981) studied sixteen FFL classes in Scotland (see discussion in Chapter 2). They correlated various dimensions of teaching events with selected (five to six per class) pupils' test scores on comprehension, narration, and structure tests. The significant findings were strong positive correlations between pupils' performance and 1) the teachers' use of metalanguage (i.e., talk about the language and grammar) and 2) the amount to which the teachers had the pupils speaking (as opposed to listening, reading, following commands, etc.). No specific activity in these largely grammar-drill type of classes was significantly correlated with pupil attainment, however. The nature of the effect of teachers' use of metalanguage on pupil performance was unexplored in discussion.

A third longitudinal study, of 14 adult ESL classes (six different teachers) in the United States, was conducted by McDonald, Stone, and Yates (1977). Correlations were calculated between student improvement based on various pre- and posttests, separated by about five months, and different observed behaviors. These relationships were then analyzed by factor analysis. The rather complicated results suggested two major types of teaching style along two dimensions: a structured style involving either "question-answer-corrective feedback-prompt-answer," or "model-practice-corrective feedback-model-practice," and a less structured style involving "direct-read," "free response," and games, discussions, and group work. Although the authors caution that there was great intrateacher, class-to-class, and student-related variability, multiple regression procedures revealed that a more structured style was related to improvements in formal, literary decoding skills, while the less structured style was more conducive to students' improvement in oral proficiency. McDonald et al. suggest that less proficient learners would benefit most from the former style.

These three observational studies present mixed results, with the latter two suggestive of a positive effect of formal instruction on certain L2 learning outcomes. Firmer findings of this sort may require more explicit classroom experimentation.

Explicit grammar instruction

As suggested in Chapter 2, a large number of context (program)-product studies in L2 classrooms have investigated the comparative effects of explicit versus implicit (pattern practice or inductive) grammar instruction on learners' achievement. A thorough review of these studies and the issues involved is beyond the scope of this book, in part because classroom process variables have typically not been observed closely or manipulated (thereby leaving some doubt as to the true differentials in instructional treatments), but also because the issues have been extensively reviewed elsewhere (see Scherer and Wertheimer 1964; Smith 1970; Levin 1972; Seliger 1975; Krashen 1982; Beretta, in press).

Because of the failure of several of the large-scale "methods comparison" studies to verify the consistency of the methodologies in classroom practice, the Swedish GUME project (Levin 1972; von Elek and Oskarsson 1975) focused on specific differences in rule presentation with very controlled instructional exercises. The difference in method was primarily that between explicit presentation and explanation of rules and implicit practice of rules. The researchers found some differential effects for explicit over implicit rule instruction, but only for selected groups of learners: adults and females, and an "accelerated" adolescent group. They did not follow up on this line of research to determine the long-term effects of maintenance of explicit instruction, however. Recall Krashen's (1982) critique of methods comparison studies noted in Chapter 2, that the learning effects of favored methods have tended to diminish over time.

Although evaluation research continues to be conducted to compare among *program* types (e.g., California State Department of Education 1984; the immersion program review in Genesee 1985; and J. D. Ramirez et al. 1986, which does have an observational component), it is perhaps a telling comment on researchers' goals that there have been increasingly fewer attempts to compare learning outcomes between grossly categorized "methods." More narrowly focused research on particular instructional variables seems necessary to ascertain the specific formal or social-interaction factors that lead to successful L2 acquisition.

Summary

The direction of results in the few large-scale classroom studies favors slightly a focus on form or explicit talk about grammar. Yet formal instruction may not be able to circumvent natural acquisitional sequences; it may only contribute to increases in the rate of acquisition through sequences, or to the acquisition of target language forms that are not affected by universal processing principles. What remains undetermined, of course, is the precise extent of effect of formal instruction on acquisition of the wide range of TL phonological, grammatical, or pragmatic rules, and the relevance of such instruction to learners of different ages, learning styles, or aptitudes. Research on outcomes of learner production and teacher-learner interaction, to be reviewed next, suggests furthermore that other factors in classroom learning may contribute greatly to acquisition; in fact, some of these factors may underlie or interact with the effects noted in this section.

Learner behavior and learning outcomes

The potential for certain learner behaviors to affect target language development has already been considered, largely in the form of correlations between production and performance. Recall, for example, the findings of Strong (1983) and Peck (1985) in Chapter 4, as well as a finding in the study by Mitchell et al. (1981; see their second finding cited in the foregoing section on formal grammar instruction). In their study, amount of student speech was significantly correlated with pupils' achievement test scores; this finding was based on correlations between class mean scores for speech production and achievement. However, these results indicate only a correlation, in which the prior proficiency of the learners may be the factor that leads to greater production, as argued in Chapter 4. There is little research designed to test a directional effect of learner production on improvement in target language proficiency. Longitudinal observation of children is of course a costly research enterprise, and the detailed analysis of verbal production is still more time-consuming. Still, several studies have results bearing on this question.

Learner production

D. Johnson's (1983) study, discussed in Chapter 4, revealed positive relationships between amount of learners' verbal interaction with peers and their improvement (measured by posttest scores with pretest scores partialed out) over the seven-week period of the study, although the effects were not significant. The "interaction" measure was in fact a frequency count of number of utterances directed to NS interlocutors, not interaction in the narrower sense of negotiation of meaning. Yet the failure to obtain effects may be a result of 1) the short duration of the study, since there was likely great variability among the children (5 to 9 years old; raw scores are not provided, however), and 2) the different treatments provided the children, for treatment effects were evidently confounded with the amount of interaction the children had (the treatment group maintained higher levels of interaction with native-speaking children than the controls).

The year-long study by Saville-Troike (1984) responds to these two criticisms. As was pointed out in Chapter 4, this study adopted a measure of interaction similar to that employed by Johnson. Nineteen beginning ESL learners in grades 2 to 6 were observed in both ESL classrooms and in play activities throughout the year. The duration of the study and the frequency of observation (every 30 seconds for one full school day a week) apparently rebuts the first criticism, while the fact that no special treatment was provided eliminates the second as plausible. Saville-Troike found low and nonsignificant correlations between the observed calculation of total use of English (interaction) and a year-end measure of reading achievement (a subtest of the Comprehensive Test of Basic Skills – CTBS – in English). Yet significant positive correlations were noted between interaction and year-end rankings on the Northwest Syntax Screening Test, and on the learners' mean length of T-unit in interview production.[4]

Regardless of what degree or type of acquisition may have been obtained as a result of the learners' verbal production in the target language, interpretation of these results is difficult for two reasons: 1) the characteristics of the verbal interaction, the functions or negotiations, were not distinguished in the encompassing measure of quantity, and 2) the great (uncontrolled and largely unanalyzed) variability among the learners in age and language background (both Indo-European and Asian languages were represented) likely contributes a number of factors to their variability in acquisition of the TL, such as age-related differences in language learning aptitude and social interaction. The lack of qualitative analysis of the interactions and the extra variability reduce the possibility of employing an interaction measure to discriminate among learning outcomes.

Chesterfield et al.'s (1983) study, discussed in Chapter 4, resembles Johnson's and Saville-Troike's in the measures taken of learner production throughout the year. Since they do not provide the complete raw data, it is difficult to judge the strength of their findings, yet there were several significant and high positive rank order correlations between the preschool children's verbal interactions in English and increases in ESL proficiency, as measured by change in MLU of in-class speech. The results again appeared to favor interaction with peers in one location and with teachers in the other (where Spanish was more dominant among the children). These supporting results are somewhat vitiated again by the use of rank order correlations and simple increment in interaction and proficiency measures (cf. footnotes 1 and 2, Chapter 4).

One relatively simple finding with positive implications of a causal relationship between production measures and proficiency improvement was obtained by A. Ramirez and Stromquist (1979), who did pre- and

---

4 For all these achievement measures, there were no initial pretests because the learners were selected for having beginning-level proficiency and little prior L2 exposure, so Saville-Troike evidently assumes (possibly erroneously) that nonerror variance on the posttest is attributable to L2 acquisition.

posttesting of grades 1 to 3 Spanish-speaking ESL children, in 18 classes of prespecified lessons on three grammar points. Two proficiency measures were taken: oral production of various grammatical points and the learners' aural comprehension of speech incorporating points from the lessons. The researchers report that the class aural comprehension posttest scores adjusted for pretest scores discriminated between the highest and lowest achieving classes on classroom observation measures of students' total production of replies, and also of expected replies (i.e., correct responses). The grammar production measure also discriminated between high and low, and middle and low, classes in terms of total replies produced. Because of the use of postlesson scores adjusted for prior knowledge on a pretest, these findings suggest a directional effect of the amount of in-class student replies and correct replies on their successful acquisition of learning points. The difference between these results and D. Johnson's (1983) or Saville-Troike's (1984) findings is perhaps attributable to the more lesson-specific nature of Ramirez and Stromquist's analysis, as well as the control over initial subject differences. Such detailed analysis of acquisition of specific points by means of practice is evidently needed.

Learner initiation and interaction

Whether learners' initiating behavior influences acquisition has already been addressed in Chapter 4 in the discussion of Seliger's and Day's research, where insufficient evidence was available to support a positive relationship. D. Johnson's (1983) study, described in the preceding section, also calculated the number of learners' initiations over the seven-week program, and found no relationship between this measure and improvement on the proficiency pre- and posttests.

With regard to learners' negotiating behaviors in classroom interaction, there is only one study indicating that such measures would relate to proficiency, although this evidence is correlational instead of causal. Naiman et al. (1978) observed the interactive behaviors of elaboration, clarification, and mutual correction, and found the proportion of these to all student responses to be positively correlated ($p < .05$) with their standardized measures of comprehension. In a stepwise regression, this set of behaviors was also among the best five predictors of students' proficiency on the comprehension test for grade 10 students and on the imitation test for grade 12 students. It was, moreover, positively correlated with the classroom initiating behavior "student callout," which, however, did not appear to be as strong a predictor alone. Such evidence can still be interpreted as indicating the greater alertness to communicative negotiation of more proficient learners, but it is interesting that these measures ranked so high in the stepwise regression.

Studies which reveal a more directional effect of negotiated interaction on learners' TL acquisition have not been done on learners in interaction with one another, but rather in interaction with NS interlocutors, so they will be reviewed in the section on classroom interaction.

Learning strategies

O'Malley et al.'s (1985b) study of the effect of learning strategies on development is suggestive of a possibly productive area for further research. They applied their analysis of students' learning strategies (O'Malley et al. 1985a; see the discussion of this study in Chapter 4) in a training experiment with 75 ESL high school students. The eight-day experiments provided one hour per day of instruction in different combinations of learning strategies for listening, speaking, or vocabulary. The comparison of interest was whether students trained in all three types of strategy (metacognitive, cognitive, and socio-affective) would be superior to those trained with two types or none. The trend for development on listening tests administered during the training period was in favor of strategy training, but on the posttests (adjusted for pretest scores) there was no significant difference. There was a significant effect on the adjusted speaking posttest scores, with the trend again favoring strategy training, but O'Malley et al. do not show which strategy groups were significantly different from the nonstrategy controls. Several factors, such as the short duration of the experiment and difficulty in some tasks, may have limited their findings of significant differences.

Summary

The rather weak findings in general for the influence of learner behavior on learning outcomes, whether production, initiation, or negotiation, probably do not indicate the true relationships but rather reflect inadequate research on the topic. Yet the failure to find a strong influence with the most investigated factor, total amount of learner production (interaction in Johnson's and Saville-Troike's studies), may indicate the weakness of this measure to discriminate the *quality* of learners' production. It may be true that overall amount of learner use of the target language in school situations will not result in improved proficiency. There are possibly more important effects arising from the quality of learners' interaction with NSs or peers, namely, the appropriateness of the input (which we have seen has not been adequately investigated) and the degree of interactive negotiation with interlocutors. The next section addresses this latter possibility.

Classroom interaction and learning outcomes

While the preceding analysis of learning outcomes has uncovered several likely contributors to successful L2 development, the interaction phenomena discussed in Chapter 5 – teachers' direct address to learners and choice of language, questioning behavior, and feedback – may be the most critical factors influencing learning. A survey of the research on these phenomena and their potential for promoting TL acquisition follows.

Speech addressed to learners

The effect of amount of speech directly addressed to learners on their L2 development was investigated by Snow and Hoefnagel-Höhle (1982). Their study of 13 kindergarten, primary, and secondary Dutch as a second language learners (L1 English) showed few relationships between the amount of speech directed to individual learners and outcomes on tests of comprehension and production. Even when the children's improvement over time was compared with the quantity of classroom input (for six subjects with longitudinal data), no distinct relationships held. It should be remarked, however, that very little classroom time was included in the sample (30 minutes per child), the number of subjects was small, with the same problem of great variability in age seen in Saville-Troike's (1984) study, and out-of-class exposure was not controlled.

In a study of eight beginning FFL university classes, Omaggio (1982) found significant rank order correlations between teachers' "personalized" speech to learners (this qualitative assessment of speech involved a composite of several affectively supportive behaviors like those in Moskowitz's FLint system – see Table 2.3) and ratings of the teachers' effectiveness by supervisors and students. It is unfortunate that more specific measures of learners' improvement in proficiency were not obtained, because as we have seen, rank order correlations ($N = 8$) may obscure the presumably quantitative relationships underlying the rankings, not to mention the uncertain relationship between rated effectiveness and true effectiveness.

Language of input

A similar issue arises concerning the influence of teacher choice of language on learner language in bilingual classrooms. To what extent will the teacher's dominant language, or differential use of the L1 and L2 for classroom functions, lead learners to use one or the other? The only evidence of this available is indirect: Legarreta's (1979) study of language use in bilingual classrooms (see Chapter 5). The balance of student use of the L1 and L2 matched that of the teacher's use in four out of the five classrooms Legarreta observed. As is typically the case in a correlational analysis, it is not clear from Legarreta's results whether the students' use was dependent on the teachers', or the reverse. Nevertheless, the longitudinal study of three L1 Spanish elementary school children by Bruck and Schultz (1977) suggests that a gradual tendency for a teacher to use her dominant language for instructional tasks (whether the L1 or the L2) will result in a similar shift in the learners' preferences for language use.

The results just discussed in the previous section on interaction and learner production do not appear to support this, however. In Chesterfield et al.'s (1983) study, certain factors in the classroom other than the teachers' language choice, such as peer language preferences, seemed to influence amount of language use by the children. These superficial conflicts may be reconciled, however, by the age factor. As children mature, they become influenced differently by peer and adult pressures, more sensitive to social norms requiring target language or dominant language use. Chesterfield et al.'s children were between three and a half and four years old, whereas Legarreta's and Bruck and Schultz's observations were in kindergarten (age 5) and grade 1 (age 6), respectively. In Wong-Fillmore's (1980) study of adolescents, there appears to be a systematic positive relationship between the bilingual teacher's balance of language use in different situations and that of the Chinese learner. These results are, of course, only important to the extent that L1 or L2 use is considered productive of development in either or both languages, at present an undecided question.

Questions and learner production

Another factor in interaction was that of questioning strategies as means of eliciting more or less learner speech. Among their other results (see the section on explicit grammar instruction), Mitchell et al.'s (1981) correlational study of FFL classrooms had found a high positive correlation between learner proficiency and "speaking," yet low correlations with activities such as "imitation," "drill/exercise," and "transposition" (i.e., reading aloud or dictation). It is difficult to determine what constituted the speaking activities observed, for questioning was not independently coded, and learners' speaking activities were likely comprised of freer responses to questions as well as more drill-like interaction. But this leaves open the possibility that more communicative speaking activities, not coded as such, would be of greater value. This issue cannot be decided until more extensive analyses are conducted on such data.

As seen in Chapter 5, Long and Sato (1983) had found that the dominant type of questioning in six ESL teachers' lessons to adults in the United States was "display" questioning, that is, questions for which the answer is already known to the teacher. This is unlike the dominant use of "referential" questions, for which the response is not known, in nonclassroom NS-NNS conversations. Aside from the possibility that display questions tend to elicit short answers, learners supply the information for didactic purposes only, so it is plausible that they would have less communicative involvement in producing a display response, and thus less motivational drive for using the target language. This question of attitude and motivation related to questioning or question type has not been researched.[5]

In connection with a study by Long et al. (1984) in high school ESL classrooms, Brock (1986) conducted an instructional experiment on the effects of these two types of questions on learners' TL production. Brock trained two teachers in the use of referential questions and encouraged them to use these to discuss a reading passage and vocabulary lesson. Two other teachers received no training. The distribution of referential and display questions in the two groups' lessons to university-level ESL students were significantly different. The treatment teachers obviously used more referential than display questions (173 to 21), quite the reverse of the control teachers (24 to 117). But more important, Brock found that the learners responded with significantly longer and more syntactically complex utterances to referential questions than to display questions (mean length = 10 words vs. 4.23 words, respectively; mean complexity = 1.19 S-nodes per communication unit versus 0.56). The treatment group students also produced significantly more sentential connectives and had significantly more instances of more than two successive turns taken by the same learner. Although Brock did not measure other qualities of the learners' speech, nor any developmental outcomes, the supposition is that learners will attain a much higher proficiency if given more opportunity to produce, and produce meaningfully, in class.

Brock's study derived from research on this same issue by Long et al. (1984). In this study, six high school ESL teachers were randomly assigned to one of three groups, two to an experimental question treatment group, two to an experimental wait-time group, and two to a control (praise feedback) group. As in Brock's study, it was hypothesized that training two of the teachers in use of referential questions would increase

---

5 Nor, for that matter, have attitudes been related to any issues of "communicative involvement" or "relevance." In arguing for the study of learner strategies, Chesterfield and Chesterfield (1985) advocated the use of "problem-solving exercises relevant to the child's world" (p. 57); it is not clear what would constitute "relevance." This matter deserves serious research, especially insofar as these concepts are fundamental to the advocacy of communicative language teaching.

their differential use over display questions, and that this would result in greater and more complex student participation measures. All teachers' class hours were videotaped at four times: in a baseline observation, in a prepared common lesson, in a second common lesson following the different training treatments, and in a fourth observation of an ordinary teacher-determined lesson.

It was found that the teachers receiving training in question types produced significantly more referential questions than the control teachers following training. Contrary to expectations, however, with the experimental question group and control groups combined, referential questions did not elicit significantly more student speech (in turns, utterances, or words per utterance) than did display questions; there was, instead, a consistent tendency (significant in comparisons at two times) for display questions to elicit more student turns and a tendency (significant in one comparison) for referential questions to elicit slightly more student utterances.

In regard to teachers' strategies in questioning learners, the wait-time treatment was hypothesized to have similar positive effects on learners' participation, consistent with L1 educational research (Rowe 1974) and with Holley and King's (1971) suppositions on learners' self-corrections (see discussion in Chapter 5). The results for the wait-time training group showed them to maintain significantly longer wait-time (comparing durations of more than three seconds against those of less than three seconds) in the observations following training. As for effects on production, however, extra wait-time did not result in longer student utterances.

In addition to anticipating immediate improvements in learner TL production as a result of different questioning behavior, researchers must be concerned with mastery of lesson content, whether that content constitutes knowledge about the TL or other subject matter taught via the L2 (an increasingly common approach to language instruction). In a meta-analysis of L1 teacher questioning research (see Rosenthal 1984 and Wolf 1986 for expositions of meta-analytical techniques), Redfield and Rousseau (1981:237) found "that gains in achievement can be expected when higher cognitive questions assume a predominant role during classroom instruction." Since referential questions may tend more to be higher cognitive level questions, one might expect effects for referential question use. Long et al. (1984) compared the relative mastery of lesson content in the prepared lessons for the groups (on criterion-referenced multiple choice quizzes). Although differences between experimental and control groups were not statistically significant after treatment, scores on the second prepared lesson following treatment showed both experimental groups *reversing* an advantage that the control group had had over them before the training sessions.

These initial results for questioning techniques that are intended to produce learner output are encouraging. Added to them is a further finding by A. Ramirez and Stromquist (1979), in their study of correlations between classroom interaction and lesson content mastery. The highest coefficient of regression on improvement in lesson-specific content was for the teachers' use of "guided questions," in effect display questions for which the desired information was presented immediately before the question. On the other hand, this teacher behavior showed no relationship to improvement in learners' L2 *production*. Nor did Ramirez and Stromquist find any significant relationship between "free response" questioning (not necessarily the same as referential questions) and learners' development.

QUESTIONS AS INTERACTIVE MODIFICATIONS

A final set of phenomena associated with questioning, which Long (1981a, 1983b) has advocated as critical for promotion of L2 acquisition, is that of interactive modifications used in negotiation of meaning – including comprehension checks, confirmation checks, and clarification requests. In Chapter 5 it was seen that these are associated in various ways with interactive tasks in which information must be shared or negotiated, and the argument is that such behaviors best allow learners to obtain appropriate intake from their interlocutors' (TL) input.

There are unfortunately no classroom-based studies of improved comprehensibility or learning resulting from interactive negotiation of meaning (but see the related experimental listening – one-way speech – studies discussed at the beginning of this chapter). Still, an experimental study of NS to NNS speech in a direction-following task has bearing on this matter. Pica, Doughty, and Young (1986) had nine NNSs perform several assembly tasks under one of two conditions: an NS presenting simplified instructions with no interaction, and an NS presenting unsimplified instructions with learner interaction and questioning permitted. The latter group ($N = 4$) was superior to the former. A separate analysis of the several tasks in the interaction condition showed that those which elicited modificational features from the learners tended to be better understood, although a measure of redundancy provided by the NS in the instructions proved to be confounded with these interactional features.

Feedback and learning outcomes

The last interactive phenomenon under consideration here is that of error correction, which was discussed at length in Chapter 5. A meta-analysis of research on several L1 instructional qualities including corrective feedback (Lysakowski and Walberg 1982) found "large and consistent effects" of feedback on learning. The L2 research, however, is limited to specific relationships between feedback and learning, so primarily the fourth question from Chapter 5 will be considered (How should learners' errors be corrected?) in an attempt to compare the results of relevant studies on how feedback affects learning outcomes.

Hendrickson (1978) cites a UCLA M.A. thesis by Margaret Robbins which experimented with weekly error explanations (apparently from composition errors) for a group of ESL learners for one trimester. They were to correct their errors and provide explanations for them. Yet this group did not reduce their verb errors over the period of the study. Hendrickson also summarizes research on composition error correction not involving classroom activities (the large amount of research on writing is regrettably beyond the scope of this book), with no concrete findings as to preferred correcting techniques. Brock et al. (1986) studied the effect of feedback in conversational interactions using the Chun et al. (1982) data (see Chapter 4) and found no differential effect for feedback judged to be explicit from that judged implicit.

On the other hand, there is some evidence of feedback on error resulting in learners' ability to correct. In addition to proposals about instructional exercises intended to reduce errors, Fanselow (1977b:590) argues for greater "redundancy, contrasts and explicit information" in teachers' feedback, isolation of the error, delaying the feedback, and various other suggestions.

In his French immersion classroom study (1977a), Chaudron tested some of these notions by comparing the effects of different types of repetitions – simple repetitions versus those with emphasis, or reduction or expansion of the learners' errors (see these types in Table 5.3). He found an advantage for repetitions of student errors with reduction or emphasis (either questioning tone or stress) to result in correct student responses, and the combination of these modifications was still more successful. Reduction of the learner's utterance to isolate the item in error increased the rate of student correct responses by about 15 percentage points (from 20% to 35%, and 42% to 59%), and adding emphasis increased rate of correct responses by over 20 percentage points (from 20% to 42%, and from 35% to 59%). It would appear that some localization of the error and clear, explicit provision of an alternative model can at least result in immediate learner revision of the error.

Two other studies found that teacher treatment aided learners in supplying correct responses. Although she did not quantify the differences by type of correction, Salica (1981) found that the ESL students supplied correct responses to 64% of teacher corrective treatments. Similarly, Wren (1982), who had tutorial conversations with one of her own advanced ESL students, found the learner able to correct 83% of her utterances after Wren treated the errors, as opposed to only a 14% rate of self-correction.

Despite these positive findings, these studies risk being accused of discovering only immediate effects that result from learners being good parrots. This would be a legitimate criticism if it were not for the sort of differential effect revealed in Chaudron's study, suggesting that some conditions can promote better parrotting, and for another differential effect found in Crookes and Rulon's (1985) study of experimental NS-NNS game conversations.

Using data collected by Long (1980b), Crookes and Rulon analyzed the amount of feedback on error provided by the NS in 16 dyads performing three tasks – a free conversation, an Odd-Man-Out game (discussing which of four words is distinct from the other three, and why), and a Spot-the-Difference game (each participant having the same picture, with slight differences). The researchers hypothesized that 1) the game tasks would generate more feedback and negotiation than the free conversation, and 2) the NNS would incorporate (repeat, re-use in later contexts) the NS feedback more in the information-exchange tasks. The first hypothesis proved true, with the game tasks resulting in four to five times as many NS feedback utterances per NNS errorful utterance as the conversation: the need for communication overrode the natural rule against other-correction. The second hypothesis was only partly true; only the Odd-Man-Out task resulted in significantly more instances of incorporation of NS feedback in the NNSs' utterances. The researchers speculate that this occurred principally because of the greater amount of unfamiliar lexical material in this task, so that the NNS was able to acquire a number of new words during the game. This speculation is in accord with unquantified observations made both by Bruton and Samuda (1980) in classroom group problem-solving discussions among adult ESL learners, and by several of the NS-NNS conversational interaction studies, which found lexical difficulties and collaborative lexical search to be the most readily engaged negotiations (Gaskill 1980; Schwartz 1980; Brock et al. 1986).

Although this last finding supports the potential effectiveness of certain types of corrective feedback, the primary conclusion to be drawn from it may be that learners will most readily incorporate corrective feedback in meaningful collaborative tasks, where appropriate use of the target language will mean success rather than failure to meet the goals of the activity. This is of course a major foundation stone of communicative language teaching, which deserves more extensive study.

These error feedback studies indicate only short-term incorporation of feedback information. Yet A. Ramirez and Stromquist (1979) also found that teachers' overt correction of grammatical errors (not, however, pronunciation errors) was significantly correlated with pupils' improvement on both lesson content comprehension (recall that the lessons were on grammar points) and ESL production tests.

Summary

The research reviewed here concerning the TL learning effects of interaction in L2 classrooms is obviously limited in its conclusions, yet highly suggestive for further research. Some of the more interesting and fruitful areas for future classroom-oriented research have appeared here, especially the influence of particular question types, negotiation for meaning, and information-rich feedback on error. It should be evident, however, that the investigation of these issues is a very time-consuming and difficult task, requiring careful design of classroom observations or experiments and laborious analyses of the data. It is most encouraging, however, to note the increase in studies focused on this area in the past five years.

Conclusion

It should be clear from this review that there is substance to the view that classroom instruction will aid L2 acquisition. For example, there is some support for hypotheses which predict a differential effect on instructed L2 learning from variations in teachers' speech characteristics. There is evidence, for example, that teachers' adjustment of their rate of speech downward for beginning-level students may enhance comprehensibility. Other input variables, such as repetition or redundancy of target language forms, may have at least short-term influence on learners' comprehension, and the overall frequency in input may be related to learners' development. This latter relationship is no doubt constrained by the focus of the instructional tasks using those forms, as Felix (1981) and Lightbown (1983) have illustrated, and by the predominance of universal sequences in acquisition.

While the quality and quantity of comprehensible input is surely important, most theorists and researchers would be reluctant to stop there in ascribing benefits of instruction. Many would look to pedagogical behaviors, such as correction, questioning, and formal explanation, for the source of positive effects. Several of these behaviors do indeed seem to have an influence on learners' development. It appears that some degree of formal analysis and focus on the code can be beneficial to learning, considering the following results: 1) the differential learning resulting from different teaching styles seen in McDonald et al.'s (1977) study, 2) the significant relationships between formal-language talk and attainment in Mitchell et al. (1981), 3) the outcome for overt correction and vocabulary explanation in A. Ramirez and Stromquist (1979), 4) the positive effect for explicit grammar teaching with some groups in von Elek and Oskarsson (1975), and 5) the differential outcome for some tasks and feedback to promote incorporation of feedback in Crookes and Rulon (1985) and Chaudron (1977a). While such a conclusion can easily be biased by the nature of the tests used to study proficiency (discrete-point, formally analytical) or measures used to study incorporation (short-term), the narrative measures in Mitchell et al. and the production measures in Ramirez and Stromquist are not vulnerable to this criticism.

In addition to these issues, there remain unresolved a large number of questions regarding the effects of instruction and classroom interaction on L2 learners. If any one conclusion is to be drawn from the preceding review of learning outcomes, it is that much more research remains to be conducted to determine what aids learners' target language development in classrooms: how comprehensibility, comprehension, learner production and practice, formal instruction, and interaction lead to greater second language competence.

7 Directions for research and teaching

To conclude this review, the major findings of the research will be summarized, and implications for further research and teaching in second language classrooms will be suggested. Despite the obvious increase in amount of classroom-oriented research in recent years, few of the suggestions offered here can be made with great confidence, for the existing research is difficult to synthesize. It has been shown that research is a) lacking in consistent measures of classroom processes and products, b) sometimes inadequate in design to address critical research questions, c) inexplicit or incomplete in quantitative or qualitative analysis, and d) in need of greater theoretical specification of the constructs and relationships to be investigated. A discussion of these methodological issues is warranted before future directions are suggested.

Methodological issues

Observation instruments

The discussion in this book has frequently called attention to the non-comparability of measures of classroom processes. Although a large number of observation instruments have been developed through the years, they have resulted from quite different theoretical positions and research goals: it is rare for any researcher, or team of researchers, to adopt a prior system. This has resulted in many studies of similar phenomena that lack true comparability (e.g., quantity of teacher speech, questioning, feedback). Baseline units of observation (often unreported) differ to such an extent that results could be extremely distorted. For example, recall Strong's argument that measures of teacher L1/L2 language use in classrooms should be done on the basis of duration rather than, say, number of utterances, turns, or moves. Analysis on the basis of frequency of discourse unit could overestimate use of one language or another if the language happened to be used more for frequent, short utterances or turns, or with greater silent periods in between utterances when a sign system is used in observation (see Table 2.1 and discussion on it). On the other hand, the duration of certain features of discourse may be an inappropriate measure, for time may have no direct psychological relationship to learning in the case of many acts, such as explanations, commands, replies.

The choice of baseline measure is also important because in many cases, as was suggested in Chapter 2, analyses based on moves appear to be confounded with functions of teacher and student behavior. There should preferably be an independent formal distinction for segmenting discourse (such as the utterance, in the sense defined in Table 2.4), which then would serve as the denominator for various other functional events and analyses. For this reason, some studies of classroom "interaction" which observe move- or turn-level units too easily obscure the functional import of within-move or within-turn behaviors.

It has also been noted on occasion that the *omission* of baseline units of analysis, in either reporting or comparing among events, leaves the reader of such research incapable of independently judging the conclusions offered.

The more important issue, of which these comments are only an indication, is the construction of descriptively adequate categories of classroom behaviors and events. It is entirely possible that, with their diverse goals, different researchers can arrive at quite different systems for the analysis of classroom interaction, some based on low-inference behaviors or discourse units, others based on high-inference categories; some derived from cognitive psychological perspectives, others from sociological analyses. Thus, the difference between some types of feedback discussed in Chapter 5 (e.g., "repetition with change and emphasis" versus "explicit") is one of low-inference versus high-inference categories. Or the difference between closed versus open questions on the one hand, and display versus referential questions on the other, is substantially a difference between a semantic (linguistic) view and a communicative (sociological) view of meaning in interaction.

The initial concern with the proliferation of such diverse categories (aside from possibly unnecessary duplication of trivially different systems) is one of reliability in classifying or analyzing events. Very few of the studies reviewed in this book have reported reliability estimates of their observational or discourse analyses. But furthermore, as was pointed out in Chapter 2, the ultimate issue is one of validity of the constructs used to describe and interpret classroom interaction. Only theoretically motivated categories that further prove to relate to learning outcomes or other research questions should be maintained as measures of L2 teaching and acquisition. The apparent lack of correlation between a category such as interaction – in the form of learner verbal exchanges with others – and learners' achievement may be due to the invalidity of the measure, for it probably encompasses too many different social functions and psychological events.

In general, the details and critique of such potential weaknesses in instrumentation have been omitted from this survey, for the sake of attempting to reveal the consistency or inconsistency across studies, and thereby discovering the most valid categories by comparison. It is hoped that the preceding and current chapters will aid in determining the measures and constructs that remain worthy of further research. Observation instruments and discourse analytical systems are much needed in classroom research, especially in order to have common means to evaluate different educational contexts; this is particularly necessary insofar as governments, administrators, teachers, and researchers wish to judge the most effective instructional programs and methods (cf. J. D. Ramirez et al. 1986; Richards and Rodgers 1986:161–3). As noted in the discussion of methods comparison studies, observational corroboration of teaching treatments in programs or experimental instruction is indispensable to assuring the validity of the findings.

Design

Only a brief comment is necessary concerning adequate research design. Among the many factors which contribute to good research design (e.g., proper sampling procedures, size of sample, and randomization – virtually none of which has been adequately incorporated in the studies reviewed here, often for reasons beyond the researchers' control), two major points have arisen frequently in the foregoing: the control of treatment effects by means of control groups and/or pretest measures, and analysis of outcomes by means of posttest measures, including long-term effects.

Regarding the first point, it was evident in Tables 3.1 and 4.1 that many studies of teacher talk or learner behavior had not adequately controlled for the variable of interest, for there was variation between the comparison groups not only on the factor of interest (e.g., L2 learners vs. L1 learners), but also on the mode of discourse (instruction vs. discussion) and on the subjects studied (e.g., teachers vs. other NSs). With an issue such as teacher speech modification, we should consider those studies which control for teachers, and preferably maintain the same teachers, in instruction with NSs and NNSs.

Similarly, in Day's study (1984; see the section on initiation in Chapter 4), it was clearly seen how not only a larger sample, but also better control over posttreatment variation by means of regression procedures with pretreatment placement levels (still not an entirely appropriate control, however), led to a serious questioning of Seliger's (1977) early research results. By the same token, the findings of Saville-Troike (1984) regarding learners' achievement must be taken with caution, because of insufficient control over learners' initial abilities or age differences.

On the second point, the problem is obvious to most L2 teachers and researchers. There is a pronounced unavailability of appropriate measures of L2 progress, whether in overall proficiency or, more particularly, with regard to whatever learning point is pertinent to the research goals − whether it be comprehension of teacher speech, acquisition of the definite article, pragmatic competence, or subject matter understanding.

The solution to these problems and others is, first of all, better knowledge and application of rigorous design and procedures among L2 researchers. A second solution is perhaps a more difficult one to achieve: making available more resources for the entire discipline of L2 teaching and research − live classrooms for observation and experimentation, adequately trained teachers, funds for research assistants to conduct analysis of the extra control classes needed, and perhaps especially, appropriate instrumentation for measurement of learner proficiency. The advantages and drawbacks of the test instruments employed in the various classroom studies have been intentionally omitted from discussion here, for those issues would lead too far from the primary goals of this book. Yet the possible lack of validity of any achievement or developmental measures cited in this research constrains the strength of any findings proposed. Researchers must always indicate the reliability and validity of measures obtained with their test instruments.

Statistics and reporting

It barely needs repeating here that much classroom research has demonstrated marked misuse, frequent underuse, and occasional unwarranted overuse of various statistical procedures. Rank order correlations have been most often mentioned in the preceding chapters, yet chi-square tests are probably more commonly used and abused. It was noted in regard to Table 3.7, distribution of sentence type, that while percentages were displayed for ease of comparison across studies, the chi-square statistics were based on raw frequencies in the studies. There are, however, too many studies which evidently have (inappropriately) calculated chi-square tests on the basis of percentages. Another problem noted is the failure to apply or interpret proper post hoc measures following significant analysis of variance. Such comparisons are critical for the reader, in order to understand the vital differences in effects. For instance, if only one teacher, student, or small group is contributing the major proportion of variance on a factor, the finding of a significant treatment effect may be seriously limited.

A point related to this is that the studies reviewed here have too rarely reported the critical statistics that a reader needs to interpret statistical tests. The typical presentation in the L2 literature of percentages, correlations, *t*-tests, and *F*-tests without means and standard deviations, much less raw data, is inexcusable. Without knowledge of raw score distributions, for instance, Pearson correlation coefficients have ambiguous interpretations. On the other hand, some studies have failed to extract important summary statistics, especially means and percentages, and without precise knowledge of the raw data, such as baseline rates or individual scores, interpretation of true differences is left to speculation. For example, at various times in this book (e.g., Tables 3.4 to 3.6, Table 5.2), means and percentages have been estimated based on insufficiently reported data.

The procedure adopted in reviewing classroom research was intended to balance many of these problems against the potentially useful information that each study contributes. By contrasting the strengths and weaknesses in comparable studies, the major emphasis was on the variability or consistency in research results. The research has not allowed, however, the sort of meta-analysis of research that the more rigorous L1 educational literature permits. For this, L2 classroom research needs many more studies on each issue, using similar categories of analysis. There is thus a very important role for classroom research in the future.

Theory and second language classrooms

One last remark on methodology is in order. Although efforts are well underway (see the texts on SLA cited in Chapter 1), attempts to construct a general theory of L2 acquisition have not fully clarified the role of instruction. The discussion in Chapters 1 and 6 regarding formal instruction is only part of the matter, for classrooms can also obviously provide L2 learners with a variety of opportunities to acquire and practice the target language. The purpose of this book has been to help elucidate which are the principal variables of interest and what might be the relationships among them, so that an explanatory theory can be developed. As Long (1985a) argued, research which follows a well-developed theory is in the end more powerful and efficient as a guide to further research and to practical applications in teaching.

Implications for research and teaching

To aid in the following summary, the findings of L2 classroom research will be grouped according to the components of the Model for the Study of Classroom Teaching shown in Figure 1.1 (Dunkin and Biddle 1974). Teacher "presage" variables will be included as a rubric, for several studies have a bearing on such variables, even though the issue of teacher characteristics independent of classroom processes has not been specifically focused on in this review. Following a brief summary of these findings, various context variables and their influence on classroom processes will be considered, followed by process variables. Both will be studied with regard to their influence upon other processes and their relationships to learning products.

Presage variables

The most common teacher variable included in these studies was the distinction between native- and nonnative-speaking teachers. Since this variable tends to be coincident with a second language versus a foreign language context in these studies, however, it is difficult to separate the independent contribution of each variable. Lucas's (1975) study of teacher feedback in West Germany and Israel and Yoneyama's (1982) in Japan, and the studies of teacher talk in Peru (Milk 1985) and Japan (Ishiguro 1986) provide the best contrasts on this variable. Felix's (1981) study also involved nonnative-speaking teachers, but there is no study like his to contrast with. The evidence here is merely that NNSs tend to be slightly more concerned with formal language instruction and correction (a priority which may be confounded with the FL program demands) and that they tend, just as NSs, to adjust their speech to L2 learners in measures of length of utterance and syntactic complexity.

Pica and Long (1986) studied experienced and inexperienced, and regular and visiting, teachers. Their findings suggest no surprising differential adjustments between the groups in speech to the learners, other than that visiting teachers tended to ask more questions and make fewer statements.

Other studies have made occasional distinctions between teachers and aides, and between teachers and nonteachers, but other than the sort of teacher-talk adjustments to be summarized in the section on process variables, no specific findings merit noting here.

Context variables

FOREIGN LANGUAGE VERSUS SECOND LANGUAGE CONTEXTS

As was discussed in Chapter 1, there are important differences between foreign language and second language contexts with regard to the availability of authentic target language input and opportunities to communicate. The classroom research reviewed here has not, however, revealed particular classroom processes that appear dependent on the contextual contrast, besides the matter of a noticeable focus on target language form (in Felix 1981 and Yoneyama 1982, for instance). However, this focus also has been noted in second language contexts. There are good reasons to suspect that programmatic and teacher training decisions play a greater role in determining the particular classroom processes in either context. Nonetheless, the possibility remains that learners' greater exposure to the target language outside school in second language contexts permits teachers to be more communicatively effective in classrooms. Such exposure might help to preclude learners' development of unusual grammatical and pragmatic rules, such as those exemplified in Kasper's (1982) study of the influence of TL input limited to inauthentic, dated, or overly formal material. In addition to more extensive comparison between foreign and second language contexts, research on the issue of exposure to authentic language activities and input in foreign language classrooms is greatly needed.

PROGRAM CONTEXTS

Within second language contexts, there were generally stable findings, in spite of programmatic differences, of a dominance of teacher talk in classrooms (about 65% to 75% of total talk). However, it has been found that program differences can result in different degrees of L1 versus L2 use. The dominance of the L2 in immersion programs and ESL classes with mixed L1 students contrasts with a greater balance between L1 and L2 use in many bilingual programs (albeit with some exceptions, such as Nystrom et al. 1984). Despite a rough balance in use of language, there was also evidence of differential functions for use of the L1 in most of these cases, however: for translation, clarifying explanations, some managerial directives, some social contact, and praise, for example (e.g., Townsend and Zamora 1975; Legarreta 1977; Milk 1982). On the other hand, J. D. Ramirez et al. (1986) found no systematic variability in functional differences for L1 and L2 across three program types.

Other program effects, such as a focus on form versus focus on communication, were observed in the comparison among studies of corrective feedback in Chapter 5, and in Fröhlich et al.'s (1985) comparison of one ESL and three FSL programs in Canada. Several of the differences found between Fröhlich et al.'s programs are likely attributable to the practice of teaching other subject matter, especially in the immersion and extended French programs. On the other hand, they found the ESL program to be the highest in the proportion of "genuine requests" made. The difficulty in making such comparisons is in determining which programs are initially likely to be focusing on form and what behaviors constitute a validation of such a focus. More concerted efforts are called for to construct theoretically appropriate measures of classroom behavior exhibiting formal or functional operations.

CLASSROOM ORGANIZATION

An important variable that has gained much recent attention is that of group work. As has been seen in Chapters 4 and 5, studies comparing group work in L2 classrooms with teacher-fronted activities have found equivalency between them, or superiority of group work on important process variables such as content coverage, amount of interaction or production, accuracy of production, and so on (Pica and Doughty 1985; Rulon and McCreary 1986). Teacher-fronted activities still have a potential advantage, however, for the extent and accuracy of input provided, or the appropriate sort of feedback (assuming teachers are trained and sensitive to learners' developmental progress). Contrasts between different learner and teacher groupings need more exploratory and replicational studies, for the size and homogeneity of groups may be a crucial factor.

For instance, there is the likelihood in homogeneous or even mixed bilingual education classes that children will congregate in monolingual groups. This may be no disadvantage, as Strong's (1983, 1984) and Chesterfield et al.'s (1983) findings suggest, for the children still grow increasingly aware of the need to use, and become proficient in, the target language in various contexts. Proponents of bilingual education for minority children generally advocate strongly the need for learners to maintain their mother tongue through the initial years of L2 learning (see especially Cummins 1981). In the case of adult ESL classes, however, linguistically homogeneous groups may not serve the same goals, although careful comparisons between group tasks conducted in the L1 and L2 remain to be examined in research.

Size of group may be important, considering Gaies's (1983b) finding of greater "feedback" acts in triads than dyads (although the inclusion of NSs in some of these small groups may be a confounding factor) and because, as will be seen, the group task may be a more important contributor to differences in type and amount of participation.

TASK AND ACTIVITY AS CONTEXT

As was noted in Chapter 2 and elsewhere, there has been little consistency throughout the classroom-oriented research in the choice of descriptors of task and activity types. Research in classrooms has been limited by not having an agreed-upon set of activity types (see Chapter 2), so little comparison was possible among studies, in part because researchers have not even reported differential findings (though see Politzer 1970; Mitchell et al. 1981). Until there is greater uniformity, the research will be difficult to consolidate into immediate implications. Moreover, while the pedagogical literature on language abounds with various proposals for communicative language activities, it appears to have avoided a concise taxonomy of types.

However, recent experimental research on interaction tasks (e.g., Long 1980b; Gaies 1983b; Gass and Varonis 1985; Pica et al. 1985; Doughty and Pica 1986; Duff 1986; see also theoretical commentary in Long 1985c; Crookes 1986) appears to be converging on a way of describing tasks, especially in terms of the extent of information available to and needed by each participant in order to complete the task goal. The indications from this research are that communicative games and information gap tasks in which each interactant has information necessary for completion (two-way tasks) can substantially promote the number of turns taken by each, as well as the number of interactive behaviors, such as confirmation checks and referential questions.

On the other hand, as Duff (1986) demonstrated, a task such as a debate, in which each participant has a separate agenda, can lead to more extensive turns and more complex language. And among different information gap tasks, the level of content may bring about a differential in the incorporation of feedback information, as Crookes and Rulon (1985) found when comparing Spot the Difference and Odd Man Out. Much more extensive research on these issues would obviously be of great benefit to program and materials developers.

LEARNER VARIABLES AS CONTEXT

One important learner variable that has not been adequately investigated in the preceding studies is age. The precise effects of age on learner participation has not been controlled for in live classroom research, despite interesting implications in the experimental literature on communication task interaction (e.g., Scarcella and Higa 1981, who found that adolescents initiated more conversation and exhibited more interactive behaviors than children). While age differences are generally a concern in SLA research (cf. Krashen, Scarcella, and Long 1982), the lack of adequate comparisons in classroom-oriented research is surprising, although it doubtless is partially due to limited access to multiple classroom contexts for many researchers.

Learner proficiency as an independent factor has been more fully studied, as in the case of teacher-talk studies and learner production in classrooms (Chapters 3 and 4). Despite some discrepancies in findings, the evidence here is fairly clear on at least one point, that teachers adjust their speech to simpler, shorter utterances, less complex vocabulary, and so on, in talk to lower-level learners. The greater frequency of questions in classrooms as compared with NS-NNS or NS-NS conversations, however, is not specifically evidence for adjustment to lower proficiency learners, for only one study actually found this contrast between classroom speech to NSs and NNSs (Mizon 1981), where several factors are confounded with the addressee variable (foreign vs. second, the precise tasks conducted, and NS vs. NNS teacher).

Learner proficiency also has been shown to correlate positively with amount of production in classrooms (Naiman et al. 1978; Strong 1983, 1984) and, as Strong argued, possibly with the efficiency with which learners can benefit from input. Of course, it has been emphasized that this correlation may only be a context-process relationship rather than a process-product one. Without the latter, still-uninvestigated relationship that Strong proposes, or Swain's principle of comprehensible output, it remains undetermined whether greater proficiency *results from* productivity in classrooms.

Process variables

Chapters 5 and 6 correspond in content to the two issues of process-process and process-product relationships, yet few of the studies reviewed there adequately explored learners' longitudinal development and target language achievement. The stronger findings relate to products internal to the classroom interaction, which of course have some bearing on long-term learning outcomes. These will be briefly considered with respect to learner comprehension and production.

COMPREHENSION

Classroom-oriented research has not adequately investigated the comprehensibility of teacher talk, although the existing experimental studies of learner comprehension of target language lecture-style information indicate a relationship between redundancy in input and learner comprehension (see the section on input and comprehension in Chapter 6). This redundancy refers either to repetition or rephrasing of information. While these studies only suggest an immediate effect, it is plausible to argue that repetition and rephrasing can have a more long-term effect on acquisition. As Snow (1972:564) postulated in regard to L1 acquisition:

Hearing adults paraphrase their own utterances could be a valuable demonstration ... to a child whose vocabulary and grammar are still so small .... Furthermore, if the child has figured out the meaning of the sentence, he needs less time to interpret its paraphrase and thus can spend more time decoding grammatically less important units of the paraphrase.

Slower speech and pauses may also aid learner comprehension, possibly for reasons similar to those just cited. Moreover, while too simple syntax may be a hindrance (see Speidel et al.'s 1985 results with children listening to first and second dialect passages, as well as the studies on reading comprehension cited in Chapter 6), the matter of appropriate modification of syntax for learners' level of development remains an important topic for study.

The finding of White and Lightbown (1984) with regard to the failure of teachers' extended rephrasing of questions, and the suggestions in Chapters 5 and 6 regarding clarity of feedback, constitute strong evidence that teachers' attempts to modify input to promote comprehensibility risk making the learners' task more complex (see also Chaudron 1982, 1983a, for examples with vocabulary elaboration, topic reference, and explanations). In both cases, questions and feedback, the suggestion is instead that brief, explicit rephrasings and informative contrasts would be more beneficial for learner comprehension, ability to reply to the question, or incorporation of the feedback.

PRODUCTION

Arguments for the benefits of learner production in classrooms are not restricted to the notion of practice effects, for as Swain (1985) proposed, the learners' production must additionally be comprehensible, in the sense that it communicates meaningfully to others – the supposition being that this would also render it more meaningful to the learner. A small amount of evidence was presented in Chapter 6 in support of some learner production in classrooms leading to learning, in the form of lesson-specific L2 rule acquisition related to correct replies to questions (A. Ramirez and Stromquist 1979; recall that the questions were display-type questions on the lesson content, but the authors controlled for pretreatment knowledge on the targeted items). There was also a trend in Long et al.'s (1984) study of question type and wait-time, for the treatment groups to surpass the controls in lesson content knowledge. While a number of process variables may contribute to learners producing more in classrooms (especially referential questions in contrast to display, as in Brock 1986), the long-term effects of such processes demand investigation.

The study of interactive features in L2 classrooms has yet to demonstrate clear effects either on immediate or on long-term acquisition of the target language, yet the arguments that they do so are not easily denied. Classroom-oriented research has initially demonstrated the frequency of such acts as comprehension checks and clarification requests relative to certain tasks and groupings, yet the argument needs further support in the form of demonstration of effects on learners' incorporation of L2 syntax and lexis by means of such interaction, just as intimations of incorporation in certain feedback types have been evident.

FORMAL INSTRUCTION

The question of formal instruction in L2 classrooms has been dealt with at length in Chapter 6. Suffice it to say here that the instructional behaviors which a teacher enlists to call learners' attention to their progress may include metatalk about the target language, and certain learners will benefit greatly from such an analysis. This is an essential role of the well-trained L2 teacher: to interpret learners' TL production in class in the light of knowledge of SLA universals, and to intervene at appropriate moments to urge the learners' developing rule systems along. The extent to which formal analysis, or communicative practice, or other TL input via materials and peer group interaction, will help learners progress remains to be explored in full. The suggestions of the stage-appropriate literature (Pienemann 1985) must be taken seriously and followed up with careful instructional experimentation. To do so, however, teachers and researchers need to work more closely with test and materials developers, in order to construct the optimum input and evaluation procedures for such studies to demonstrate the validity of this perspective.

Also, research on the relationship between learner strategies in the classroom and learning outcomes is barely beginning. Any interventions that teachers or researchers might have in such strategies, if these are indeed manipulable (as O'Malley et al. 1985b implies), may contribute to learners' developing metalinguistic awareness, and thereby formal knowledge, of the TL. However, because of the wide diversity of possible phenomena, many of which would probably not aid conscious knowledge, the caution for further research on learner strategies is that it be fully attentive to developments in cognitive psychology and educational learning theory, to ensure that the phenomena adopted for study hold promise as valid constructs and productive learning strategies.

The value of second language instruction

The purpose of this book has been to attempt to elucidate the critical issues and findings of research in and about second language classrooms. While the studies reviewed here clearly are not always as rigorous or convincing as we would like, the past ten years of classroom-oriented research is impressive in the breadth and depth of study of a variety of issues, when virtually every study was groundbreaking in one respect or another – methodology, research questions, population studied, analytical techniques applied.

At the same time, second language instruction has been gaining in importance, as more people throughout the world find the need to acquire one or more second languages. There is a diversification in the specific purposes of language instruction, an increase in language schools and programs, and an expansion in training programs for second language teachers, researchers, and program developers. For these reasons alone, second language classroom research has an important role to play.

Although first language education and acquisition research has led the way at many points in methods and issues, second language researchers have inevitably had to pose rather different questions, given the fact that the subjects (and the eventual beneficiaries) of our research are a unique population. We are dealing with individuals who are usually cognitively and linguistically far more sophisticated than their L2 resources would suggest, which results in a discrepancy between the way we tend to interact with them (simplifying our speech as if they were children, structuring their environment with TL form-related questions and activities), and how we would interact with a native speaker of the same age. But fortunately, L2 learners are usually well aware of their needs and are willing to put aside their natural expectations for social interaction in order to discover the target language communicative system. So second language learners often prove to be highly cooperative and inquisitive, pushing teachers and researchers beyond the intended purpose of their instruction or investigative goals.

This context makes the study of L2 classrooms a rewarding experience. If it were not so, many individuals would not be devoting endless hours to designing research, observing, transcribing, counting, analyzing, and reporting findings. But the intrinsic reward in discovering the processes and potential products of classroom instruction, which has been the principal task of the past decade and more of development in the field, would not be fulfilling if researchers and the teaching professionals they collaborate with did not have confidence in future research. We need to proceed, assured that the further study of second language classrooms will lead to more concrete knowledge about how to help learners achieve full competence in a communicative system that is mastered by every child and adult of the target language community, who have learned it naturally, without classroom instruction.

References

Adams, Raymond. 1972. Observational studies of teacher role. *International Review of Education* 18:440–459.

Agard, F. B., and H. B. Dunkel. 1948. *An investigation of second language teaching*. Boston: Ginn and Co.

Allen, J. P. B., Maria Fröhlich, and Nina Spada. 1984. The communicative orientation of language teaching: an observation scheme. In J. Handscombe, R. A. Orem, and B. Taylor, eds. *On TESOL '83: the question of control*, 231–252. Washington, D.C.: TESOL.

Allwright, Richard L. 1975a. Problems in the study of the language teacher's treatment of learner error. In M. K. Burt and H. C. Dulay, eds. *On TESOL '75: new directions in second language learning, teaching and bilingual education*, 96–109. Washington, D.C.: TESOL.

ed. 1975b. *Working papers: language teaching classroom research*. Essex: University of Essex, Department of Language and Linguistics.

1980. Turns, topics and tasks: patterns of participation in language teaching and learning. In D. Larsen-Freeman, ed. *Discourse analysis in second language acquisition research*, 165–187. Rowley, Mass.: Newbury House.

1983. Classroom-centered research on language teaching and learning: a brief historical overview. *TESOL Quarterly* 17:191–204.

1984. The importance of interaction in classroom language learning. *Applied Linguistics* 5:156–171.

Allwright, Richard L., and Kathleen M. Bailey. In press. *Focus on the classroom*. Cambridge: Cambridge University Press.

Annett, John. 1969. *Feedback and human behavior*. Harmondsworth: Penguin.

Bailey, Kathleen M. 1980. An introspective analysis of an individual's language learning experience. In S. D. Krashen and R. Scarcella, eds. *Research in second language acquisition: selected papers of the Los Angeles Second Language Research Forum*, 58–65. Rowley, Mass.: Newbury House.

1983. Competitiveness and anxiety in second language learning: looking at and through the diary studies. In H. W. Seliger and M. H. Long, eds. *Classroom oriented research in second language acquisition*, 67–102. Rowley, Mass.: Newbury House.

1985. Classroom-centered research on langauge teaching and learning. In M. Celce-Murcia, ed. *Beyond basics: issues and research in TESOL*, 96–121. Rowley, Mass.: Newbury House.

Bailey, Kathleen M., and Robert Ochsner. 1983. A methodological review of the diary studies: windmill tilting or social science? In K. M. Bailey, M. H. Long, and S. Peck, eds. *Second language acquisition studies*, 188–198. Rowley, Mass.: Newbury House.

Bailey, Leona G. 1975. An observational method in the foreign language classroom: a closer look at interaction analysis. *Foreign Language Annals* 8:335–344.

Baker, Keith A., and Adriana A. de Kanter. 1981. *Effectiveness of bilingual education: a review of the literature.* Final draft report. Office of Technical and Analytic Systems, Office of Planning and Budget, U.S. Department of Education, Washington, D.C.

Bales, Robert F. 1950. *Interaction process analysis: a method for the study of small groups.* Cambridge, Mass.: Addison-Wesley.

Barkman, Bruce. 1978. Classroom interaction. In P. M. Lightbown and B. Barkman. *Interactions among learners, teachers, texts, and methods of English as a second language. Progress Report 1977–78*, 71–85. Montreal: Concordia University.

Barnes, Douglas. 1969. Language in the secondary classroom. In D. Barnes, J. Britton, and H. Rosen, eds. *Language, the learner and the school*, 11–77. Harmondsworth: Penguin.

Barnes, Douglas, James Britton, and Harold Rosen. 1969. *Language, the learner and the school.* Harmondsworth: Penguin.

Bellack, Arno A., Herbert M. Kliebard, Ronald T. Hyman, and Frank L. Smith, Jr. 1966. *The language of the classroom.* New York: Teachers College Press.

Beretta, Alan. In press. Language teaching program evaluation: retrospect and prospect. In R. K. Johnson, ed. *Program design and evaluation in language teaching.* Cambridge: Cambridge University Press.

Bialystok, Ellen. 1982. On the relationship between knowing and using forms. *Applied Linguistics* 3:181–206.

Bialystok, Ellen, and Maria Fröhlich. 1978. Variables of classroom achievement in second language learning. *Modern Language Journal* 62:327–335.

Bialystok, Ellen, Maria Fröhlich, and Joan Howard. 1978. *The teaching and learning of French as a second language in two distinct learning settings. Project report.* Toronto: Modern Language Centre, Ontario Institute for Studies in Education.

Biddle, Bruce J. 1967. Methods and concepts in classroom research. *Review of Educational Research* 37:337–357.

Blau, Eileen K. 1982. The effect of syntax on readability for ESL students in Puerto Rico. *TESOL Quarterly* 16:517–528.

Bradshaw, Julie. 1986. Teaching as a context for learning: correcting pronunciation. Unpublished manuscript.

Breen, Michael P. 1985. The social context for language learning – a neglected situation? *Studies in Second Language Acquisition* 7:135–158.

Brock, Cindy A. 1986. The effects of referential questions on ESL classroom discourse. *TESOL Quarterly* 20:47–59.

Brock, Cindy, Graham Crookes, Richard R. Day, and Michael H. Long. 1986. The differential effects of corrective feedback in native speaker-nonnative speaker conversation. In R. R. Day, ed. *Talking to learn: conversation in second language acquisition*, 229–236. Rowley, Mass.: Newbury House.

Brooks, Nelson. 1964. *Language and language learning: theory and practice.* 2nd ed. New York: Harcourt, Brace and World.

Brophy, Jere E., and Thomas L. Good. 1974. *Teacher-student relationships: causes and consequences.* New York: Holt, Rinehart and Winston.

Brown, Cheryl. 1985. Two windows on the classroom world: diary studies and participant observation differences. In P. Larson, E. L. Judd, and D. S. Messerschmitt, eds. *On TESOL '84: a brave new world for TESOL*, 121–134. Washington, D.C.: TESOL.

Brown, Gillian, and George Yule. 1983. *Discourse analysis.* Cambridge: Cambridge University Press.

Brown, James Dean. 1983. An exploration of morpheme group interactions. In K. Bailey, M. H. Long, and S. Peck, eds. *Second language acquisition studies*, 25–40. Rowley, Mass.: Newbury House.

Brown, Roger. 1973. *A first language.* Cambridge, Mass.: Harvard University Press.

Brown, Ron. 1985. *A comparison of the comprehensibility of modified and unmodified ESL reading materials.* M.A. in ESL thesis, University of Hawaii at Manoa, Honolulu.

Bruck, Margaret, and Jeffrey Schultz. 1977. An ethnographic analysis of the language use patterns of bilingually schooled children. *Working Papers on Bilingualism*, No. 13, 59–91. Toronto: Ontario Institute for Studies in Education.

Bruton, Anthony, and Virginia Samuda. 1980. Learner and teacher roles in the treatment of oral error in group work. *RELC Journal* 11:49–63.

Buckheister, Patrick E., and John F. Fanselow. 1984. Do you have the key? In J. Handscombe, R. A. Orem, and B. P. Taylor, eds. *On TESOL '83: the question of control*, 223–229. Washington, D.C.: TESOL.

Burstall, Claire, M. Jamieson, S. Cohen, and M. Hargreaves. 1974. *Primary French in the balance.* Windsor, Berkshire: NFEP Publishing.

Burt, Marina K., and Carol Kiparsky. 1974. Global and local mistakes. In J. H. Schumann and N. Stenson, eds. *New frontiers in second language learning*, 71–80. Rowley, Mass.: Newbury House.

California State Department of Education. 1984. *Studies on immersion education: a collection for United States educators.* Sacramento: California State Department of Education.

Capelle, G. C., R. J. Jarvella, and E. Revelle. n.d. Development of computer-assisted observational systems for teacher-training. Center for Research on Language and Language Behavior, University of Michigan.

Carrasco, Robert L. 1981. Expanded awareness of student performance: a case study in applied ethnographic monitoring in a bilingual classroom. In H. T. Trueba, G. P. Guthrie, and K. H-P. Au, eds. *Culture and the bilingual classroom: studies in classroom ethnography*, 153–177. Rowley, Mass.: Newbury House.

Carroll, John B. 1975. *The teaching of French as a foreign language in eight countries.* New York: Wiley.

Carton, Aaron S. 1966. The "method of inference" in foreign language study. Office of Research and Evaluation, Division of Teacher Education, City University of New York.

Cathcart, Ruth. 1983. Functional analysis of language data. Paper presented at the 17th Annual TESOL Convention, Toronto, Canada. (mimeo)

1986a. Input generation by young second language learners. *TESOL Quarterly* 20:515–530.

1986b. Situational differences and the sampling of young L2 children's school language. In R. R. Day, ed. *Talking to learn: conversation in second language acquisition*, 118–140. Rowley, Mass.: Newbury House.

Cathcart, Ruth, and Judy Winn-Bell Olsen. 1976. Teachers' and students' preferences for correction of classroom errors. In J. Fanselow and R. Crymes, eds. *On TESOL '76*, 41–53. Washington, D.C.: TESOL.

Cathcart, Ruth, Michael A. Strong, and Lily Wong-Fillmore. 1979. The social and linguistic behavior of good language learners. In C. A. Yorio, K. Perkins, and J. Schachter, eds. *On TESOL '79: the learner in focus*, 267–274. Washington, D.C.: TESOL.

Cazden, Courtney B. 1986. Classroom discourse. In M. C. Wittrock, ed. *Handbook of research on teaching*, 432–463. New York: Macmillan.

Cazden, Courtney B., Robert L. Carrasco, A. A. Maldonado, and Frederick Erickson. 1980. The contribution of ethnographic research to bilingual bicultural education. In J. E. Alatis, ed. *Current issues in bilingual education*, 64–80. Washington, D.C.: Georgetown University Press.

Cazden, Courtney B., Vera P. John, and Dell Hymes, eds. 1972. *Functions of language in the classroom*. New York: Teachers College Press.

Cervantes, Raoul. 1983. Say it again Sam: the effect of exact repetition on listening comprehension. ESL 670 term paper, University of Hawaii at Manoa, Honolulu. (mimeo)

Chamberlain, Alan, and Teodoro Llamzon, eds. 1982. *Studies in classroom interaction*. SEAMEO Regional Language Centre, Occasional Papers No. 20. Singapore: RELC.

Chaudron, Craig. 1977a. A descriptive model of discourse in the corrective treatment of learners' errors. *Language Learning* 27:29–46.

1977b. *The context and method of oral error correction in second language learning*. Qualifying Research Paper, Ontario Institute for Studies in Education, Toronto.

1979. Complexity of teacher speech and vocabulary explanation/elaboration. Paper presented at the 13th Annual TESOL Convention, Boston, March 2. (mimeo)

1980. Review article: those dear old golden rule days... *Journal of Pragmatics* 4:157–172.

1982. Vocabulary elaboration in teachers' speech to L2 learners. *Studies in Second Language Acquisition* 4:170–180.

1983a. Foreigner talk in the classroom – an aid to learning? In H. W. Seliger and M. H. Long, eds. *Classroom oriented research in second language acquisition*, 127–143. Rowley, Mass.: Newbury House.

1983b. Simplification of input: topic reinstatements and their effects on L2 learners' recognition and recall. *TESOL Quarterly* 17:437–458.

1983c. Research on metalinguistic judgments: a review of theory, methods, and results. *Language Learning* 33:343–377.

1984. The effects of feedback on students' composition revisions. *RELC Journal* 15:1–14.

1985a. Intake: on models and methods for discovering learners' processing of input. *Studies in Second Language Acquisition* 7:1–14.

1985b. Comprehension, comprehensibility, and learning in the second language classroom. *Studies in Second Language Acquisition* 7:216–232.

1986a. Teachers' priorities in correcting learners' errors in French immersion classes. In R. R. Day, ed. *Talking to learn: conversation in second language acquisition*, 64–84. Rowley, Mass.: Newbury House. Reprinted from *Working Papers on Bilingualism* No. 12, 1977.

1986b. The role of simplified input in classroom language. In G. Kasper, ed. *Learning, teaching and communication in the foreign language classroom*, 99–110. Aarhus, Denmark: Aarhus University Press.

1987. The role of error correction in second language teaching. In B. K. Das, ed. *Patterns of Classroom Interaction in Southeast Asia*, 17–50. Singapore: SEAMEO Regional Language Centre.

Chenoweth, N. Ann, Richard R. Day, Ann E. Chun, and Stuart Luppescu. 1983. Attitudes and preferences of nonnative speakers to corrective feedback. *Studies in Second Language Acquisition* 6:79–87.

Chesterfield, Ray, and Kathleen Barrows Chesterfield. 1985. Natural order in children's use of second language learning strategies. *Applied Linguistics* 6:45–59.

Chesterfield, Ray, Kathleen Barrows Chesterfield, Katherine Hayes-Latimer, and Regino Chávez. 1983. The influence of teachers and peers on second language acquisition in bilingual preschool programs. *TESOL Quarterly* 17:401–419.

Chun, Ann E., Richard R. Day, N. Ann Chenoweth, and Stuart Luppescu. 1982. Errors, interaction, and correction: a study of native-nonnative conversations. *TESOL Quarterly* 16:537–547.

Cicourel, Aaron V., K. H. Jennings, S. H. M. Jennings, K. C. W. Leiter, Robert Mackay, Hugh Mehan, and D. R. Roth. 1974. *Language use and school performance*. New York: Academic Press.

Clark, Herbert H. 1973. The language-as-fixed-effect fallacy: a critique of language statistics in psychological research. *Journal of Verbal Learning and Verbal Behavior* 12:335–359.

Clyne, Michael G. ed. 1981. Foreigner talk. *International Journal of the Sociology of Language* 28.

1985. Medium or object — different contexts of (school-based) second language acquisition. In K. Hyltenstam and M. Pienemann, eds. *Modelling and assessing second language acquisition*, 197–212. San Diego: College-Hill Press.

Cooley, William W., Gaea Leinhardt, and Janet McGrail. 1977. How to identify effective teaching. *Anthropology and Education Quarterly* 8:119–126.

Courchêne, Robert. 1980. The error analysis hypothesis, the contrastive analysis hypothesis, and the correction of error in the second language classroom. *TESL Talk* 11/2:3–13, 11/3:10–29.

Crookes, Graham. 1986. *Task classification: a cross-disciplinary review*. Technical Report No. 4. Honolulu: Center for Second Language Classroom Research, Social Science Research Institute, University of Hawaii at Manoa.

Crookes, Graham, and Kathryn A. Rulon. 1985. *Incorporation of corrective feedback in native speaker/non-native speaker conversation*. Technical Report No. 3. Honolulu: Center for Second Language Classroom Research, Social Science Research Institute, University of Hawaii at Manoa.

Cummins, James. 1981. The role of primary language development in promoting educational success for language minority students. In California State Department of Education, ed. *Schooling and language minority students: a theoretical framework*, 3–49. Los Angeles: California State University at Los Angeles.

Dahl, Deborah A. 1981. The role of experience in speech modifications for second language learners. *Minnesota Papers in Linguistics and Philosophy of Language* 7:78–93.

Davies, Alan, C. Criper, and A. P. R. Howatt, eds. 1984. *Interlanguage.* Edinburgh: Edinburgh University Press.

Day, Richard R. 1984. Student participation in the ESL classroom or some imperfections in practice. *Language Learning* 34/3:69–102.

1985. The use of the target language in context and second language proficiency. In S. M. Gass and C. G. Madden, eds. *Input and second language acquisition*, 257–271. Rowley, Mass.: Newbury House.

ed. 1986. *Talking to learn: conversation in second language acquisition.* Rowley, Mass.: Newbury House.

Day, Richard R., N. Ann Chenoweth, Ann E. Chun, and Stuart Luppescu. 1984. Corrective feedback in native-nonnative discourse. *Language Learning* 34/2:19–45.

Dinsmore, David. 1985. Waiting for Godot in the EFL classroom. *ELT Journal* 39:225–234.

Doughty, Cathy, and Teresa Pica. 1986. Information gap tasks: do they facilitate second language acquisition? *TESOL Quarterly* 20:305–325.

Downes, Nancy. 1981. Foreigner talk inside and outside the classroom. Department of Linguistics, University of Pittsburgh. (mimeo)

Dressler, Wolfgang U., ed. 1978. *Current trends in textlinguistics.* Berlin: Walter de Gruyter.

Duff, Patsy. 1986. Another look at interlanguage talk: taking task to task. In R. R. Day, ed. *Talking to learn: conversation in second language acquisition*, 147–181. Rowley, Mass.: Newbury House.

Dunkin, Michael J., and Bruce J. Biddle. 1974. *The study of teaching.* New York: Holt, Rinehart and Winston.

Early, Margaret. 1985. *Input and interaction in content classrooms: foreigner talk and teacher talk in classroom discourse.* Unpublished Ph.D. dissertation, University of California at Los Angeles.

Edmondson, Willis J. 1980. Some problems concerning the evaluation of foreign language classroom discourse. *Applied Linguistics* 1:271–287.

1985. Discourse worlds in the classroom and in foreign language learning. *Studies in Second Language Acquisition* 7:159–168.

Ellis, Rod. 1980. Classroom interaction and its relation to second language learning. *RELC Journal* 11:29–48.

1984a. Can syntax be taught? A study of the effects of formal instruction on the acquisition of WH questions by children. *Applied Linguistics* 5:138–155.

1984b. *Classroom second language development.* Oxford: Pergamon Press.

1985a. Teacher-pupil interaction in second language development. In S. Gass and C. Madden, eds. *Input in second language acquisition*, 69–85. Rowley, Mass.: Newbury House.

1985b. *Understanding second language acquisition.* Oxford: Oxford University Press.

Enright, D. Scott. 1984. The organization of interaction in elementary classrooms. In J. Handscombe, R. A. Orem, and B. P. Taylor, eds. *On TESOL '83: the question of control*, 23–38. Washington, D.C.: TESOL.

Erickson, Frederick. 1977. Some approaches to inquiry in school-community ethnography. *Anthropology and Education Quarterly* 8:58–69.

Faerch, Claus. 1985. Meta talk in FL classroom discourse. *Studies in Second Language Acquisition* 7:184–199.

1986. Rules of thumb and other teacher-formulated rules in the foreign language classroom. In G. Kasper, ed. *Language, teaching and communication in the foreign language classroom*, 125–143. Aarhus, Denmark: Aarhus University Press.

Faerch, Claus, and Gabriele Kasper. 1980. Processes and strategies in foreign language learning and communication. *The Interlanguage Studies Bulletin–Utrecht* 5:47–118.

eds. 1983. *Strategies in interlanguage communication*. London: Longman.

eds. 1985a. Foreign language learning under classroom conditions: a special issue. *Studies in Second Language Acquisition* 7/2.

1985b. Repair in learner-native speaker discourse. In E. Glahn and A. Holmen, eds. *Learner discourse*, 11–23. Anglica et Americana 22, Department of English, University of Copenhagen, Copenhagen.

1986. The role of comprehension in second language learning. *Applied Linguistics* 7:257–274.

Fanselow, John F. 1977a. Beyond 'Rashomon' – conceptualizing and describing the teaching act. *TESOL Quarterly* 11:17–39.

1977b. The treatment of error in oral work. *Foreign Language Annals* 10:583–593.

Felix, Sascha W. 1981. The effect of formal instruction on second language acquisition. *Language Learning* 31:87–112.

Felix, Sascha W., and Angela Hahn. 1985. Natural processes in classroom second-language learning. *Applied Linguistics* 6:223–238.

Flanders, Ned A. 1960. Interaction analysis in the classroom: a manual for observers, University of Michigan, Ann Arbor.

1970. *Analyzing teaching behavior*. Reading, Mass.: Addison-Wesley.

Freed, Barbara F. 1980. Talking to foreigners versus talking to children: similarities and differences. In R. C. Scarcella and S. D. Krashen, eds. *Research in second language acquisition*, 19–27. Rowley, Mass.: Newbury House.

1981. Foreigner talk, baby talk, native talk. In M. G. Clyne, ed. Foreigner talk. *International Journal of the Sociology of Language* 28:19–39.

Freudenstein, Reinhold. 1976. How to analyze a foreign language lesson. Paper presented at the 10th annual TESOL Convention, New York. (mimeo)

Frick, Ted, and Melvyn I. Semmel. 1978. Observer agreement and reliabilities of classroom observational measures. *Review of Educational Research* 48:157–184.

Fröhlich, Maria, Nina Spada, and Patrick Allen. 1985. Differences in the communicative orientation of L2 classrooms. *TESOL Quarterly* 19:27–57.

Fujimoto, Donna, Jan Lubin, Yoshi Sasaki, and Michael H. Long. 1986. The effect of linguistic and conversational adjustments on the comprehensibility of spoken second language discourse. Department of ESL, University of Hawaii at Manoa, Honolulu. (mimeo)

Gaies, Stephen J. 1977a. The nature of linguistic input in formal second language learning: linguistic and communicative strategies in ESL teachers' classroom language. In H. D. Brown, C. A. Yorio, and R. H. Crymes, eds. *On TESOL '77: teaching and learning English as a second language: trends in research and practice*, 204–212. Washington, D.C.: TESOL.

1977b. *A comparison of the classroom language of ESL teachers and their speech among peers: an exploratory syntactic analysis.* Unpublished Ph.D. dissertation, Indiana University, Bloomington.

1983a. The investigation of language classroom processes. *TESOL Quarterly* 17:205–217.

1983b. Learner feedback: an exploratory study of its role in the second language classroom. In H. W. Seliger and M. H. Long, eds. *Classroom oriented research in second language acquisition*, 190–212. Rowley, Mass.: Newbury House.

Gaskill, William H. 1980. Correction in native speaker-nonnative speaker conversation. In D. Larsen-Freeman, ed. *Discourse analysis in second language research*, 125–137. Rowley, Mass.: Newbury House.

Gass, Susan M., and Carolyn G. Madden, eds. 1985. *Input in second language acquisition.* Rowley, Mass.: Newbury House.

Gass, Susan, and Evangeline Marlos Varonis. 1985. Task variation and non-native/non-native negotiation of meaning. In S. M. Gass and C. G. Madden, eds. *Input and second language acquisition*, 149–161. Rowley, Mass.: Newbury House.

Genesee, Fred. 1985. Second language learning through immersion: a review of U.S. programs. *Review of Educational Research* 55:541–561.

Glahn, Esther, and Anne Holmen, eds. 1985. *Learner discourse.* Anglica et Americana 22, Department of English, University of Copenhagen, Copenhagen.

Green, Judith L. 1983. Research on teaching as a linguistic process: a state of the art. *Review of Research in Education* 10, 151–252. Washington, D.C.: American Educational Research Association.

Green, Judith L., and Cynthia Wallat, eds. 1981. *Ethnography and language in educational settings.* Norwood, N.J.: Ablex Publishing.

Grimes, Joseph E. 1975. *The thread of discourse.* The Hague: Mouton.

Gumperz, John J., and Dell Hymes, eds. 1972. *Directions in sociolinguistics: the ethnography of communication.* New York: Holt, Rinehart and Winston.

Guthrie, Larry F. 1984. Contrasts in teachers' language use in a Chinese-English bilingual classroom. In J. Handscombe, R. A. Orem, and B. P. Taylor, eds. *On TESOL '83: the question of control*, 39–52. Washington, D.C.: TESOL.

Håkansson, Gisela. 1986. Quantitative aspects of teacher talk. In G. Kasper, ed. *Learning, teaching and communication in the foreign language classroom*, 83–98. Aarhus, Denmark: Aarhus University Press.

Halliday, Michael A. K. 1961. Categories of the theory of grammar. *Word* 17:241–292.

Hamayan, Else V., and G. Richard Tucker. 1980. Language input in the bilingual classroom and its relationship to second language achievement. *TESOL Quarterly* 14:453–468.

Hatch, Evelyn Marcussen. 1974. Second language learning – universals? *Work-*

ing Papers on Bilingualism/Travaux de recherches sur le bilinguisme, No. 3, 1–17. Toronto: Ontario Institute for Studies in Education.

1978. Discourse analysis and second language acquisition. In E. M. Hatch, ed. *Second language acquisition: a book of readings*, 401–435. Rowley, Mass.: Newbury House.

1983. *Psycholinguistics: a second language perspective*. Rowley, Mass.: Newbury House.

Heltoft, Anne Marie, and Kirsten Paaby. 1978. *Tampen braender: en analyse af undervisning som samtale*. Copenhagen: Hans Reitsels.

Hendrickson, James M. 1978. Error correction in foreign language teaching: recent theory, research, and practice. *Modern Language Journal* 62:387–398.

Henzl, Vera M. 1973. Linguistic register of foreign language instruction. *Language Learning* 23:207–222.

1979. Foreign talk in the classroom. *International Review of Applied Linguistics* 17:159–167.

Hernandez, Hilda. 1983. English-as-a-second-language lessons in bilingual classrooms: a discourse analysis. Paper presented at the 17th Annual TESOL Convention, Toronto, March 15–20. (mimeo)

Hoge, Robert D. 1985. The validity of direct observation measures of pupil classroom behavior. *Review of Educational Research* 55:469–483.

Holley, Freda M., and Janet K. King. 1971. Imitation and correction in foreign language learning. *Modern Language Journal* 55:494–498.

Holmes, Janet. 1983. The structure of teachers' directives. In J. C. Richards and R. W. Schmidt, eds. *Language and communication*, 89-114. London: Longman.

Hughes, David C. 1973. An experimental investigation of the effects of pupil responding and teacher reacting on pupil achievement. *American Educational Research Journal* 10:21–37.

Hunt, Kellogg W. 1966. Recent measures in syntactic development. *Elementary English* 43:732–739.

Hyltenstam, Kenneth. 1983. Teacher talk in Swedish as a second language classrooms: quantitative aspects and markedness conditions. In S. W. Felix and H. Wode, eds. *Language development at the crossroads*, 173–188. Tübingen, West Germany: Gunter Narr.

Hyltenstam, Kenneth, and Manfred Pienemann, eds. 1985. *Modelling and assessing second language acquisition*. San Diego: College-Hill Press.

Hyman, Ronald T., ed. 1974. *Teaching: vantage points for study*, 2nd ed. Philadelphia: Lippincott.

Hymes, Dell. 1962. The ethnography of speaking. In T. Gladwin and W. C. Sturtevant, eds. *Anthropology and human behavior*, 13–53. Washington, D.C.: Anthropological Society of Washington.

1964. Introduction: toward ethnographies of communication. In J. J. Gumperz and D. Hymes, eds. *The ethnography of communication*, 1–34. Washington, D.C.: American Anthropological Association.

1967. Models of the interaction of language and social settings. *Journal of Social Issues* 23:8–28.

1977. Qualitative/quantitative research methodologies in education: a linguistic perspective. *Anthropology and Education Quarterly* 8:165–176.

1981. Ethnographic monitoring. In H. T. Trueba, G. P. Guthrie, and K. H-P. Au, eds. *Culture and the bilingual classroom*, 56–68. Rowley, Mass.: Newbury House.

Ishiguro, Toshiaki. 1986. *Simplification and elaboration in foreign language teacher talk and its source*. Unpublished Ph.D. dissertation, Stanford University, Stanford, Ca.

Jarvis, Gilbert A. 1968. A behavioral observation system for classroom foreign-language skill acquisition activities. *Modern Language Journal* 52:335–341.

Johnson, Donna M. 1983. Natural language learning by design: a classroom experiment in social interaction and second language acquisition. *TESOL Quarterly* 17:55–68.

Johnson, Patricia. 1981. Effects on reading comprehension of language complexity and cultural background of a text. *TESOL Quarterly* 15:169–181.

Kasper, Gabriele. 1982. Teaching-induced aspects of interlanguage discourse. *Studies in Second Language Acquisition* 4:99–113.

1985. Repair in foreign language teaching. *Studies in Second Language Acquisition* 7:200–215.

ed. 1986. *Learning, teaching and communication in the foreign language classroom*. Aarhus, Denmark: Aarhus University Press.

Kelch, Ken. 1985. Modified input as an aid to comprehension. *Studies in Second Language Acquisition* 7:81–90.

Kirk, Roger. 1982. *Experimental design: procedures for the behavioral sciences*, 2nd ed. Monterey, Ca.: Brooks/Cole.

Klein, Wolfgang. 1986. *Second language acquisition*. Cambridge: Cambridge University Press.

Kliefgen, Jo Anne. 1985. Skilled variation in a kindergarten teacher's use of foreigner talk. In S. M. Gass and C. G. Madden, eds. *Input in second language acquisition*, 59–68. Rowley, Mass.: Newbury House.

Kocher, Sue, and Lynn Potter. 1985. Interaction patterns in multiethnic "SLEP" classrooms. M.A. in ESL scholarly paper, University of Hawaii at Manoa. (mimeo)

Kramsch, Claire J. 1985. Classroom interaction and discourse options. *Studies in Second Language Acquisition* 7:169–183.

Krashen, Stephen D. 1977. Some issues relating to the Monitor Model. In H. D. Brown, C. A. Yorio, and R. H. Crymes, eds. *On TESOL '77: teaching and learning English as a second language: trends in research and practice*, 144–158. Washington, D.C.: TESOL.

1982. *Principles and practice in second language acquisition*. Oxford: Pergamon Press.

1983. Newmark's 'ignorance hypothesis' and current second language acquisition theory. In S. Gass and L. Selinker, eds. *Language transfer in language learning*, 135–153. Rowley, Mass.: Newbury House.

Krashen, Stephen D., Robin C. Scarcella, and Michael H. Long, eds. 1982. *Child-adult differences in second language acquisition*. Rowley, Mass.: Newbury House.

Kuhn, Thomas S. 1970. *The structure of scientific revolutions*. Chicago: University of Chicago Press.

Kulhavy, Raymond W. 1977. Feedback in written instruction. *Review of Educational Research* 47:211–232.

Kumaravadivelu, B. n.d. Patterns of interaction in English as a first and second language classroom discourse. University of Michigan, Ann Arbor. (mimeo)

Lado, Robert. 1957. *Linguistics across cultures.* Ann Arbor: University of Michigan Press.

Laosa, Luis M. 1979. Inequality in the classroom: observational research on teacher-student interaction. *Aztlan* 8:51–67.

Larsen-Freeman, Diane E. 1975. The acquisition of grammatical morphemes by adult ESL students. *TESOL Quarterly* 9:409–420.

1976. ESL teacher speech as input to the learner. *Workpapers in Teaching English as a Second Language* 10:45–49. Los Angeles: University of California at Los Angeles.

ed. 1980. *Discourse analysis in second language research.* Rowley, Mass.: Newbury House.

Larsen-Freeman, Diane, and Michael H. Long. In press. *Introduction to second language acquisition research.* London: Longman.

Legarreta, Dorothy. 1977. Language choice in bilingual classrooms. *TESOL Quarterly* 11:9–16.

Levin, Lennart. 1972. *Comparative studies in foreign language teaching.* Stockholm: Almqvist and Wiksell.

Levine, Harold G., Ronald Gallimore, Thomas S. Weisner, and Jim L. Turner. 1983. Teaching participant-observation methods: a skills-building approach. *Anthropology and Education Quarterly* 11:38–54.

Lightbown, Patsy A. 1983. Exploring relationships between developmental and instructional sequences in L2 acquisition. In H. W. Seliger and M. H. Long, eds. *Classroom oriented research in second language acquisition,* 217–243. Rowley, Mass.: Newbury House.

Loban, Walter. 1976. *Language development: kindergarten through grade twelve.* Research Report No. 18, NCTE Committee on Research. Urbana, Ill.: National Council of Teachers of English.

Long, Michael H. 1977. Teacher feedback on learner error: mapping cognitions. In H. D. Brown, C. A. Yorio, and R. H. Crymes, eds. *On TESOL '77: teaching and learning English as a second language: trends in research and practice,* 278–293. Washington, D.C.: TESOL.

1980a. Inside the "black box": methodological issues in classroom research on language learning. *Language Learning* 30:1–42.

1980b. *Input, interaction and second language acquisition.* Ph.D. dissertation, University of California at Los Angeles.

1981a. Input, interaction and second language acquisition. In H. Winitz, ed. *Native language and foreign language acquisition. Annals of the New York Academy of Sciences* 379:259–278.

1981b. Questions in foreigner talk discourse. *Language Learning* 31:135–157.

1983a. Does second language instruction make a difference? A review of research. *TESOL Quarterly* 17:359–382.

1983b. Native speaker/non-native speaker conversation and the negotiation of comprehensible input. *Applied Linguistics* 4:126–141.

1985a. Input and second language acquisition theory. In S. M. Gass and

C. G. Madden, eds. *Input in second language acquisition*, 377–393. Rowley, Mass.: Newbury House.

1985b. *Bibliography of research on second language classroom processes and classroom second language acquisition*. Technical Report No. 2. Honolulu: Center for Second Language Classroom Research, Social Science Research Institute, University of Hawaii at Manoa.

1985c. A role for instruction in second language acquisition: task-based language teaching. In K. Hyltenstam and M. Pienemann, eds. *Modelling and assessing second language development*, 77–99. San Diego: College-Hill Press.

In press. Instructed interlanguage development. In L. Beebe, ed. *Issues in second language acquisition: multiple perspectives*. Rowley, Mass.: Newbury House.

Long, Michael H., Leslie Adams, Marilyn McLean, and Fernando Castaños. 1976. Doing things with words: verbal interaction in lockstep and small group classroom situations. In J. F. Fanselow and R. Crymes, eds. *On TESOL '76*, 137–153. Washington, D.C.: TESOL.

Long, Michael H., Cindy A. Brock, Graham Crookes, Carla Deicke, Lynn Potter, and Shu-qiang Zhang. 1984. *The effect of teachers' questioning patterns and wait-time on pupil participation in public high school classes in Hawaii for students of limited English proficiency*. Technical Report No. 1. Honolulu: Center for Second Language Classroom Research, Social Science Research Institute, University of Hawaii at Manoa.

Long, Michael H., and Patricia A. Porter. 1985. Group work, interlanguage talk, and second language acquisition. *TESOL Quarterly* 19:207–228.

Long, Michael H., and Charlene J. Sato. 1983. Classroom foreigner talk discourse: forms and functions of teachers' questions. In H. W. Seliger and M. H. Long, eds. *Classroom-oriented research in second language acquisition*, 268–285. Rowley, Mass.: Newbury House.

Lörscher, Wolfgang. 1986. Conversational structures in the foreign language classroom. In G. Kasper, ed. *Learning, teaching and communication in the foreign language classroom*, 11–22. Aarhus, Denmark: Aarhus University Press.

Lucas, Esther. 1975. *Teachers' reacting moves following errors made by pupils in post-primary English as a second language classes in Israel*. M.A. thesis, School of Education, Tel Aviv University.

Lysakowski, Richard S., and Herbert J. Walberg. 1982. Instructional effects of cues, participation, and corrective feedback: a quantitative synthesis. *American Educational Research Journal* 19:559–578.

MacFarlane, John M. 1975. Focus analysis. In R. L. Allwright, ed. *Working papers: language teaching classroom research*, 131–145. Essex: University of Essex, Department of Language and Linguistics.

Mackey, William F. 1978. Cost-benefit quantification of language teaching behavior. *Die Neueren Sprachen* 77:2–32.

Malcolm, Ian. 1986a. Classroom interaction analysis: using a sociolinguistic model. Paper presented at the RELC Regional Seminar on Patterns of Classroom Interaction in Southeast Asia, Singapore, April 21–25. (mimeo)

1986b. Continuities in communicative patterns in cross-cultural classrooms.

Paper presented at the RELC Regional Seminar on Patterns of Classroom Interaction in Southeast Asia, Singapore, April 21–25. (mimeo)

Mannon, Tracy Marie. 1986. *Teacher talk: a comparison of a teacher's speech to native and non-native speakers.* M.A. in TESL thesis, University of California at Los Angeles.

McCutcheon, Gail. 1981. On the interpretation of classroom observations. *Educational Researcher* 10:5–10.

McDonald, Frederick J., Meredith K. Stone, and Allen Yates. 1977. *The effects of classroom interaction patterns and student characteristics on the acquisition of proficiency in English as a second language.* Princeton, N.J.: Educational Testing Service.

McEwen, N. Z. 1976. *An exploratory study of the multidimensional nature of teacher-student verbal interaction in second language classrooms.* Unpublished Ph.D. dissertation, University of Alberta, Canada.

McLaughlin, Barry, Tammi Rossman, and Beverly McLeod. 1983. Second language learning: an information-processing perspective. *Language Learning* 33:135–158.

McTear, M. F. 1975. Structure and categories of foreign language teaching sequences. In R. L. Allwright, ed. *Working papers: language teaching classroom research*, 97–130. Essex: University of Essex, Department of Language and Linguistics.

Medley, Donald M., and H. E. Mitzel. 1963. Measuring classroom behavior by systematic observation. In N. L. Gage, ed. *Handbook of research on teaching*, 247–328. Chicago: Rand McNally.

Mehan, Hugh. 1974. Accomplishing classroom lessons. In A. Cicourel et al., eds. *Language use and school performance*, 76–142. New York: Academic Press.

1979. *Learning lessons: social organization in the classroom.* Cambridge, Mass.: Harvard University Press.

Meisel, Jürgen, Harald Clahsen, and Manfred Pienemann. 1981. On determining developmental stages in second language acquisition. *Studies in Second Language Acquisition* 3:109–135.

Milk, Robert D. 1982. Language use in bilingual classrooms: two case studies. In M. Hines and W. Rutherford, eds. *On TESOL '81*, 181–191. Washington, D.C.: TESOL.

1985. Can foreigners do "foreigner-talk"?: A study of the linguistic input provided by nonnative teachers of EFL. Paper presented at the 19th Annual TESOL Convention, New York, April 8. (mimeo)

Miller, James R., Peter G. Polson, and Walter Kintsch. 1984. Problems of methodology in cognitive science. In W. Kintsch, J. R. Miller, and P. G. Polson, eds. *Method and tactics in cognitive science*, 1–18. Hillsdale, N.J.: Lawrence Erlbaum Assoc.

Mitchell, Rosamond. 1985. Process research in second-language classrooms. *Language Teaching* 18:330–352.

Mitchell, Rosamond, and Richard Johnstone. 1984. The routinisation of "communicative" methodology. Paper presented to the 7th World Congress of Applied Linguistics, Brussels, August. (mimeo)

Mitchell, Rosamond, Brian Parkinson, and Richard Johnstone. 1981. *The foreign language classroom: an observational study.* Stirling Educational Monographs No. 9. Stirling: Department of Education, University of Stirling, Scotland.

Mizon, Suzanne. 1981. *Teacher talk: a case study from the Bangalore/Madras communicational ELT project.* M.A. thesis, University of Lancaster, England.

Mohatt, Gerald V., and Frederick Erickson. 1981. Cultural differences in teaching styles in an Odawa school: a sociolinguistic approach. In H. T. Trueba, G. P. Guthrie, and K. H-P. Au, eds. *Culture and the bilingual classroom: studies in classroom ethnography,* 105–119. Rowley, Mass.: Newbury House.

Morrison, Donald M., and Graham Low. 1983. Monitoring and the second language learner. In J. C. Richards and R. W. Schmidt, eds. *Language and communication,* 228–250. London: Longman.

Moskowitz, Gertrude. 1967. The FLint system: an observational tool for the foreign language class. In A. Simon and E. G. Boyer, eds. *Mirrors for behavior: an anthology of classroom observation instruments,* section 15, 1–15. Philadelphia: Center for the Study of Teaching, Temple University.

1968. The effects of training foreign language teachers in interaction analysis. *Foreign Language Annals* 1:218–235.

1970. *The foreign language teacher interacts.* Minneapolis: Association for Productive Teaching.

1971. Interaction analysis – a new modern language for supervisors. *Foreign Language Annals* 5:211–221.

1976. The classroom interaction of outstanding foreign language teachers. *Foreign Language Annals* 9:135–143, 146–157.

Naiman, Neil, Maria Fröhlich, H. H. Stern, and Angie Todesco. 1978. *The good language learner.* Toronto: Ontario Institute for Studies in Education.

Nearhoof, O. 1965. Teacher-pupil interaction in the foreign language classroom: a technique for self-evaluation. Unpublished paper cited in F. M. Grittner, *Teaching foreign languages,* 2nd ed., 330–332. New York: Harper and Row, 1977.

Nerenz, Anne G., and Constance K. Knop. 1982. A time-based approach to the study of teacher effectiveness. *Modern Language Journal* 66:243–254.

Nunnally, Jum C. 1978. *Psychometric theory,* 2nd ed. New York: McGraw-Hill.

Nystrom, Nancy J. 1983. Teacher-student interaction in bilingual classrooms: four approaches to error feedback. In H. W. Seliger and M. H. Long, eds. *Classroom oriented research in second language acquisition,* 169–188. Rowley, Mass.: Newbury House.

Nystrom, Nancy J., Samuel C. Stringfield, and Louis F. Miron. 1984. Policy implications of teaching behavior in bilingual and ESL classrooms. Paper presented at the 18th Annual TESOL Convention, Houston, March 6–9. (mimeo)

Oller, John W., Jr., and Jack C. Richards. 1973. *Focus on the learner: pragmatic perspectives for the language teacher.* Rowley, Mass.: Newbury House.

Omaggio, Alice C. 1982. The relationship between personalized classroom talk and teacher effectiveness ratings: some research results. *Foreign Language Annals* 14:255–269.

O'Malley, J. Michael, Anna Uhl Chamot, Gloria Stewner-Manzanares, Lisa

Kupper, and Rocco P. Russo. 1985a. Learning strategies used by beginning and intermediate ESL students. *Language Learning* 35:21–46.

O'Malley, J. Michael, Anna Uhl Chamot, Gloria Stewner-Manzanares, Rocco P. Russo, and Lisa Kupper. 1985b. Learning strategy applications with students of English as a second language. *TESOL Quarterly* 19:557–584.

Peck, Sabrina. 1985. Signs of learning: child nonnative speakers in tutoring sessions with a child native speaker. Department of English — ESL, University of California, Los Angeles. (mimeo)

Peterson, Penelope L., Louise Cherry Wilkinson, and Maureen T. Hallinan, eds. 1983. *The social context of instruction: group organization and group processes.* Orlando, Fla.: Academic Press.

Philips, Susan. 1972. Participation structures and communicative competence: Warm Springs children in community and classroom. In C. Cazden, V. P. John, and D. H. Hymes, eds. *Functions of language in the classroom,* 370–394. New York: Teachers College Press.

Pica, Teresa. 1983. Adult acquisition of English as a second language under different conditions of exposure. *Language Learning* 33:465–497.

Pica, Teresa, and Cathy Doughty. 1985. Input and interaction in the communicative language classroom: a comparison of teacher-fronted and group activities. In S. M. Gass and C. G. Madden, eds. *Input and second language acquisition,* 115–132. Rowley, Mass.: Newbury House.

Pica, Teresa, Cathy Doughty, and Richard Young. 1986. Making input comprehensible: do interactional modifications help? *I. T. L. Review of Applied Linguistics* 72:1–25.

Pica, Teresa, and Michael H. Long. 1986. The linguistic and conversational performance of experienced and inexperienced teachers. In R. R. Day, ed. *Talking to learn: conversation in second language acquisition,* 85–98. Rowley, Mass.: Newbury House.

Pienemann, Manfred. 1984. Psychological constraints on the teachability of languages. *Studies in Second Language Acquisition* 6:186–214.

1985. Learnability and syllabus construction. In K. Hyltenstam and M. Pienemann, eds. *Modelling and assessing second language development,* 23–75. San Diego: College-Hill Press.

Politzer, Robert L. 1970. Some reflections on "good" and "bad" language teaching behaviors. *Language Learning* 20:31–43.

1980. Foreign language teaching and bilingual education: research implications. *Foreign Language Annals* 13:291–297.

1983. An exploratory study of self-reported language learning behaviors and their relation to achievement. *Studies in Second Language Acquisition* 6:54–68.

Politzer, Robert L., and Mary McGroarty. 1985. An exploratory study of learning behaviors and their relationship to gains in linguistic and communicative competence. *TESOL Quarterly* 19:103–123.

Politzer, Robert L., and Louis Weiss. 1969. *Characteristics and behaviors of the successful foreign language teacher.* Technical Report No. 5. Stanford, Ca.: Stanford Center for Research and Development in Teaching.

Porter, Patricia. 1986. How learners talk to each other: input and interaction in task-centered discussions. In R. R. Day, ed. *Talking to learn: conversation in second language acquisition,* 200–222. Rowley, Mass.: Newbury House.

Ramirez, Arnulfo G., and Nelly P. Stromquist. 1979. ESL methodology and student language learning in bilingual elementary schools. *TESOL Quarterly* 13:145–158.

Ramirez, J. David, Sandra D. Yuen, Dena R. Ramey, and Barbara Merino. 1986. *First year report: longitudinal study of immersion programs for language minority children.* Arlington, Va.: SRA Technologies.

Reber, Arthur S. 1976. Implicit learning of synthetic languages: the role of instructional set. *Journal of Experimental Psychology: Human Learning and Memory* 2:88–94.

Redfield, Doris L., and Elaine Waldman Rousseau. 1981. A meta-analysis of experimental research on teacher questioning behavior. *Review of Educational Research* 51:237–245.

Rehbein, Jochen. 1984. Reparative Handlungsmuster und Ihre Verwendung im Fremdsprachenunterricht. *ROLIG papir* 30. Roskilde, Denmark: Roskilde University Center.

Reichardt, Charles S., and Thomas D. Cook. 1979. Beyond qualitative *versus* quantitative methods. In T. D. Cook and C. S. Reichardt, eds. *Qualitative and quantitative methods in evaluation research*, 7–32. Beverly Hills, Ca.: Sage Publications.

Richards, Jack C. 1986. Focus on the learner. University of Hawaii at Manoa, Honolulu. (mimeo)

Richards, Jack C., and Theodore S. Rodgers. 1986. *Approaches and methods in language teaching: a description and analysis.* New York: Cambridge University Press.

Riley, Philip. 1977. Discourse networks in classroom interaction: some problems in communicative language teaching. Paper presented at the BAAL seminar, University of Bath, England. (mimeo)

Rosenshine, Barak. 1976. Classroom instruction. In N. L. Gage, ed. *The psychology of teaching methods*, 335–371. Chicago: National Society for the Study of Education.

Rosenshine, Barak, and Norma Furst. 1973. The use of direct observation to study teaching. In R. Travers, ed. *Second handbook of research on teaching*, 122–183. Chicago: Rand McNally.

Rosenthal, Robert. 1984. *Meta-analytic procedures for social research.* Beverly Hills, Ca.: Sage Publications.

Rothfarb, S. H. 1970. Teacher-pupil interaction in the FLES class. *Hispania* 53:256–260.

Rowe, Mary Budd. 1974. Pausing phenomena: influence on the quality of instruction. *Journal of Psycholinguistic Research* 3:203–224.

Rubin, Joan. 1981. The study of cognitive processes in second language learning. *Applied Linguistics* 2:127–131.

Rudes, Blair A., Milton R. Goldsamt, and Edward J. Cervenka. 1983. *Issues in applying ethnography to bilingual classroom settings.* Los Angeles: Evaluation, Dissemination and Assessment Center, California State University at Los Angeles.

Rulon, Kathy, and Jan McCreary. 1986. Negotiation of content: teacher-fronted and small group interaction. In R. R. Day, ed. *Talking to learn: conversation in second language acquisition*, 182–199. Rowley, Mass.: Newbury House.

Rutherford, William E. 1982. Markedness in second language acquisition. *Language Learning* 32:85–108.

Salica, Christine. 1981. *Testing a model of corrective discourse*. M.A. in TESL thesis, University of California, Los Angeles.

Sato, Charlene. 1982. Ethnic styles in classroom discourse. In M. Hines and W. Rutherford, eds. *On TESOL '81*, 11–24. Washington, D.C.: TESOL.

Saville-Troike, Muriel. 1984. What *really* matters in second language learning for academic achievement? *TESOL Quarterly* 18:199–219.

Scarcella, Robin C., and Corrine Higa. 1981. Input, negotiation, and age differences in second language acquisition. *Language Learning* 31:409–437.

Schachter, Jacquelyn. 1983a. Nutritional needs of language learners. In M. A. Clarke and J. Handscombe, eds. *On TESOL '82: Pacific perspectives on language learning and teaching*, 175–189. Washington, D.C.: TESOL.

1983b. A new account of language transfer. In S. Gass and L. Selinker, eds. *Language transfer in language learning*, 98–111. Rowley, Mass.: Newbury House.

1984. A universal input condition. In W. E. Rutherford, ed. *Language universals and second language acquisition*, 167–183. Philadelphia: John Benjamins.

Schegloff, Emmanuel A., Gail Jefferson, and Harvey Sacks. 1977. The preference for self-correction in the organization of repair in conversation. *Language* 53:361–382.

Scherer, George A. C., and Michael Wertheimer. 1964. *A psycholinguistic experiment in foreign language teaching*. New York: McGraw-Hill.

Schinke-Llano, Linda. 1983. Foreigner talk in content classrooms. In H. W. Seliger and M. H. Long, eds. *Classroom oriented research in second language acquisition*, 146–164. Rowley, Mass.: Newbury House.

Schmidt, Richard W., and Sylvia Nagem Frota. 1986. Developing basic conversational ability in a second language: a case study of an adult learner of Portuguese. In R. R. Day, ed. *Talking to learn: conversation in second language acquisition*, 237–326. Rowley, Mass.: Newbury House.

Schumann, Francine M. 1980. Diary of a language learner: a further analysis. In R. C. Scarcella and S. D. Krashen, eds. *Research in second language acquisition*, 51–57. Rowley, Mass.: Newbury House.

Schumann, Francine M., and John H. Schumann. 1977. Diary of a language learner: an introspective study of second language learning. In H. D. Brown, C. A. Yorio, and R. H. Crymes, eds. *On TESOL '77: teaching and learning English as a second language: trends in research and practice*, 241–249. Washington, D.C.: TESOL.

Schwartz, Joan. 1980. The negotiation for meaning in repair in conversations between second language learners of English. In D. Larsen-Freeman, ed. *Discourse analysis in second language research*, 138–153. Rowley, Mass.: Newbury House.

Scollon, Ronald T. 1974. *One child's language from one to two: the origins of construction*. Ph.D. dissertation, University of Hawaii.

Scollon, Ronald T., and Suzanne B. K. Scollon. 1979. *Linguistic convergence: an ethnography of speaking at Fort Chipewyan, Alberta*. New York: Academic Press.

Searle, John R. 1969. *Speech acts*. Cambridge: Cambridge University Press.

Seliger, Herbert W. 1975. Inductive and deductive method in language teaching: a re-examination. *International Review of Applied Linguistics* 13:1–18.

1977. Does practice make perfect? A study of interaction patterns and L2 competence. *Language Learning* 27:263–278.

Seliger, Herbert W., and Michael H. Long, eds. 1983. *Classroom oriented research in second language acquisition*. Rowley, Mass.: Newbury House.

Selinker, Larry. 1972. Interlanguage. *IRAL* 10:219–231.

Shapiro, Frances. 1979. What do teachers actually *do* in language classrooms? Paper presented at the 13th Annual TESOL Convention, Boston, February 27–March 4. (mimeo)

Shaw, Peter Ambler. 1983. *The language of engineering professors: a discourse and registral analysis of a speech event*. Unpublished Ph.D. dissertation, University of Southern California, Los Angeles.

Shrum, Judith L., and Virginia Tech. 1985. Wait-time and the use of target or native languages. *Foreign Language Annals* 18:305–313.

Simon, Anita, and G. E. Boyer, eds. 1970. *Mirrors for behavior*. Philadelphia: Research for Better Schools.

Sinclair, J. McH., and Malcolm Coulthard. 1975. *Towards an analysis of discourse*. London: Oxford.

Smith, Philip D. 1970. *A comparison of the cognitive and audiolingual approaches to foreign language instruction: the Pennsylvania Foreign Language Project*. Philadelphia: Center for Curriculum Development.

Snow, Catherine E. 1972. Mothers' speech to children learning language. *Child Development* 43:549–565.

Snow, Catherine E., and Marian Hoefnagel-Höhle. 1982. School-aged second language learners' access to simplified linguistic input. *Language Learning* 32:411–430.

Spada, Nina M. 1986. The interaction between types of content and type of instruction: some effects on the L2 proficiency of adult learners. *Studies in Second Language Acquisition* 8:181–199.

1987. Relationships between instructional differences and learning outcomes: a process-product study of communicative language teaching. *Applied Linguistics* 8:137–161.

Speidel, Gisela E. 1984. Conversation and language learning in the classroom. Center for the Development of Early Education, Kamehameha Schools, Honolulu. (mimeo)

Speidel, Gisela E., Roland G. Tharp, and Linda Kobayashi. 1985. Is there a comprehension problem for children who speak nonstandard English? A study of children with Hawaiian-English backgrounds. *Applied Psycholinguistics* 6:83–96.

Stern, H. H. 1983. *Fundamental concepts of language teaching*. Oxford: Oxford University Press.

Steyaert, Marcia. 1977. A comparison of the speech of ESL teachers to native speakers and non-native learners of English. Paper presented at the winter meeting of the Linguistic Society of America, Chicago. (mimeo)

Stodolsky, Susan S. 1984. Teacher evaluation: the limits of looking. *Educational Researcher* 13:11–18.

Stokes, A. 1975. Error and teacher-student interaction. In R. L. Allwright, ed. *Working papers: language teaching classroom research*, 52–63. Essex: University of Essex, Department of Languages and Linguistics.

Stratton, Harley. 1986. Repair and error in the language classroom. Paper

presented at the RELC Regional Seminar on Patterns of Classroom Interaction in Southeast Asia, Singapore, April 21–25. (mimeo)
Strong, Michael. 1983. Social styles and the second language acquisition of
Spanish-speaking kindergartners. *TESOL Quarterly* 17:241–258.
1984. Integrative motivation: cause or result of successful second language
acquisition? *Language Learning* 34:1–14.
1986. Teacher language to limited English speakers in bilingual and submersion classrooms. In R. R. Day, ed. *Talking to learn: conversation in
second language acquisition*, 53–63. Rowley, Mass.: Newbury House.
Stubbs, Michael. 1983. *Discourse analysis: the sociolinguistic analysis of natural
language*. Chicago: University of Chicago Press.
Stubbs, Michael, and Sara Delamont, eds. 1976. *Explorations in classroom
observation*. New York: Wiley.
Swaffar, Janet K., Katherine Arens, and Martha Morgan. 1982. Teacher classroom practices: redefining method as task hierarchy. *Modern Language
Journal* 66:24–33.
Swain, Merrill. 1981. Time and timing in bilingual education. *Language Learning* 31:1–15.
1985. Communicative competence: some roles of comprehensible input and
comprehensible output in its development. In S. M. Gass and C. G. Madden,
eds. *Input in second language acquisition*, 235–253. Rowley, Mass.: Newbury House.
Swain, Merrill, and Sharon Lapkin. 1982. *Evaluating bilingual education: a
Canadian case study*. Avon, England: Multilingual Matters.
Tikunoff, William J., and Beatrice A. Ward, eds. 1977. Special issue: exploring
qualitative/quantitative research methodologies in education. *Anthropology and Education Quarterly* 8/2.
Townsend, Darryl R., and Gloria L. Zamora. 1975. Differing interaction pat-
terns in bilingual classrooms. *Contemporary Education* 46:196–202.
Trueba, Henry T. 1979. Bilingual education models: types and designs. In
H. T. Trueba and C. Barnett-Mizrahi, eds. *Bilingual multicultural education
and the professional: from theory to practice*, 54-73. Rowley, Mass.: Newbury House.
Trueba, Henry T., Grace Pung Guthrie, and Kathryn Hu-Pei Au, eds. 1981.
Culture and the bilingual classroom: studies in classroom ethnography.
Rowley, Mass.: Newbury House.
Trueba, Henry T., and Pamela G. Wright. 1981. A challenge for ethnographic
researchers in bilingual settings: analyzing Spanish/English classroom interaction. *Journal of Multilingual and Multicultural Development* 2:243–
257.
Tsui, Amy Bik-May. 1985. Analyzing input and interaction in second language
classrooms. *RELC Journal* 16:8–32.
Ullmann, Rebecca, and E. Geva. 1983. Classroom observation in the L2 setting:
a dimension of program evaluation. Modern Language Centre, Ontario
Institute for Studies in Education. (mimeo)
van Dijk, Teun A. 1972. *Some aspects of text grammars*. The Hague: Mouton.
1977. *Text and context*. London: Longman.
ed. 1985. *Handbook of discourse analysis, Vols. 1–4*. New York: Academic
Press.

van Lier, Leo A. W. 1982. *Analyzing interaction in second-language classrooms.* Ph.D. Dissertation, University of Lancaster, Lancaster, England.

1984. Discourse analysis and classroom research: a methodological perspective. *International Journal of the Sociology of Language* 49:111–133.

In press. *The classroom and the language learner: ethnography and second language classroom research.* London: Longman.

Varonis, Evangeline Marlos, and Susan Gass. 1985. Nonnative/nonnative conversations: a model for negotiation of meaning. *Applied Linguistics* 6:71–90.

Vigil, Neddy A., and John Oller. 1976. Rule fossilization: a tentative model. *Language Learning* 26:281–295.

von Elek, Tibor, and Mats Oskarsson. 1975. *Comparative methods experiments in foreign language teaching.* Department of Educational Research. Gothenburg, Sweden: Molndal School of Education.

Walmsley, J. B. 1978. "Cloud-Cuckoo-Land" or: feedback as the central component in foreign-language teaching. *Studies in Second Language Acquisition* 2/2:29–42.

Wesche, Marjorie Bingham. 1977. Learning behaviors of successful adult students on intensive language training. Paper presented at the first Los Angeles Second Language Acquisition Research Forum, Los Angeles. (mimeo)

Wesche, Marjorie Bingham, and Doreen Ready. 1985. Foreigner talk in the university classroom. In S. M. Gass and C. G. Madden, eds. *Input in second language acquisition,* 89–114. Rowley, Mass.: Newbury House.

White, Joanna, and Patsy M. Lightbown. 1984. Asking and answering in ESL classes. *Canadian Modern Language Review* 40:228–244.

Wilkinson, Louise Cherry, ed. 1982. *Communicating in the classroom.* New York: Academic Press.

Willing, Ken. 1985. *Learning styles in adult migrant education.* Report of the Program Development Project on Identifying and Accommodating Different Learning Styles. Sydney: Australian Migrant Education Project.

Wilson, Stephen. 1977. The use of ethnographic techniques in educational research. *Review of Educational Research* 47:245–265.

Wittgenstein, Ludwig. 1953. *Philosophical investigations.* Oxford: Blackwell.

Wolf, Fredric M. 1986. *Meta-analysis: quantitative methods for research synthesis.* Beverly Hills, Ca.: Sage Publications.

Wong-Fillmore, Lily. 1980. Learning a second language: Chinese children in the American classroom. In J. E. Alatis, ed. *Current issues in bilingual education.* Georgetown University Round Table on Languages and Linguistics 1980, 309–325. Washington, D.C.: Georgetown University Press.

1982. Instructional language as linguistic input: second-language learning in classrooms. In L. C. Wilkinson, ed. *Communicating in the classroom,* 283–296. New York: Academic Press.

1985. When does teacher talk work as input? In S. Gass and C. Madden, eds. *Input in second language acquisition,* 17–50. Rowley, Mass.: Newbury House.

Wragg, E. C. 1970. Interaction analysis in the foreign language classroom. *Modern Language Journal* 54:116–120.

Wren, Deborah. 1982. A case study of the treatment of oral errors. *Selected Papers in TESOL* 1, 90–103. Monterey, Ca.: Monterey Institute of International Studies.

Yee, Valerie, and Mary Wagner. 1984. Teacher talk: the structure of vocabulary and grammar explanations. Department of ESL scholarly paper, University of Hawaii at Manoa, Honolulu. (mimeo)

Yoneyama, Asaji. 1982. The treatment of learners' errors by novice EFL teachers. *Bulletin of the College of Education, Human and Social Sciences* (University of Niigata) Issue 23:85–94.

Zahorik, John A. 1968. Classroom feedback behavior of teachers. *Journal of Educational Research* 62:147–150.

Zamel, Vivian. 1981. Cybernetics: a model for feedback in the ESL classroom. *TESOL Quarterly* 15:139–150.

Zhang, Shu-qiang. 1985. *The differential effects of source of corrective feedback on ESL writing proficiency.* M.A. in ESL thesis, University of Hawaii at Manoa, Honolulu.

Zobl, Helmut. 1984. The wave model of linguistic change and the naturalness of interlanguage. *Studies in Second Language Acquisition* 6:160–185.

1985. Grammars in search of input and intake. In S. M. Gass and C. G. Madden, eds. *Input in second language acquisition,* 329–344. Rowley, Mass.: Newbury House.

Index

References to programs or levels of instruction (adult, university, bilingual education, etc.) include discussion of studies conducted on such populations, without necessarily specific comment on the levels or programs per se.

Abbreviations: *n.*, footnote on page; *t.*, table on page; *f.*, figure on page